DIALECTICAL LOGIC
Essays on its History and Theory

E.V. ILYENKOV

Translated by

H. Campbell Creighton

AAKAR

DIALECTICAL LOGIC
Essays on its History and Theory
E.V. ILYENKOV

© Aakar Books
First Indian Edition, 2008
Reprinted 2010
ISBN 978-81-89833-39-8

Published by
AAKAR BOOKS
28 E Pocket IV, Mayur Vihar Phase I, Delhi-110 091
Phone : 011-2279 5505 Telefax : 011-2279 5641
aakarbooks@gmail.com; www.aakarbooks.com

Printed at
Mudrak, 30 A Patparganj, Delhi-110 091

CONTENTS

The task, bequeathed to us by V. I. Lenin, of creating a Logic (with a capital 'L'), i.e. of a systematically developed exposition of dialectics understood as the logic and theory of knowledge of modern materialism, has become particularly acute today. The clearly marked dialectical character of the problems arising in every sphere of social life and scientific knowledge is making it more and more clear that only Marxist-Leninist dialectics has the capacity to be the method of scientific understanding and practical activity, and of actively helping scientists in their theoretical comprehension of experimental and factual data and in solving the problems they meet in the course of research.

In the past ten or fifteen years quite a few works have been written devoted to separate branches that are part of the whole of which we still only dream; they can justly be regarded as paragraphs, even chapters, of the future *Logic*, as more or less finished blocks of the building being erected. One cannot, of course, cement these 'blocks' mechanically into a whole; but since the task of a systematic exposition of dialectical logic can only be solved by collective efforts, we must at least determine the most general principles of joint work. In the essays presented here we attempt to concretise some of the points of departure of such a collective work.

In philosophy, more than in any other science, as Hegel remarked with some regret in his *Phenomenology of Mind*, 'the end of final result seems ... to have absolutely expressed the complete fact itself in its very nature; contrasted with that the mere process of bringing it to light would seem, properly speaking, to have no essential significance'.[1]

That is very aptly put. So long as dialectics (dialectical logic) is looked upon as a simple tool for proving a previously accepted thesis (irrespective of whether it was initially advanced as the rules of mediaeval disputes required, or only disclosed at the end of the argument, in order to create the illusion of not being preconceived, that is, of saying 'Look, here is what we have obtained although we did not assume it'), it will remain something of 'no essential significance'. When dialectics is converted into a simple tool for proving a previously accepted (or given) thesis, it becomes a sophistry only outwardly resembling dialectics, but empty of content. And if it is true that real dialectical logic takes on life not

---

[1] G. W. F. Hegel. *The Phenomenology of Mind.* Translated by J. B. Baillie (London, 1931) p 67.

in 'naked results', and not in the 'tendency' of the movement of thought, but only in the form of 'the result along with the process of arriving at it',[2] then, during the exposition of dialectics as Logic, we must reckon with this truth. For it is impossible to go to the other extreme, taking the view that we had allegedly not set ourselves any aim determining the means and character of our activity from the very outset in the course of our analysis of the problem, but had set out swimming at random. And we are therefore obliged, in any case, to say clearly, at the very beginning, what the 'object' is in which we want to discover the intrinsically necessary division into parts.

Our 'object' or 'subject matter' in general, and on the whole, is thought, thinking; and dialectical Logic has as its aim the development of a scientific representation of thought in those necessary moments, and moreover in the necessary sequence, that do not in the least depend either on our will or on our consciousness. In other words Logic must show how thought develops if it is scientific, if it reflects, i.e. reproduces in concepts, an object existing outside our consciousness and will and independently of them, in other words, creates a mental reproduction of it, reconstructs its self-development, recreates it in the logic of the movement of concepts so as to recreate it later in fact (in experiment or in practice). Logic then is the theoretical representation of such thinking.

----

[2] *Ibid.*, p 69.

From what we have said it will be clear that we understand thought (thinking) as the ideal component of the real activity of social man transforming both external nature and himself by his labour.

Dialectical Logic is therefore not only a universal scheme of subjective activity creatively transforming nature, but is also at the same time a universal scheme of the changing of any natural or socio-historical material in which this activity is fulfilled and with the objective requirements of which it is always connected. That, in our opinion, is what the real gist of Lenin's thesis on the identity (not 'unity' only, but precisely identity, full coincidence) of dialectics, logic, and the theory of knowledge of the modern, scientific, i.e. materialist, world outlook consists in. This approach preserves as one of the definitions of dialectics that given by Frederick Engels ('dialectics, however, is nothing more than the science of the general laws of the motion and development of nature, human society, and thought',[3] i.e. of natural and socio-historical development, and not of 'specifically subjective' laws and forms of thought).

We think that one can unite dialectics and materialism in precisely that way, and show that Logic, being dialectical, is not only the science of 'thinking' but also the science of the development of all things, both material and 'spiritual'.

---

[3] Frederick Engels. *Anti-Dühring*. Translated by Emile Burns (Progress Publishers, Moscow, 1975) pp 168-169.

Understood in that way Logic can also be the genuine science of thought, the materialist science of the reflection of the movement of the world in the movement of concepts. Otherwise it is inevitably transformed, as has happened to it in the hands of Neopositivists, into a purely technical discipline, a description of systems of manipulations with the terms of language.

The concretisation of the general definition of Logic presented above must obviously consist in disclosing the concepts composing it, above all the concept of thought (thinking). Here again a purely dialectical difficulty arises, namely, that to define this concept fully, i.e. concretely, also means to 'write' Logic, because a full description cannot by any means be given by a 'definition' but only by 'developing the essence of the matter'.

The concept 'concept' itself is also very closely allied with the concept of thought. To give a 'definition' of it here would be easy, but would it be of any use? If we, adhering to a certain tradition in Logic, tend to understand by 'concept' neither 'sign' nor 'term defined through other terms', and not simply a 'reflection of the essential or intrinsic attributes of things' (because here the meaning of the insidious words 'essential' and 'intrinsic' comes to the fore), but the gist of the matter, then it would be more correct, it seems to us, to limit ourselves in relation to definition rather to what has been said, and to start to consider 'the gist of the matter', to begin with abstract, simple definitions accepted as far as possible by everyone, in order to arrive at the 'concrete', or in this case at a Marxist-Leninist understanding of the essence of Logic and its concretely developed 'concept'. Everything we have said determines the design and plan of our book. At first glance it may seem that it is, if not wholly, then to a considerable degree, a study in the history of philosophy. But the 'historical' collisions of realising the 'matter of Logic' is not an end-in-itself for us, but only the factual material through which the clear outlines of the 'logic of Matter' gradually show through,[4] those very general outlines of dialectics as Logic which, critically corrected and materialistically rethought by Marx, Engels, and Lenin, also characterise our understanding of this science.

[4] See Karl Marx. Contribution to the Critique of Hegel's Philosophy of Law. In: Karl Marx and Frederick Engels. *Collected Works*, Vol. 3 (1843-44) (Lawrence and Wishart, London, 1975) p 18.

PART ONE

FROM THE HISTORY OF DIALECTICS

ESSAY ONE

The Problem of the Subject Matter and Sources of Logic

The most promising means of resolving any scientific problem is the historical approach to it. In our case this approach proves a very essential one. The fact is that what are now called logic are doctrines that differ considerably in their understanding of the boundaries of this science. Each of them, of course, lays claim not so much simply to the title as to the right to be considered the sole modern stage in the development of world logical thought. That, therefore, is why we must go into the history of the matter.

The term 'logic' was first introduced for the science of thinking by the Stoics, who distinguished by it only that part of Aristotle's actual teaching that corresponded to their own views on the nature of thinking. The term itself was derived by them from the Greek word *logos* (which literally means 'the word'), and the science so named was very closely related to the subject matter of grammar and rhetoric. The mediaeval scholastics, who finally shaped and canonised the tradition, simply converted logic into a mere instrument *(organon)* for conducting verbal disputes, a tool for interpreting the texts of the Holy Writ, and a purely formal apparatus. As a result not only did the official interpretation of logic become discredited, but also its very name. The emasculated 'Aristotelean logic' therefore also became discredited in the eyes of all leading scientists and philosophers of the new times, which is the reason why most of the philosophers of the sixteenth to eighteenth centuries generally avoided using the term 'logic' as the name for the science of thought, intellect, and reason.

Recognition of the uselessness of the official, formal, scholastic version of logic as the *organon* of real thought and of the development of scientific knowledge was the *leitmotif* of all the advanced, progressive philosophers of the time. 'The logic now in use serves rather to fix and give stability to the errors which have their foundation in commonly received notions than to help the search after truth. So it does more harm than good,' Francis Bacon said.[1] 'I observed in respect to Logic,' said Descartes, 'that the syllogisms and the greater part of the other teaching served better in explaining to others those things that one knows (or like the art of Lully, in enabling one to speak without judgment of those things of which one is ignorant) than in learning what is new.'[2] John Locke suggested that 'syllogism, at

---

[1] Francis Bacon. Novum Organum. In: *The Works of Francis Bacon*, Vol. IV (New York, 1968) pp 48-49.

[2] René Descartes. Discourse on Method. Translated by E. T. Haldane and G. R. T. Ross. In: *Great Books of the*

best, is but the Art of fencing with the little knowledge we have, without making any Addition to it. . .'³. On this basis Descartes and Locke considered it necessary to classify all the problems of the old logic in the sphere of rhetoric. And insofar as logic was preserved as a special science, it was unanimously treated not as the science of thinking but as the science of the correct use of words, names, and signs. Hobbes, for example, developed a conception of logic as the calculation of word signs.⁴

In concluding his *Essay Concerning Human Understanding*, Locke defined the subject matter and task of logic as follows: 'The business [of logic—*Ed.*] is to consider the nature of signs the mind makes use of for the understanding of things, or conveying its knowledge to others.'⁵ He treated logic as 'the doctrine of signs', i.e. as semeiotics.

But philosophy, fortunately, did not jell at that level. The best brains of the period understood very well that it might be all right for logic to be interpreted in that spirit, but not for the science of thinking. True, in general, the representatives of purely mechanistic views of the world and of thinking held such a view of logic. Since

Western World, Vol. 31, *Descartes. Spinoza* (Encyclopaedia Britannica Inc., Chicago, 1952) p 46.

3 John Locke. *An Essay Concerning Human Understanding*, Vol. II (London, 1710) p 299.

4 See Thomas Hobbes. *Leviathan or the Matter, Form and Power of a Commonwealth* (London, 1894) p 27.

5 John Locke. *Op. cit.*, p 339.

they interpreted objective reality in an abstract, geometrical way (i.e. only purely quantitative characteristics were considered objective and scientific), the principles of thinking in mathematical science merged in their eyes with the logical principles of thinking in general, a tendency that took final form in Hobbes.

The approach of Descartes and Leibniz was much more careful. They too took to the idea of creating a 'universal mathematics' in place of the old, ridiculed, and discredited logic; and they dreamed of instituting a universal language, a system of terms strictly and unambiguously defined, and therefore admitting of purely formal operations in it.

Both Descartes and Leibniz, unlike Hobbes, were well aware of the difficulties of principle standing in the way of realising such an idea. Descartes understood that the definition of terms in the universal language could not be arrived at by amical agreement, but must only be the result of careful analysis of the simple ideas, the bricks, from which the whole intellectual edifice of man was built; and that the exact language of 'universal mathematics' could only be something derived from 'true philosophy'. Only then would one succeed in replacing thinking about the things given in reflection or imagination (i.e. in the terminology of the day, in contemplation) and in general in people's real sense experience by a kind of calculus of terms and statements, and in drawing conclusions and inferences as infallible as the solutions of equations.

In supporting this point of Descartes', Leibniz categorically limited the field of application of the 'universal mathematics' solely to those things that belonged to the sphere of the powers of imagination. The 'universal mathematics' should also, in his view, be only (so to say) a logic of the powers of imagination. But that was precisely why all metaphysics was excluded from its province, and also such things as thought, and action, and the field of ordinary mathematics, commensurate only in reason. A very essential reservation! Thought, in any case, thus remained outside the competence of the 'universal mathematics'.

It is not surprising that Leibniz, with unconcealed irony, classified Locke's treatment of logic, by which it was understood as a special doctrine of signs, as purely nominalist. Leibniz revealed the difficulties associated with such an understanding of logic. Above all, he said, the 'science of reasoning, of judgments and inventions, seems very different from recognition of the etymologies and usage of words, which is something indeterminable and arbitrary. One must, moreover, when one wants to explain words, make an excursion into the sciences themselves as was seen in dictionaries; and one must not, on the other hand, engage in a science without at the same time giving a definition of the terms.'[6]

Instead of the threefold division of philosophy into different sciences (logic, physics, and ethics)

___

[6] G. W. Leibniz. *Neue Abhandlungen über den menschlichen Verstand* (Leipzig, 1915) p 640.

that Locke had taken over from the Stoics, Leibniz therefore suggested speaking of three different aspects, under which the same knowledge, the same truth, would function, namely theoretical (physics), practical (ethics), and terminological (logic). The old logic thus corresponded simply to the *terminological aspect of knowledge*, or, as Leibniz put it, 'arrangement by terms, as in a handbook'.[7] Such a systematisation, of course, even the best, was not a science of thought, because Leibniz had a more profound appreciation of thinking. And he classed the true doctrine of thought as metaphysics, in this sense following Aristotle's terminology and the essence of his logic, and not the Stoics.

But why should thought be investigated within the framework of 'metaphysics'? It was not a matter, of course, of indicating to which 'department' the theoretical understanding of thought 'belonged', but of a definite way of approaching the solution of an essential philosophical problem. And the difficulty constantly facing every theoretician lies in understanding what it is that links knowledge (the totality of concepts, theoretical constructions, and ideas) and its subject matter together, and whether the one agrees with the other, and whether the concepts on which a person relies correspond to something real, lying outside his consciousness? And can that, in general, be tested? And if so, how?

---

[7] G. W. Leibniz. *Neue Abhandlungen über den menschlichen Verstand* (Leipzig, 1915) pp 644-645.

The problems are really very complicated. An affirmative answer, for all its seeming obviousness, is not quite so simple to prove, and as for a negative answer, it proves possible to back it up with very weighty arguments, such as that, since an object is refracted in the course of its apprehension through the prism of the 'specific nature' of the organs of perception and reason, we know any object only in the form it acquires as a result of this refraction. The 'existence' of things outside consciousness is thus by no means necessarily rejected. One thing 'only' is rejected, the possibility of verifying whether or not such things are 'in reality' as we know and understand them. It is impossible to compare the thing as it is given in consciousness with the thing outside consciousness, because it is impossible to compare what I know with what I don't know, what I do not see, what I do not perceive, what I am not aware of. Before I can compare my idea of a thing with the thing, I must also be aware of the thing, i.e. must also transform it into an idea. As a result I am always comparing and contrasting only ideas with ideas, although I may think that I am comparing the idea with the thing.

Only similar objects, naturally, can be compared and contrasted. It is senseless to compare bushels and rods, poles, or perches, or the taste of steak and the diagonal of a square. And if, all the same, we want to compare steaks and squares, then we will no longer be comparing 'steak' and 'square' but two objects both possessing a geometrical, spatial form. The 'specific' property of the one and of the other cannot in general be involved in the comparison.

'What is the distance between the syllable A and a table? The question would be nonsensical. In speaking of the distance of two things, we speak of their difference in space. . . . Thus we equalise them as being both existences of space, and only after having them equalised *sub specie spatii* [under the aspect of space—*Ed.*], we distinguish them as different points of space. To belong to space is their unity.'[8] In other words, when we wish to establish a relation of some sort between two objects, we always compare not the 'specific' qualities that make one object 'syllable A' and the other a 'table', 'steak', or a 'square', but only those properties that express a 'third' something, different from their existence as the things enumerated. The things compared are regarded as different modifications of this 'third' property common to them all, inherent in them as it were. So if there is no 'third' in the nature of the two things common to them both, the very differences between them become quite senseless.

In what are such objects as 'concept' ('idea') and 'thing' related? In what special 'space' can they be contrasted, compared, and differentiated? Is there, in general, a 'third' thing in which they are 'one and the same', in spite of all their directly visible differences? If there is no such com-

---

[8] Karl Marx. *Theories of Surplus-Value*, Part III. Translated by Jack Cohen and S. W. Ryazanskaya (Progress Publishers, Moscow, 1971) p 143.

18

mon substance, expressed by different means in an idea and in a thing, it is impossible to establish any intrinsically necessary relationship between them. At best we can 'see' only an external relation in the nature of that which was once established between the position of luminaries in the heavens and events in personal lives, i.e. relations between two orders of quite heterogeneous events, each of which proceeds according to its own, particular, specific laws. And then Wittgenstein would be right in proclaiming logical forms to be mystical and inexpressible.

But in the case of the relationship between an idea and reality there is yet another difficulty. We know where the search for some sort of special essence can and does lead, an essence that would at once not be an idea and not material reality, but would constitute their common substance, the 'third' that appears one time as an idea and another time as being. For an idea and being are mutually exclusive concepts. That which is an idea is not being, and vice versa. How, then, in general, can they be compared? In what, in general, can the basis of their interaction be, what is that in which they are 'one and the same'?

This difficulty was sharply expressed in its naked logical form by Descartes. In its general form it is the central problem of any philosophy whatsoever, the problem of the relationship of 'thought' to the reality existing outside it and independently of it, to the world of things in space and time, the problem of the coincidence of the forms of thought and reality, i.e. the problem of truth or, to put it in traditional philosophical language, the 'problem of the identity of thought and being'.

It is clear to everyone that 'thought' and 'things outside thought' are far from being one and the same. It is not necessary to be a philosopher to understand that. Everyone knows that it is one thing to have a hundred roubles (or pounds, or dollars) in one's pocket, and another to have them only in one's dreams, only in one's *thoughts*. The *concept* obviously is only a state of the special substance that fills the brain box (we could go on, furthermore, explaining this substance as brain tissue or even as the very thin ether of the soul keeping house there, as the *structure of the brain tissue*, or even as the formal *structure of inner speech*, in the form of which thinking takes place *inside the head*); but the subject is outside the head, in the space beyond the head, and is something quite other than the *internal state of thought, ideas,* the *brain, speech,* etc.

In order to understand such self-evident things clearly, and to take them into consideration, it is not generally necessary to have Descartes' mind; but it is necessary to have its analytical rigour in order to define the fact that *thought* and the *world of things in space* are not only and not simply *different* phenomena, but are also directly *opposite*.

Descartes' clear, consistent intellect is especially needed in order to grasp the problem arising from this difficulty, namely, in what way do these two worlds (i.e. the world of concepts, of the *inner states of thought*, on the one hand, and the world of things in external space, on the other hand) nevertheless agree with one another? Descartes expressed the difficulty as follows. If the existence of things is determined through their extension and if the spatial, geometric forms of things are the sole objective forms of their existence outside the subject, then thinking is not disclosed simply through its description in forms of space. The *spatial* characteristic of thinking in general has no relation to its specific nature. The nature of thinking is disclosed through concepts that have nothing in common with the expression of any kind of spatial, geometric image. He also expressed this view in the following way: thought and extension are really two different substances, and a substance is that which exists and is defined only through itself and not through *something else*. There is nothing *common* between thought and extension that could be expressed in a special definition. In other words, in a series of definitions of thought there is not a single attribute that could be part of the definition of extension, and vice versa. But if there is no such common attribute it is also impossible to deduce being rationally from thought, and vice versa, because deduction requires a 'mean term', i.e. a term such as might be included in the series of definitions of the idea and of the existence of things outside consciousness, outside thought. Thought and being cannot in general *come into contact* with one another, since their boundary (the line or even the point of contact) would then also be exactly that which simultaneously both divides them and unites them.

In view of the absence of such a boundary, thought cannot limit the extended thing, nor the thing the mental expression. They are free, as it were, to penetrate and permeate each other, nowhere encountering a boundary. Thought as such cannot interact with the extended thing, nor the thing with thought; each revolves within itself.

Immediately a problem arises: how then are thought and bodily functions united in the human individual? That they are linked is an obvious fact. Man can consciously control his spatially determined body among other such bodies, his mental impulses are transformed into spatial movements, and the movements of bodies, causing alterations in the human organism (sensations) are transformed into mental images. That means that thought and the extended body interact in some way after all. But how? What is the nature of the interaction? How do they *determine*, i.e. *delimit*, each other?

How does it come about that a trajectory, drawn by thought in the plane of the imagination, for example a curve described in its equation, proves to be congruent with the geometrical contours of the same curve in real space? It means that the form of the curve in thought (i.e. in the form of the 'magnitude' of the algebraic signs of the equation) is identical with a corresponding curve in real space, i.e. a curve drawn on paper, in a space outside the head. It is surely *one and the same* curve, only the one is in thought and the other in real space; therefore, acting in accordance with thought (understood as the sense of words or signs), I simultaneously act in the strictest accord with the shape (in this case the geometrical contour) of a thing outside thought. How can that be, if 'the thing in thought' and 'the thing outside thought' are not only 'different' but are also absolutely opposite? For absolutely opposite means exactly this: not having anything in 'common' between them, nothing identical, not one attribute that could at once be a criterion of the concept 'thing outside thought' and of the concept 'thing in thought', or 'imagined thing'. How then can the two worlds conform with one another? And, moreover, not accidentally, but systematically and regularly, these two worlds that have absolutely nothing in *common*, nothing *identical*? That is the problem around which all Cartesians spin, Descartes himself, and Geulincx, and Malebranche, and the mass of their followers.

Malebranche expressed the principal difficulty arising here in his own witty way, as follows: during the siege of Vienna, the defenders of the city undoubtedly saw the Turkish army as 'transcendental Turks', but those killed were very real Turks. The difficulty here is clear; and from the Cartesian point of view on thought it is absolutely insoluble, because the defenders of Vienna acted, i.e. aimed and fired their cannonballs in accordance with the image of Turks that they had in their brains, in accordance with 'imagined', 'transcendental Turks', and with trajectories

23

calculated in their brains; and the shots fell among real Turks in a space that was not only outside their skulls, but also outside the walls of the fortress.

How does it come about that two worlds having absolutely nothing in common between them are in agreement, namely the world 'thought of', the world in thought, and the real world, the world in space? And why? God knows, answered Descartes, and Malebranche, and Geulincx; from our point of view it is inexplicable. Only God can explain this fact. He makes the two opposing worlds agree. The concept 'God' comes in here as a 'theoretical' construction by which to express the obvious but quite inconceivable fact of the unity, congruence, and identity perhaps, of phenomena that are absolutely contrary by definition. God is the 'third' which, as the 'connecting link', unites and brings into agreement thought and being, 'soul' and 'body', 'concept' and 'object', action in the plane of signs and words and action in the plane of real, geometrically defined bodies outside the head.

Having come directly up against the naked dialectical fact that 'thought' and 'being outside thought' are in absolute opposition, yet are nevertheless in agreement with one another, in unity, in inseparable and necessary interconnection and interaction (and thus subordinated to some higher law—and moreover, one and the same law), the Cartesian school capitulated before theology and put the inexplicable (from their point of view) fact down to God, and explained it by a 'miracle', i.e. by the direct intervention of supernatural powers in the causal chain of natural events.

Descartes, the founder of analytical geometry, could therefore not explain in any rational way whatever the reason for the algebraic expression of a curve by means of an equation 'corresponding' to the spatial image of this curve in a drawing. They could not, indeed, manage without God, because according to Descartes, actions with signs and on the basis of signs, in accordance only with signs (with their mathematical sense), i.e. actions in the ether of 'pure thought', had nothing in common with real bodily actions in the sphere of spatially determined things, in accordance with their real contours. The first were pure actions of the soul (or thinking as such), the second—actions of the body repeating the contours (spatially geometric outlines) of external bodies, and therefore wholly governed by the laws of the 'external', spatially material world.

(This problem is posed no less sharply today by the 'philosophy of mathematics'. If mathematical constructions are treated as constructions of the creative intellect of mathematicians, 'free' of any external determination and worked out exclusively by 'logical' rules—and the mathematicians themselves, following Descartes, are quite often apt to interpret them precisely so—it becomes quite enigmatic and inexplicable why on earth the empirical facts, the facts of 'external experience', keep on agreeing and coinciding in their mathematical, numerical expressions with the results obtained by purely logical calculations and by the 'pure' actions of the intellect. It is absolutely unclear. Only 'God' can help.)

In other words the identity of these absolute opposites ('thought', 'spirit', and 'extension', 'body') was also recognised by Descartes as a factual principle—without it even his idea of an analytical geometry would have been impossible (and not only inexplicable)—but it was explained by an act of God, by his intervention in the interrelations of 'thought and being', 'soul and body'. God, moreover, in Cartesian philosophy, and especially for Malebranche and Geulincx, could be understood as the purely traditional Catholic, orthodox God, ruling both the 'bodies' and the 'souls' of men from outside, from the heights of his heavenly throne, and co-ordinating the actions of the 'soul' with those of the 'body'.

Such is the essence of the famous psychophysical problem, in which it is not difficult to see the specifically concrete and therefore historically limited formulation of the central problem of philosophy. The problem of the theoretical understanding of thought (logic), consequently, and hence not of the rules of operating with words or other signs, comes down to solving the cardinal problems of philosophy, or of metaphysics, to put it in a rather old-fashioned way. And that assumes mastering the culture of the genuinely theoretical thinking represented by the classical philosophers, who not only knew how to pose problems with maximum clarity, but also knew how to solve them.

ESSAY TWO

Thought as an Attribute of Substance

An immense role in the development of logic, and in preparing the ground for modern views on its subject matter, a role far from fully appreciated, was played by Spinoza. Like Leibniz, Spinoza rose high above the mechanistic limitations of the natural science of his time. Any tendency directly to universalise partial forms and methods of thinking only useful within the bounds of mechanistic, mathematical natural science was also foreign to him.

Insofar as logic was preserved alongside the doctrine of substance, Spinoza treated it as an applied discipline by analogy with medicine, since its concern proved not to be the invention of artificial rules but the co-ordination of human intellect with the laws of thought understood as an 'attribute' of the natural whole, only as 'modes of expression' of the universal order and connection of things. He also tried to work out logical problems on the basis of this conception.

Spinoza understood thought much more profoundly and, in essence, dialectically, which is why his figure presents special interest in the history of dialectics; he was probably the only one of the great thinkers of the pre-Marxian era who knew how to unite brilliant models of acutely dialectical thought with a consistently held materialist principle (rigorously applied throughout his system) of understanding thought and its relations to the external world lying in the space outside the human head. The influence of Spinoza's ideas on the subsequent development of dialectical thought can hardly be exaggerated. 'It is therefore worthy of note that thought must begin by placing itself at the standpoint of Spinozism; to be a follower of Spinoza is the essential commencement of all Philosophy.'[1]

But orthodox religious scholasticism, in alliance with subjective idealist philosophy, has not ceased to flog Spinoza as a 'dead dog', treating him as a living and dangerous opponent. Elementary analysis reveals that the main principles of Spinoza's thought directly contradict the conception of 'thought' developed by modern positivism all along the line. The most modern systems of the twentieth century still clash in sharp antagonism in Spinoza; and that obliges us to analyse the theoretical foundation of his conception very carefully, and to bring out the principles in it that, in rather different forms of expression perhaps, remain the most precious principles of any scientific thinking to this day, and as such

---

[1] *Hegel's Lectures on the History of Philosophy.* Translated by E. S. Haldane and F. H. Simson, Vol. III (Routledge and Kegan Paul, London, 1968; Humanities Press, New York, 1974) p 257.

are very heatedly disputed by our contemporary opponents of dialectical thought.

Hegel once noted that Spinoza's philosophy was very simple and easy to understand. And in fact the principles of his thinking, which constitute the essential commencement of all Philosophy, i.e. the real foundation on which alone it is possible to erect the edifice of philosophy as a science, are brilliant precisely in their crystal clarity, free of all reservations and ambiguities.

It is not so easy, however, to bring these brilliant principles out because they are decked out in the solid armour of the constructions of formal logic and deductive mathematics that constitute the 'shell' of Spinoza's system, its (so to say) defensive coat of mail. In other words, the real logic of Spinoza's thinking by no means coincides with the formal logic of the movement of his 'axioms', 'theorems', 'scholia', and their proofs.

'Even with philosophers who gave their work a systematic form, e.g. Spinoza, the real inner structure of their system is quite distinct from the form in which they consciously presented it,' Karl Marx wrote to Ferdinand Lassalle.[2]

Our job then cannot be once more to paraphrase

---

[2] Karl Marx. Letter to Ferdinand Lassalle, May 31, 1858. In: Marx/Engels, *Werke*, Bd. 29 (Dietz Verlag, Berlin, 1973) p 561.

Marx repeated this idea eleven years later in a letter to M. M. Kovalevsky: '... It is necessary ... to distinguish between that which the author in fact offers and that which he gives only in his own representation. This is justifiable even for philosophical systems: thus what Spinoza considered the keystone of his system, and what the theoretical foundations on which Spinoza built his main work, the *Ethics*, and the conclusions that he drew from them by means of his famous 'geometric modus'. In that case it would be more proper simply to copy out the text of the *Ethics* itself once again. Our job is to help the reader to understand the 'real inner structure' of his system, which far from coincides with its formal exposition, i.e. to see the real 'cornerstone' of his reflections and to show what real conclusions were drawn from them, or could be drawn from them, that still preserve their full topicality.

That can only be done in one way, and one way only, which is to show the real problem that Spinoza's thought came up against quite independently of how he himself realised it and in what terms he expressed it for himself and for others (i.e. to set the problem out in the language of our century), and then to trace what were the real principles (once more independently of Spinoza's own formulation of them) on which he based the solution of the problem. Then it will become clear that Spinoza succeeded in finding the only formulation exact for his time of a real problem that remains the great problem of our day, only formulated in another form.

---

in fact constitutes this keystone, are two quite different things.' [This is retranslated from the Russian; the original letter, which was in English, has not come down to us, and is known only from a Russian text taken down from an oral translation by Kovalevsky himself. The letter is not included in the *Werke*, but is given in K. Marx and F. Engels. *Sochineniya*, Vol. 34 (Moscow, 1964) p 287.— *Tr.*]

We formulated this problem in the preceding essay. Spinoza found a very simple solution to it, brilliant in its simplicity for our day as well as his: the problem is insoluble only because it has been wrongly posed. There is no need to rack one's brains over how the Lord God 'unites' 'soul' (thought) and 'body' in one complex, represented initially (and by definition) as *different* and even *contrary* principles allegedly existing separately from each other before the 'act' of this 'uniting' (and thus, also being able to exist after their 'separation'; which is only another formulation of the thesis of the immortality of the soul, one of the cornerstones of Christian theology and ethics). In fact, there simply is no such situation; and therefore there is also no problem of 'uniting' or 'co-ordination'.

There are not two different and originally contrary objects of investigation—body and thought—but only *one single* object, which is the *thinking body* of living, real man (or other analogous being, if such exists anywhere in the Universe), only considered from two different and even opposing aspects or points of view. Living, real thinking man, the sole thinking body with which we are acquainted, does not consist of two Cartesian halves—'thought lacking a body' and a 'body lacking thought'. In relation to real man both the one and the other are equally fallacious abstractions, and one cannot in the end model a real thinking man from two equally fallacious abstractions.

That is what constitutes the real 'keystone' of

the whole system, a very simple truth that is easy, on the whole, to understand.

It is not a special 'soul', installed by God in the human body as in a temporary residence, that thinks, but the *body of man* itself. *Thought* is a property, a mode of existence, of the body, the same as its extension, i.e. as its spatial configuration and position among other bodies.

This simple and profoundly true idea was expressed this way by Spinoza in the language of his time: thought and extension are not two special substances as Descartes taught, but only two attributes of one and the same substance; not two special objects, capable of existing separately and quite independently of each other, but only two different and even opposite aspects under which *one and the same* thing appears, two different modes of existence, two forms of the manifestation of some third thing.

What is this third thing? Real infinite Nature, Spinoza answered. It is Nature that extends in space and 'thinks'. The whole difficulty of the Cartesian metaphysics arose because the specific difference of the real world from the world as only imagined or thought of was considered to be extension, a spatial, geometric determinateness. But extension as such just existed in imagination, only in thought. For *as such* it can generally only be thought of in the form of emptiness, i.e. purely negatively, as the complete absence of any definite geometric shape. Ascribing only spatial, geometric properties to Nature is, as Spinoza said, to think of it in an imperfect way, i.e. to deny it in advance one of its perfections. And then it is asked how the perfection removed from Nature can be restored to her again.

The same argumentation applies to thought. Thought as such is the same kind of fallacious abstraction as emptiness. In fact it is only a property, a predicate, an attribute of that very body which has spatial attributes. In other words one can say very little about thought as such; it is not a reality existing separately from, and independently of, bodies but only a mode of existence of Nature's bodies. Thought and space do not really exist by themselves, but only as Nature's bodies linked by chains of interaction into a measureless and limitless whole embracing both the one and the other.

By a simple turn of thought Spinoza cut the Gordian knot of the 'psychophysical problem', the mystic insolubility of which still torments the mass of theoreticians and schools of philosophy, psychology, physiology of the higher nervous system, and other related sciences that are forced one way or another to deal with the delicate theme of the relation of 'thought' to 'body', of 'spiritual' to 'material', of 'ideal' to 'real', and such like topics.

Spinoza showed that it is only impossible to solve the problem because it is absolutely wrongly posed; and that such posing of it is nothing but the fruit of imagination.

It is *in man* that Nature really performs, in a self-evident way, that very activity that we are accustomed to call 'thinking'. In man, in the form of man, in his person, *Nature itself* thinks, and not at all some special substance, source, or principle instilled into it from outside. In man, therefore, Nature thinks *of itself*, becomes aware of *itself*, senses *itself*, acts on *itself*. And the 'reasoning', 'consciousness', 'idea', 'sensation', 'will', and all the other special actions that Descartes described as *modi of thought*, are simply different modes of revealing a property inalienable from Nature as a whole, one of its own attributes.

But if thinking is always an action performed by a natural and so by a spatially determined body, it itself, too, is an action that is also expressed spatially, which is why there is not and cannot be the *cause and effect* relation between thinking and bodily action for which the Cartesians were looking. They did not find it for the simple reason that no such relation exists in Nature, and cannot, simply because thinking and the body are not two different things at all, existing separately and therefore capable of interacting, but *one and the same thing*, only expressed by two different modes or considered in two different aspects.

Between body and thought there is no relation of cause and effect, but the relation of an organ (i.e. of a spatially determinate body) to the mode of its own action. The thinking body cannot cause changes in thought, cannot act *on* thought, because its existence as 'thinking' *is thought*. If a thinking body does nothing, it is no longer a

34

thinking body but simply a body. But when it does act, it does not do so *on* thought, because its very activity is thought.

Thought as a spatially expressed activity therefore cannot also be secreted from the body performing it as a special 'substance' distinct from the body, in the way that bile is secreted from the liver or sweat from sweat glands. Thinking is not the *product* of an action but the *action itself*, considered at the moment of its performance, just as walking, for example, is the mode of action of the legs, the 'product' of which, it transpires, is the space walked. And that is that. The product or result of thinking may be an exclusively spatially expressed, or exclusively geometrically stated, change in some body or another, or else in its position relative to other bodies. It is absurd then to say that the one gives rise to (or 'causes') the other. Thinking does not evoke a spatially expressed change in a body but exists through it (or within it), and vice versa; any change, however fine, within that body, induced by the effect on it of other bodies, is directly expressed for it as a certain change in its mode of activity, i.e. in thinking.

The position set out here is extremely important also because it immediately excludes any possibility of treating it in a vulgar materialist, mechanistic key, i.e. of identifying thought with the material processes that take place *within* the thinking body (head, brain tissue), while nevertheless understanding that thought takes place precisely through these processes.

Spinoza was well aware that what is expressed and performed in the form of structural, spatial changes within the thinking body is not at all some kind of thinking taking place outside of and independently of them, and vice versa (shifts of thinking by no means express immanent movements of the body within which they arise). It is therefore impossible either to understand thought through examination, however exact and thorough, of the spatially geometric changes in the form of which it is expressed within the body of the brain, or, on the contrary, to understand the spatial, geometric changes in the brain tissue from the most detailed consideration of the composition of the ideas existing in the brain. It is impossible, Spinoza constantly repeated, because they are *one and the same*, only expressed by two different means.

To try to explain the one by the other simply means to double the description of one and the same fact, not yet understood and incomprehensible. And although we have two full, quite adequate descriptions of *one and the same event*, equivalent to one another, the event itself falls outside both descriptions, as the 'third thing', the very 'one and the same' that was not yet understood or explained. Because the event twice described (once in the language of the 'physics of the brain' and once in the language of the 'logic of ideas') can be explained and correspondingly understood only after bringing out the *cause* evoking the event described but not understood.

Bishop Berkeley ascribed the cause to God.

And so did Descartes, Malebranche, and Geulincx. The shallow, vulgar materialist tries to explain everything by the purely mechanical actions of external things on the sense organs and brain tissue, and takes for the cause the concrete thing, the sole object, that is affecting our bodily organisation at a given moment and causing corresponding changes in our body, which we feel within ourselves and experience as our thinking.

While rejecting the first explanation as the capitulation of philosophy before religious theological twaddle, Spinoza took a very critical attitude as well toward the superficially materialist—mechanistic—explanation of the cause of thought. He very well understood that it was only a 'bit' of an explanation, leaving in the dark the very difficulty that Descartes was forced to bring in God to explain.

For to explain the event we call 'thinking', to disclose its effective *cause*, it is necessary to include it in the chain of events *within which it arises of necessity and not fortuitously*. The 'beginnings' and the 'ends' of this chain are clearly not located within the thinking body at all, but far outside it.

To explain a separate, single, sensuously perceived fact passing momentarily before our eye, and even the whole mass of such facts, as the cause of thought means to explain precisely nothing. For this very fact exerts its effect (mechanical, say, or light) on stone as well, but no action of any kind that we describe as 'thinking' is evoked in the stone. The explanation must consequently also include those relations of cause and effect that of necessity generate our own physical organisation capable (unlike a stone) of thinking, i.e. of so refracting the external influences and so transforming them within itself that they are experienced by the thinking body not at all only as changes arising within itself, but as external things, as the shapes of things outside the thinking body.

For the action produced on the retina of our eye by a ray of light reflected from the Moon is perceived by the thinking being not simply as a mechanical irritation within the eye but *as the shape of the thing itself*, as the lunar disc hanging in space outside the eye, which means that the Ego, the thinking substance or creature, directly feels not the effect produced on it by the external thing but something quite different, viz. the shape or form (i.e. the spatial, geometric configuration) and position of this external body, which has been evoked within us as a result of the mechanical or light effect. In that lies both the enigma and the whole essence of thinking as the mode of activity of a thinking body in distinction to one that does not think. It will readily be understood that one body evokes a change by its action in another body; that is fully explained by the concepts of physics. It is difficult, and from the angle of purely physical concepts (and in Spinoza's time of even 'purely' mechanical, geometric concepts) even impossible, to explain just why and how the thinking body feels and perceives the effect caused by an external body within itself *as an external body*, as its, and not as its own shape, configuration, and position in space.

Such was the enigma, in general, that Leibniz and Fichte came up against later; but Spinoza had already found a fully rational, though only general, theoretical solution. He clearly understood that the problem could only be fully and finally solved by quite concrete investigation (including anatomical and physiological) of the material mechanism by which the thinking body (brain) managed to do the trick, truly mystically incomprehensible (from the angle of purely geometric concepts). But that it did the trick—that it saw the *thing* and not the changes in the particles of the retina and brain that this body caused by its light effect within the brain—was an undoubted fact; and a fact calling for fundamental explanation and in a general way outlining paths for more concrete study in the future.

What can the philosopher say here categorically, who remains a philosopher and does not become a physiologist, or an anatomist, or a physicist? Or rather, what can he say, without plunging into a game of the imagination, without trying to construct hypothetical mechanisms in the fancy by which the trick mentioned 'might', in general, be performed? What can he say while remaining on the ground of firmly established facts known before and independently of any concrete, physiological investigation of the inner mechanisms of the thinking body, and not capable either of being refuted or made doubtful by any further probing within the eye and the skull?

In the given, partial, though very characteristic case, there is another, more general problem, namely that of the relation of philosophy as a special science to the concrete research of the natural sciences. Spinoza's position on this point cannot in principle be explained if we start from the positivist idea that philosophy has made all its outstanding achievements (and makes them) only by purely empirical 'generalisation of the progress of its contemporary natural sciences'. Because natural science did not find the answers to the problem before us either in the seventeenth century, in Spinoza's time, or even in our day, three hundred years later. Furthermore, the natural science of his day did not even suspect the existence of such a problem; and when it did, knew it only in a theological formulation. As for the 'soul' or 'spirit', and in general everything connected one way or another with 'spiritual', psychic life, the natural scientists of the time (even the great ones like Isaac Newton) found themselves prisoners of the prevailing (i.e. religious, theological) illusions. Spiritual life they gladly left to the Church, and humbly acknowledged its authority, interesting themselves exclusively in the mechanical characteristics of the surrounding world. And everything that was inexplicable on purely mechanical grounds was not subjected to scientific study at all but was left to the competence of religion.

If Spinoza had in fact tried to construct his

philosophical system by the method that our contemporary positivism would have recommended
to him, it is not difficult to imagine what he would
have produced as a 'system'. He would only have
brought together the purely mechanical and religious, mystical 'general ideas' that were guiding
all (or almost all) naturalists in his day. Spinoza
understood very clearly that religious, theological
mysticism was the inevitable complement of a
purely mechanistic (geometrical, mathematical)
world outlook, i.e. the point of view that considers
the sole 'objective' properties of the real world
to be only the spatial, geometrical forms and
relations of bodies. His greatness was that he did
not plod along behind contemporaneous natural
science, i.e. behind the one-sided, mechanistic
thinking of the coryphaei of the science of the
day, but subjected this way of thinking to well
substantiated criticism from the angle of the
specific concepts of philosophy as a special science. This feature of Spinoza's thinking was brought
out clearly and explicitly by Frederick Engels:
'It is to the highest credit of the philosophy of the
time that it did not let itself be led astray by the
restricted state of contemporary natural knowledge, and that—from Spinoza right to the great
French materialists—it insisted on explaining the
world from the world itself and left the justifica-
tion in detail to the natural science of the future.'[3]
That is why Spinoza has come down in the

---

[3] Frederick Engels. *Dialectics of Nature*. Translated by
Clemens Dutt (Lawrence and Wishart, London, 1940) p 7.

history of science as an equal contributor to its progress with Galileo and Newton, and not as their epigone, repeating after them the general ideas that could be drawn from their work. He investigated reality himself from the special, philosophical angle, and did not generalise the results and ready-made findings of other people's investigation, did, not bring together the general ideas of the science of his day and the methods of investigation characteristic of it, or the methodology and logic of his contemporary science. He understood that that way led philosophy up a blind alley, and condemned it to the role of the wagon train bringing up in the rear of the attacking army the latter's own 'general ideas and methods', including all the illusions and prejudices incorporated in them.

That is why he also developed 'general ideas and methods of thought' to which the natural science of the day had not yet risen, and armed future science with them, which recognised his greatness three centuries later through the pen of Albert Einstein, who wrote that he would have liked 'old Spinoza' as the umpire in his dispute with Niels Bohr on the fundamental problems of quantum mechanics rather than Carnap or Bertrand Russell, who were contending for the role of the 'philosopher of modern science' and spoke disdainfully of Spinoza's philosophy as an 'outmoded' point of view 'which neither science nor philosophy can nowadays accept'.[4] Spinoza's

4 Bertrand Russell. *History of Western Philosophy* (London, 1946) p 601.

understanding of thinking as the activity of that same nature to which extension also belonged is an axiom of the true modern philosophy of our century, to which true science is turning more and more confidently and consciously in our day (despite all the attempts to discredit it) as the point of view of true materialism.

The brilliance of the solution of the problem of the relation of thinking to the world of bodies in space outside thought (i.e. outside the head of man), which Spinoza formulated in the form of the thesis that thought and extension are not two substances, but only two attributes of one and the same substance, can hardly be exaggerated. This solution immediately rejected every possible kind of interpretation and investigation of thought by the logic of spiritualist and dualist constructions, so making it possible to find a real way out both from the blind alley of the dualism of mind and body and from the specific blind alley of Hegelianism. It is not fortuitous that Spinoza's profound idea only first found true appreciation by the dialectical materialists Marx and Engels. Even Hegel found it a hard nut to crack. In fact, on the decisive point, he returned again to the position of Descartes, to the thesis that pure thought is the *active cause* of all the changes occurring in the 'thinking body of man', i.e. in the matter of the brain and sense organs, in language, in actions and their results, including in that the instruments of labour and historical events.

From Spinoza's standpoint *thought before and outside of its spatial expression in the matter*

43

proper to it simply does not exist. All talk about an idea that first arises and then tries to find material suitable for its incarnation, selecting the body of man and his brain as the most suitable and malleable material, all talk of thought first arising and then 'being embodied in words', in 'terms' and 'statements', and later in actions, in deeds and their results, all such talk, therefore, from Spinoza's point of view, is simply senseless or, what is the same thing, simply the atavism of religious theological ideas about the 'incorporeal soul' as the active cause of the human body's actions. In other words, the sole alternative to Spinoza's understanding proves to be the conception that an idea can ostensibly exist first somewhere and somehow *outside the body of the thought* and independently of it, and can then 'express itself' in that body's actions.

What is thought then? How are we to find the true answer to this question, i.e. to give a scientific definition of this concept, and not simply to list all the actions that we habitually subsume under this term (reasoning, will, fantasy, etc.), as Descartes did? One quite clear recommendation follows from Spinoza's position, namely: if thought is *the mode of action of the thinking body*, then, in order to define it, we are bound to investigate the mode of action of the thinking body very thoroughly, in contrast to the mode of action (mode of existence and movement) of the non-thinking body; and in no case whatsoever to investigate the structure or spatial composition of this body in an inactive state. Because the

44

thinking body, when it is inactive, is no longer a thinking body but simply a 'body'.

Investigation of all the material (i.e. spatially defined) mechanisms by which thought is effected within the human body, i.e. anatomical, physiological study of the brain, of course, is a most interesting scientific question; but even the fullest answers to it have no direct bearing on the answer to the question 'What is thought?'. Because that is another question. One does not ask how legs capable of walking are constructed, but in what walking consists. What is thinking as the action of, albeit inseparable from, the material mechanisms by which it is effected, yet not in any way identical with mechanisms themselves? In the one case the question is about the structure of an organ, in the other about the function the organ performs. The 'structure', of course, must be such that it can carry out the appropriate function; legs are built so that they can walk and not so that they can think. The fullest description of the *structure of an organ*, i.e. a description of it in an *inactive* state, however, has no right to present itself as a description, however approximate, of the *function* that the organ performs, as a description of the *real thing* that it does.

In order to understand the mode of action of the thinking body it is necessary to consider the mode of its active, causal interaction with other bodies both 'thinking' and 'non-thinking', and not its inner structure, not the spatial geometric relations that exist between the cells of its body and between the organs located within its body.

The cardinal distinction between the mode of action of a thinking body and that of any other body, quite clearly noted by Descartes and the Cartesians, but not understood by them, is that the former actively builds (constructs) the shape (trajectory) of its own movement in space in conformity with the shape (configuration and position) *of the other body*, co-ordinating the shape of its own movement (its own activity) with the shape of the other body, *whatever it is*. The proper, specific form of the activity of a thinking body consists consequently in *universality*, in that very property that Descartes actually noted as the chief distinction between human activity and the activity of an automaton copying its appearance, i.e. of a device structurally adapted to some one limited range of action even better than a human, but for that very reason unable to do 'everything else'.

Thus the human hand can perform movements in the form of a circle, or a square, or any other intricate geometrical figure you fancy, so revealing that it was not designed *structurally* and *anatomically* in advance for any one of these 'actions', and *for that very reason* is capable of performing *any action*. In this it differs, say, from a pair of compasses, which describe circles much more accurately than the hand but cannot draw the outlines of triangles or squares. In other words, the action of a body that 'does not think' (if only in the form of spatial movement, in the form of the simplest and most obvious case) is determined by its *own inner construction*, by its 'nature', and is quite unco-ordinated with the shape of the other bodies among which it moves. It therefore either disturbs the shapes of the other bodies or is itself broken in colliding with insuperable obstacles.

Man, however, *the thinking body, builds his movement on the shape of any other body*. He does not wait until the insurmountable resistance of other bodies forces him to turn off from his path; the thinking body goes freely round any obstacle of the most complicated form. *The capacity of a thinking body to mould its own action actively to the shape of any other body*, to co-ordinate the shape of its movement in space with the shape and distribution of all other bodies, Spinoza considered to be its distinguishing sign and the specific feature of that activity that we call 'thinking' or 'reason'.

This capacity, as such, has its own gradations and levels of 'perfection', and manifests itself to the maximum in man, in any case much more so than in any other creature known to us. But man is not divided from the lower creatures at all by that impassable boundary that Descartes drew between them by his concept of 'soul' or 'spirit'. The actions of animals, especially of the higher animals, are also subsumed, though to a limited degree, under Spinoza's definition of thinking.

This is a very important point, which presents very real interest. For Descartes the animal was only an automaton, i.e. all its actions were determined in advance by ready-made structures,

47

internally inherent to it, and by the distribution of the organs located within its body. These actions, therefore, could and had to be completely explained by the following scheme: external effect—movement of the inner parts of the body— external reaction. The last represents the response (action, movement) of the body evoked by the external effect, which in essence is only transformed by the working of the inner parts of the body, following the scheme rigidly programmed in its construction. There is a full analogy with the working of a self-activating mechanism (pressure on a button—working of the parts inside the mechanism—movement of its external parts). This explanation excluded the need for any kind of 'incorporeal soul'; everything was beautifully explained without its intervention. Such in general, and on the whole, is the theoretical scheme of a reflex that was developed two hundred years later in natural science in the work of Sechenov and Pavlov.

But this scheme is not applicable to man because in him, as Descartes himself so well understood, there is a supplementary link in the chain of events (i.e. in the chain of external effect— working of the inner bodily organs according to a ready-made scheme structurally embodied in them—external reaction) that powerfully interferes with it, forces its way into it, breaking the ready-made chain and then joining its disconnected ends together in a new way, each time in a different way, each time in accordance with new conditions and circumstances in the external action not previously foreseen by any prepared scheme and this supplementary link is 'reflection' or 'consideration'. But a 'reflection' is that activity (in no way outwardly expressed) which directs *reconstruction of the very schemes of the transformation* of the initial effect into response. Here *the body itself is the object of its own activity.*

Man's 'response' mechanisms are by no means switched on just as soon as 'the appropriate button is pressed', as soon as he experiences an effect from outside. Before he responds he contemplates, i.e. he does not act immediately according to any one prepared scheme, like an automaton or an animal, but considers the scheme of the forthcoming action critically, elucidating each time how far it corresponds to the needs of the new conditions, and actively correcting, even designing all over again, the whole set-up and scheme of the future actions in accordance with the external circumstances and the forms of things.

And since the forms of things and the circumstances of actions are in principle infinite in number, the 'soul' (i.e. 'contemplation') must be capable of an infinite number of actions. But that is impossible to provide for in advance in the form of ready-made, bodily programmed schemes. Thinking is the capacity of actively building and reconstructing schemes of external action in accordance with any new circumstances, and does not operate according to a prepared scheme as an automaton or any inanimate body does.

'For while reason is a universal instrument which can serve for all contingencies, these ['bodily'—*EVI*] organs have need of some special adaptation for every particular action,' Descartes wrote.[5] For that reason he was unable to conceive of the organ of thought *bodily*, as structurally organised in space. Because, in that case, as many ready-made, structurally programmed patterns of action would have to be postulated in it as there were external bodies and combinations of external bodies and contingencies that the thinking body would generally encounter in its path, that is, in principle, an infinite number. 'From this it follows,' Descartes said, 'that it is morally impossible that there should be sufficient diversity in any machine to allow it to act in all the events of life in the same way as our reason causes us to act,'[6] i.e. each time taking account again of any of the infinite conditions and circumstances of the external action. (The adverb 'morally' in Descartes' statement, of course, does not mean impossible 'from the aspect of morals' or of 'moral principles', etc., *moralement* in French meaning 'mentally' or 'intellectually' in general.)

Spinoza counted the considerations that drove Descartes to adopt the concept of 'soul' to be quite reasonable. But why not suppose that the organ of thought, while remaining wholly corporeal and therefore incapable of having schemes of its present and future actions *ready-made* and *innate within it* together with its bodily-organised structure, was capable of active-

---

[5] René Descartes. *Op. cit.*, p 59.
[6] *Ibid.*, p 59.

ly building them anew each time in accordance with the forms and arrangement of the 'external things'? Why not suppose that the thinking thing was designed in a special way; that not having any ready-made schemes of action within it, it acted for that very reason in accordance with whatever scheme was dictated to it at a given moment by the forms and combinations of other bodies located outside it? For that was the real role or function of the thinking thing, the only functional definition of thinking corresponding to the facts that it was impossible to deduce from structural analysis of the organ in which and by means of which it (thinking) was performed. Even more so, a functional definition of thinking as action according to the shape of any *other* thing also puts structural, spatial study of the thinking thing on the right track, i.e. study in particular of the body of the brain. It is necessary to elucidate and discover in the thinking thing those very structural features that enable it to perform its specific function, i.e. to act, not according to the scheme of its own structure but according to the scheme and location of all other things, including its own body.

In that form the materialist approach to the investigation of thought comes out clearly. Such is the truly materialist, functional definition of thought, or its definition as the active function of a natural body organised in a special way, which prompts both logic (the system of functional definitions of thought) and brain physiology (a system of concepts reflecting the material structure of the organ in and by which this function is performed) to make a really scientific investigation of the problem of thought, and which excludes any possibility of interpreting thinking and the matter of its relation to the brain by the logic of either spiritualist and dualist constructions or of vulgar mechanistic ones.

In order to understand thought as a function, i.e. as the mode of action of thinking things in the world of all other things, it is necessary to go beyond the bounds of considering what goes on inside the thinking body, and how (whether it is the human brain or the human being as a whole who possesses this brain is a matter of indifference), and to examine the real system within which this function ∴ performed, i.e. the system of relations *'thinking body and its object'*. What we have in mind here, moreqver, is not any single object or other in accordance with whose form the thinking body's activity is built in any one specific case, but *any object* in general, and correspondingly any possible 'meaningful act' or action in accordance with the form of its object.

Thought can therefore only be understood through investigation of its mode of action in the system thinking body—nature as a whole (with Spinoza it is 'substance', 'God'). But if we examine a system of smaller volume and scale, i.e. the relations of the thinking body with as wide a sphere of 'things' and their forms as you like, but still limited, then we shall not arrive at what thought is *in general* (thought in the whole fullness of its possibilities associated with its nature), but only at that limited mode of thinking that happens in a given case; and we shall therefore be taking only definitions of a *partial case* of thinking, only its *modus* (in Spinoza's parlance) as scientific definitions of *thought in general.*

The whole business consists in this, that the thinking body (in accordance with its nature) is not linked at all by its structural, anatomical organisation with any partial mode of action whatsoever (with any partial form of the external bodies). It is linked with them, but only currently, at the given moment, and by no means originally or forever. Its mode of action has a clearly expressed universal character, i.e. is constantly being extended, embracing ever newer and newer things and forms of things, and actively and plastically adapting itself to them.

That is why Spinoza also defined thought as an *attribute of substance*, and not as its *modus*, not as a partial case. Thus he affirmed, in the language of his day, that the single system, within which thought was found of necessity and not fortuitously (which it may or may not be), was not a single body or even as wide a range of bodies as you wished, but only and solely *nature as a whole.* The individual body possessed thought only by virtue of chance or coincidence. The crossing and combination of masses of chains of cause and effect could lead in one case to the appearance of a thinking body and in another case simply to a body, a stone, a tree, etc. So that the individual body, even the human body, did not possess thought one whit of necessity. Only nature as a whole was that system which possessed all its perfections, including thought, of absolute necessity, although it did not realise this perfection in any single body and at any moment of time, or in any of its 'modi'.

In defining thought as an attribute Spinoza towered above any representative of mechanistic materialism and was at least two centuries in advance of his time in putting forward a thesis that Engels expressed in rather different words: 'The point is, however, that mechanism (and also the materialism of the eighteenth century) does not get away from abstract necessity, and hence not from chance either. That matter evolves out of itself the thinking human brain is for him [Haeckel] a pure accident, although necessarily determined, step by step, where it happens. But the truth is that it is in the nature of matter to advance to the evolution of thinking beings, hence, too, this always necessarily occurs wherever the conditions for it (not necessarily identical at all places and times) are present.'[7]

That is what distinguishes materialism, sensible and dialectical, from mechanistic materialism that knows and recognises only one variety of 'necessity', namely that which is described in the language of mechanistically interpreted physics and mathematics. Yes, only Nature as a whole, understood as an infinite whole in space and time, *generating* its own partial forms from itself, pos-

7 Frederick Engels. *Dialectics of Nature*, p 228.

sesses at any moment of time, though not at any point of space, *all the wealth of its attributes*, .i.e. those properties that are reproduced in its make-up of necessity and not by a chance, miraculous coincidence that might just as well not have happened.

Hence it inevitably follows logically, as Engels said, 'that matter remains eternally the same in all its transformations, that none of its attributes can ever be lost, and therefore, also, that with the same iron necessity that it will exterminate on the earth its highest creation, the thinking mind, it must somewhere else and at another time again produce it.'[8]

That was Spinoza's standpoint, a circumstance that seemingly gave Engels grounds for replying categorically and unambiguously to Plekhanov when he asked: 'So *in your opinion old Spinoza was right in saying that thought and extension were nothing but two attributes of one and the same substance?*' "Of course," answered Engels, "*old Spinoza was quite right*".[9]

Spinoza's definition means the following: in man, as in any other possible thinking creature, the same matter thinks as in other cases (other modi) only 'extends' in the form of stones or any other 'unthinking body'; that thought in fact cannot be separated from world matter and counterposed to it itself as a special, incorporeal

---

[8] *Ibid.*, p 25.
[9] G. V. Plekhanov. Bernstein and Materialism. In: *Sochineniya*, Vol. XI (Moscow-Petrograd, 1923) p 22.

'soul', and it (thought) is matter's own perfection. That is how Herder and Goethe, La Mettrie and Diderot, Marx and Plekhanov (all great 'Spinozists') and even the young Schelling, understood Spinoza.

Such, let us emphasise once more, is the general, methodological position that later allowed Lenin to declare that it was reasonable to assume, as the very foundation of matter, a property akin to sensation though not identical with it, the property of reflection. Thought, too, according to Lenin, is the highest form of development of this universal property or attribute, extremely vital for matter. And if we deny matter this most important of its attributes, we shall be thinking of matter itself 'imperfectly', as Spinoza put it, or simply, as Engels and Lenin wrote, incorrectly, one-sidedly, and mechanistically. And then, as a result, we should continually be falling into the most real Berkeleianism, into interpreting nature as a complex of our sensations, as the bricks or elements absolutely specific to the animated being from which the whole world of ideas is built (i.e. the world as and how we know it). Because Berkeleianism too is the absolutely inevitable complement making good of a one-sided, mechanistic understanding of nature. That is why Spinoza too said that substance, i.e. the universal world matter, did not possess just the single attribute of 'being extended' but also possessed many other properties and attributes as inalienable from it (inseparable from it though separable from any 'finite' body).

Spinoza said more than once that it was impermissible to represent *thought as attribute* in the image and likeness of *human thought*; it was only the universal property of substance that was the basis of any 'finite thought', including human thought, but in no case was it identical with it. To represent thought in general in the image and likeness of existing human thought, of its *modus*, or 'particular case', meant simply to represent it incorrectly, in 'an incomplete way', by a 'model', so to say, of its far from most perfected image (although the most perfected known to us).

With that Spinoza also linked his profound theory of truth and error, developed in detail in the *Ethica ordine geometrico demonstrata (Ethics)*, *Tractatus de intellectus emendatione, Tractatus theologico-politicus*, and in numerous letters.

If the mode of action of the *thinking* body as a whole is determined in the form of an 'other', and not of the immanent structure of 'this' body, the problem arises, how ever are we to recognise error? The question was posed then with special sharpness because it appeared in ethics and theology as the problem of 'sin' and 'evil'. The criticism of Spinozism from the angle of theology was invariably directed at this point; Spinoza's teaching took all the sense out of the very distinguishing of 'good and evil', 'sin and righteousness', 'truth and error'. In fact, in what then did they differ?

Spinoza's answer again was simple, like any fundamentally true answer. Error (and hence 'evil' and 'sin') was not a characteristic of ideas and actions as regards their own composition, and was not a positive attribute of them. The erring man also acted in strict accordance with a thing's form, but the question was what the thing was. If it were 'trivial', 'imperfect' in itself, i.e. fortuitous, the mode of action adapted to it would also be imperfect. And if a person transferred this mode of action to another thing, he would slip up.

Error, consequently, only began when a mode of action that was limitedly true was given universal significance, when the relative was taken for the absolute. It is understandable why Spinoza put so low a value on acting by abstract, formal analogy, formal deduction based on an abstract universal. What was fixed in the abstract "idea" was what most often struck the eye. But it, of course, could be a quite accidental property and form of the thing; and that meant that the narrower the sphere of the natural whole with which the person was concerned, the greater was the measure of error and the smaller the measure of truth. For that very reason the *activity* of the thinking body was in direct proportion to the *adequateness of its ideas*. The more passive the person, the greater was the power of the nearest, purely external circumstances over him, and the more his mode of action was determined by the chance form of things; conversely, the more actively he extended the sphere of nature determining his activity, the more adequate were his ideas. The complacent position of the philistine was therefore the greatest sin.

Man's thinking could achieve 'maximum perfection' (and then it would be identical with thought as the attribute of substance) only in one case, when his actions conformed with all the conditions that the infinite aggregate of interacting things, and of their forms and combinations, imposed on them, i.e. if they were built in accordance with the absolutely universal necessity of the natural whole and not simply with some one of its limited forms. Real earthly man was, of course, still very, very far from that, and the attribute of thought was therefore only realised in him in a very limited and 'imperfect' (finite) form; and it would be fallacious to build oneself an idea of thinking as an attribute of substance in the image and likeness of finite human thought. On the contrary one's finite thought must be built in the image and likeness of *thought in general*. For finite thought the philosophical, theoretical definition of thinking as an attribute of substance poses some sort of ideal model, to which man can and must endlessly approximate, though never having the power to bring himself up to it in level of 'perfection'.

That is why the idea of substance and its all-embracing necessity functioned as the principle of the constant *perfecting or improvement of intellect*. As such it had immense significance. Every 'finite' thing was correctly understood only as a 'fading moment' in the bosom of infinite substance; and not one of its 'partial forms', however often encountered, should be given universal significance.

In order to disclose the really general, truly universal forms of things in accordance with which the 'perfected' thinking body should act, another criterion and another mode of knowledge than formal abstraction was required. The idea of substance was not formed by abstracting the attribute that belonged equally to extension and thought. The abstract and general in them was only that they *existed*, existence in general, i.e. an absolutely empty determination in no way disclosing the nature of the one or the other. The really general (infinite, universal) relation between thought and spatial, geometric reality could only be understood, i.e. the idea of substance arrived at, through real understanding of their mode of interaction within nature. Spinoza's whole doctrine was just the disclosure of this 'infinite' relation.

Substance thus proved to be an absolutely necessary condition, without assuming which it was impossible in principle to understand the mode of the interaction between the thinking body and the world within which it operated as a thinking body. This is a profoundly dialectical point. Only by proceeding from the idea of substance could the thinking body understand both itself and the reality with and within which it operated and about which it thought; any other way it could not understand either the one or the other and was forced to resort to the idea of an outside power, to a theologically interpreted 'God', to a miracle. But, having once understood the mode of its actions (i.e. thought), the thinking body just so comprehended substance as the absolutely necessary condition of interaction with the external world.

Spinoza called the mode of knowledge or cognition described here 'intuitive'. In creating an adequate idea of itself, i.e. of the form of its own movement along the contours of external objects, the thinking body thus also created an adequate idea of the forms and contours of the objects themselves. Because *it was one and the same form, one and the same contour.* In this understanding of the intuitive there was nothing resembling subjective introspection. Rather the contrary. On Spinoza's lips intuitive knowledge was a synonym of rational understanding by the thinking body of the laws of its own actions within nature. In giving itself a rational account of what and how it did in fact operate, the thinking body at the same time formed a true idea of the object of its activity.

From that there followed the consistent materialist conclusion that 'the true definition of any one thing neither involves nor expresses anything except the nature of the thing defined'.[10] That is why there can only be one correct definition (idea) in contrast and in opposition to the plurality and variety of the individual bodies of the same nature. These bodies are as real as the unity (identity) of their 'nature' expressed by the definition in the 'attribute of thought' and by

---

[10] Benedict de Spinoza. *Ethics.* Translated by W. H. White. In: *Great Books of the Western World*, Vol. 31, *Descartes, Spinoza*, p 357.

real diversity in the 'attribute of extension'. *Variety and plurality* are clearly understood here as *modes of realisation* of their own opposition, i.e. of the *identity and unity of their 'nature'*. That is a distinctly dialectical understanding of the relation between them, in contrast to the feeble eclectic formula (often fobbed off dialectics) that 'both unity and plurality', 'both identity and difference' equally really exist. Because eclectic pseudodialectics, when it comes down to solving the problem of knowledge and of 'definition' or 'determination', arrives safely at exactly the contrary (compared with Spinoza's solution), at the idea that 'the definition of a concept' is a verbally fixed form of expression in consciousness, in the idea of a real, sensuously given variety.

Talk of the objective identity, existing outside the head, of the nature of a given range of various and opposing single phenomena thus safely boils down to talk about the purely formal unity (i.e. similarity, purely external identity) of sensuously contemplated, empirically given things, of isolated facts, formally subsumed under 'concept'. And it then generally becomes impossible to consider the 'definition of the concept' as the determination of the *nature of the defined thing*. The starting point then proves to be not the 'identity and unity' of the phenomena but in fact the 'variety and plurality' of isolated facts allegedly existing originally quite 'independently' of one another, and later only formally united, tied together as it were with string, by the 'unity of the concept' and the 'identity of the name'. So the sole result proves to be the identity in consciousness (or rather in name) of the initially heterogeneous facts, and their purely verbal 'unity'.

Hence it is not difficult to understand why Neopositivists are dissatisfied with Spinoza and attack the *logical* principle of his thinking. 'Spinoza's metaphysic is the best example of what may be called "logic monism"—the doctrine, namely, that the world as a whole is a single substance, none of whose parts are logically capable of existing alone. The ultimate basis for this view is the belief that every proposition has a single subject and a single predicate, which leads us to the conclusion that relations and plurality must be illusory.'[11]

The alternative to Spinoza's view, in fact, is the affirmation that any 'part' of the world is not only 'capable' of 'existing' independently of all other parts, but must do so. As another authority of this trend postulated it, 'the world is the totality of facts, not of things', by virtue of which 'the world divides into facts', and so 'any one can either be the case or not be the case, and everything else remain the same'.[12]

Thus, according to the 'metaphysic of Neopositivism', the external world must be considered some kind of immeasurable *accumulation,* a simple *conglomeration,* of 'atomic facts' absolutely independent of each other, the 'proper de-

---

[11] Bertrand Russell. *Op. cit.*, pp 600-601.
[12] Ludwig Wittgenstein. *Tractatus Logico-Philosophicus* (London, 1955) p 31.

termination' of each of which is bound to be absolutely independent of the determination of any other fact. The determination (definition, description) remains 'correct' even given the condition that there are no other facts in general. In other words, 'a scientific consideration of the world' consists in a purely formal, verbal uniting of a handful of odd facts by subsuming them under one and the same term, under one and the same 'general'. The 'general', interpreted only as the 'meaning of the term or sign', always turns out to be something quite arbitrary or 'previously agreed upon', i.e. 'conventional'. The 'general' (unity and identity) as the sole result of the 'scientific logical' treatment of the 'atomic facts', is consequently not the result at all, but a previously established, conventional *meaning of the term,* and nothing more.

Spinoza's position, of course, had no connection with this principle of 'logical analysis' of the phenomena given in contemplation and imagination. For him the 'general', 'identical', 'united' were by no means illusions created only by our speech (language), by its subject-predicate structure (as Russell put it), but primarily the real, general nature of things. And that nature must find its verbal expression in a correct definition of the concept. It is not true, moreover, that 'relations and plurality must be illusory' for Spinoza, as Russell said. That is not at all like Spinoza, and the affirmation of it is on Russell's conscience, that he should have stooped so low to discredit the 'concept of substance' in the eyes of 'modern science' as 'incompatible with modern logic and with scientific method'.[13]

One thing, however, is beyond doubt here: what Russell called 'modern logic and scientific method' really is incompatible with the logic of Spinoza's thinking, with his principles of the development of scientific definitions, with his understanding of 'correct definitions'. For Spinoza 'relations and plurality' were not 'illusory' (as Russell described them) and 'identity and unity' were not illusions created solely by the 'subject-predicate structure' (as Russell himself thought). Both the one and the other were wholly real, and both existed in 'God', i.e. *in the very nature of things,* quite irrespective of whatever the verbal structures of the so-called 'language of science' were.

But for Bertrand Russell, both the one and the other were equally illusions. 'Identity' (i.e. the principle of substance, of the general nature of things), was an illusion created by language and 'relations and plurality' were illusions created by our own sensuality. But what, in fact, is independent of our illusions? I do not know and I don't want to know; I don't want to know because I cannot, Russell answered. I know only what is the 'world' given to me in my sensations and perceptions (where it is something 'plural') and in my language (where it is something 'identical' and related). But what is there besides this 'world'? God only knows, answered Russell, word

---

[13] Bertrand Russell. *Op. cit.,* p 601.

for word repeating Bishop Berkeley's thesis, though not risking to affirm categorically after him that 'God' in fact 'knew' it, because it was still not known if God himself existed.

There we have the polar contrast of the positions of Spinoza and of Berkeley and Hume (whom the Neopositivists are now trying to galvanise back to life). Berkeley and Hume also primarily attacked the whole concept of substance, trying to explain it as the product of an 'impious mind'. Because there is a really unpersuasive alternative here, namely two polar and mutually exclusive solutions of one and the same problem—the problem of the relation of 'the world in consciousness' (in particular in 'correct definition') to the 'world outside consciousness' (outside 'verbal definition'). For here a choice must be made: either nature, including man as part of it, must be understood through the logic of the 'concept of substance', or it must be interpreted as a complex of one's sensations.

But let us return to consideration of Spinoza's conception. Spinoza well understood all the sceptical arguments against the possibility of finding a single one correct definition of the thing that we are justified in taking as a definition of the nature of the thing itself and not of the specific state and arrangement of the organs within ourselves, in the form of which this thing is represented 'within us'. In considering different variants of the interpretation of one and the same thing, Spinoza drew the following direct conclusion: 'All these things sufficiently show that every one judges things by the constitution of his brain, or rather accepts the affections of his imagination in the place of things.'[14] In other words, we have within us, in the form of ideas, not the thing itself and its proper form, but only the inner state that the effect of the external things evoked in our body (in the corpus of the brain).

Therefore, in the ideas we directly have of the external world, two quite dissimilar things are muddled and mixed up: the form of our own body and the form of the bodies outside it. The naive person immediately and uncritically takes this hybrid for an external thing, and therefore judges things in conformity with the specific state evoked in his brain and sense organs by an external effect in no way resembling that state. Spinoza gave full consideration to the Cartesians' argument (later taken up by Bishop Berkeley), that toothache was not at all identical in geometric form to a dentist's drill and even to the geometric form of the changes the drill produced in the tooth and the brain. The brain of every person, moreover, was built and tuned differently, from which we get the sceptical conclusion of the plurality of truths and of the absence of a truth one and the same for all thinking beings. 'For every one has heard the expressions: So many heads, so many ways of thinking; Each is wise in his own manner; Differences of brains are not less common than differences of taste;—all which maxims show that men decide upon matters ac-

---

[14] Spinoza. *Op. cit.*, p 372.

cording to the constitution of their brains, and imagine rather than understand things.'[15]

The point is this, to understand and correctly determine the thing itself, its proper form, and not the means by which it is represented inside ourselves, i.e. in the form of geometric changes in the body of our brain and its microstructures. But how is that to be done? Perhaps, in order to obtain the pure form of the thing, it is simply necessary to 'subtract' from the idea all its elements that introduce the arrangement (disposition) and means of action of our own body, of its sense organs and brain into the pure form of the thing?

But (1) we know as little of how our brain is constructed and what exactly it introduces into the composition of the idea of a thing as we know of the external body itself; and (2) the thing in general cannot be given to us in any other way than through the specific changes that it has evoked in our body. If we 'subtract' everything received from the thing in the course of its refraction through the prism of our body, sense organs, and brain, we get pure nothing. 'Within us' there remains nothing, no idea of any kind. So it is impossible to proceed that way.

However differently from any other thing man's body and brain are built they all have something in common with one another, and it is to the finding of this something common that the activity of reason is in fact directed, i.e. the real activity of our body that we call 'thinking'.

---

[15] Spinoza. *Op. cit.*, p 372.

In other words an adequate idea is only the conscious state of our body *identical in form with the thing outside the body*. This can be represented quite clearly. When I describe a circle with my hand on a piece of paper (in real space), my body, according to Spinoza, comes into a state fully identical with the form of the circle outside my body, into a state of real *action* in the form of a circle. My body (my hand) really describes a circle, and the awareness of this state (i.e. of the form of my own action in the form of the thing) is also the idea, which is, moreover, 'adequate'.

And since 'the human body needs for its preservation many other bodies by which it is, as it were, continually regenerated'[16], and since it 'can move and arrange external bodies in many ways'[17], it is in the activity of the human body in the shape of another external body that Spinoza saw the key to the solution of the whole problem. Therefore 'the human mind is adapted to the perception of many things, and its aptitude increases in proportion to the number of ways in which its body can be disposed.'[18] In other words, the more numerous and varied the means it has 'to move and arrange external bodies', the more it has 'in common' with other bodies. Thus the body, knowing how to be in a state of movement along the contours of a circle, in that way knows

---

[16] *Ibid.*, p 380.
[17] *Ibid.*
[18] *Ibid.*

how to be in a state in common with the state and arrangement of all circles or external bodies moving in a circle.

In possessing consciousness of my own state (actions along the shape of some contour or other), I thus also possess a quite exact awareness (adequate idea) of the shape of the external body. That, however, only happens where and when I actively determine myself, and the states of my body, i.e. its actions, in accordance with the shape of the external body, and not in conformity with the structure and arrangement of my own body and its 'parts'. The more of these actions I know how to perform, the more perfect is my thinking, and the more adequate are the ideas included in the 'mind' (as Spinoza continued to express it, using the language normal to his contemporaries), or simply in the *conscious states of my body,* as he interpreted the term 'mind' on neighbouring pages.

Descartes' dualism between the world of external objects and the inner states of the human body thus disappeared right at the very start of the explanation. It is interpreted as a difference within one and the same world (the world of bodies), as a difference in their mode of existence ('action'). The 'specific structure' of the human body and brain is here, for the first time, interpreted not as a barrier separating us from the world of things, which are not at all like that body, but on the contrary as the same property of universality that enables the thinking body (in contrast to all others) to be in the very same states as things, and to possess forms in common with them.

Spinoza himself expressed it thus: 'There will exist in the human mind an adequate idea of that which is common and proper to the human body, and to any external bodies by which the human body is generally affected—of that which is equally in the part of each of these external bodies and in the whole is common and proper.

'Hence it follows that the more things the body has in common with other bodies, the more things will the mind be adapted to perceive.'[19]

Hence, also it follows that 'some ideas or notions exist which are common to all men, for . . . all bodies agree in some things, which . . . must be adequately, that is to say, clearly and distinctly, perceived by all.'[20] In no case can these 'common ideas' be interpreted as specific forms of the human body, and they are only taken for the forms of external bodies by mistake (as happened with the Cartesians and later with Berkeley), despite the fact that 'the human mind perceives no external body as actually existing, unless through the ideas of the affections of its body'.[21]

The fact is that the 'affections of one's body' are quite objective, being the actions of the body in the world of bodies, and not the results of the action of bodies on something unlike them, 'in-

---

[19] Spinoza. *Op. cit.*, pp 386, 387.
[20] *Ibid.*, p 386.
[21] *Ibid.*, p 384.

71

corporeal'. Therefore, 'he who possesses a body fit for many things possesses a mind of which the greater part is eternal'.[22]

From all that it follows that 'the more we understand individual objects, the more we understand God,'[23] i.e. the general universal nature of things, world substance; the more individual things our activity embraces and the deeper and more comprehensively we determine our body to act along the shape of the external bodies themselves, and the more we become an active component in the endless chain of the causal relations of the natural whole, the greater is the extent to which the power of our thinking is increased, and the less there is of the 'specific constitution' of our body and brain mixed into the 'ideas' making them 'vague and inadequate' (ideas of the imagination and not of 'intellect'). The more active our body is, the more universal it is, the less it introduces 'from itself', and the more purely it discloses the real nature of things. And the more passive it is, the more the constitution and arrangement of the organs within it (brain, nervous system, sense organs, etc.) affect ideas.

Therefore the real composition of psychic activity (including the logical component of thought) is not in the least determined by the structure and arrangement of the parts of the human body and brain, but by the external conditions of universally human activity in the world of other bodies.

---

[22] Spinoza. *Op. cit.*, p 462.
[23] *Ibid.*, p 458.

This functional determination gives an exact orientation to structural analysis of the brain, fixes the general goal, and gives a criterion by which we can distinguish the structures through which thinking is carried on within the brain from those that are completely unrelated to the process of thought, but govern, say, digestion, circulation of the blood, and so on.

That is why Spinoza reacted very ironically to all contemporaneous 'morphological' hypotheses, and in particular to that of the special role of the 'pineal gland' as primarily the organ of the 'mind'. On this he said straight out: since you are philosophers, do not build speculative hypotheses about the structure of the body of the brain, but leave investigation of what goes on inside the thinking body to doctors, anatomists, and physiologists. You, as philosophers, not only can, but are bound to, work out for doctors and anatomists and physiologists the functional determination of thinking and not its structural determination, and you must do it strictly and precisely, and not resort to vague ideas about an 'incorporeal mind', 'God', and so on.

But you can find the functional determination of thought only if you do not probe into the *thinking body* (the brain), but carefully examine the real composition of its objective activities among the other bodies of the infinitely varied universum. Within the skull you will not find anything to which a functional definition of thought could be applied, because thinking is a function of external, objective activity. And you must there-

73

fore investigate not the anatomy and physiology of the brain but the 'anatomy and physiology' of that 'body' whose active function *in fact* is thought, i.e. the 'inorganic body of man', the 'anatomy and physiology' of the world of his culture, the world of the 'things' that he produces and reproduces by his activity.

The sole 'body' that thinks from the necessity built into its special 'nature' (i.e. into its specific structure) is *not the individual brain at all,* and not even the whole man with a brain, heart, and hands, and all the anatomical features peculiar to him. Of necessity, according to Spinoza, only substance possesses thought. Thinking has its necessary premise and indispensable condition (*sine qua non*) in all nature as a whole.

But that, Marx affirmed, is not enough. According to him, only nature of necessity thinks, nature that has achieved the stage of man socially producing his own life, nature changing and knowing itself in the person of man or of some other creature like him in this respect, universally altering nature, both that outside him and his own. A body of smaller scale and less 'structural complexity' will not think. Labour is the process of changing nature by the action of social man, and is the 'subject' to which thought belongs as 'predicate'. But nature, the universal matter of nature, is also its substance. Substance, having become the subject of all its changes in man, the cause of itself (*causa sui*).

Logic and Dialectics

The most direct path to the creation of dialectical logic, as we have already said, is 'repetition of the past', made wise by experience, repetition of the work of Marx, Engels, and Lenin, or critical, materialist rethinking of the achievements that humanity owes in the realm of the Higher Logic to classical German philosophy of the end of the eighteenth and beginning of the nineteenth centuries, to the process of spiritual maturing, striking in its rapidity, associated with the names of Kant, Fichte, Schelling, and Hegel.

The 'matter of logic' then underwent, in a very short historical period, the most prodigious 'flight of imagination' since antiquity, marked in itself by an inner dialectic so tense that even simple acquaintance with it still cultivates dialectical thinking.

First of all we must note that it was German classical philosophy that clearly recognised and sharply expressed the fact that all problems of philosophy as a special science somehow or other turned on the question of *what thought was and what were its interrelations with the external world.* Understanding of this fact, already matured earlier in the systems of Descartes and Locke, Spinoza and Leibniz, was now transformed into the consciously established jumping-off point of all investigations, into the basic principle of a critical rethinking of the results of the preceding development. Philosophy, completing in Kant a more than two-century cycle of investigation, entered on a fundamentally new stage of understanding and resolving of its special problems.

The need to examine and analyse the path critically was not of course dictated only by the inner needs of philosophy itself, by the striving to completeness and orderliness (although the philosophers themselves so expressed it), but mainly by the powerful pressure of outside circumstances, the crisis-ridden, pre-revolutionary state of all intellectual culture. The intense conflict of ideas in all spheres of intellectual life, from politics to natural science, willy-nilly involved in ideological struggle, more and more insistently impelled philosophy to dig down ultimately to the very roots and sources of what was happening, to understand where the general cause of the mutual hostility between people and ideas was hidden, to find and point out to people the rational way out of the situation that had arisen.

Kant was the first to attempt to embrace within the framework of a single conception all the main opposing principles of the thought of the time which was approaching a catastrophic collision. In trying to unite and reconcile those principles within one system he only, against his will, exposed more clearly the essence of the problems which were unresolvable by the tried and known methods of philosophy.

The actual state of affairs in science presented itself to Kant as a war of all against all; in the image of that 'natural' state which, following Hobbes, he characterised (as applied to science) as 'a state of injustice and violence'.[1] In this state scientific thought ('reason') 'can establish and secure its assertions only through *war*...'. In that case 'the disputes are ended by a victory to which both sides lay claim, and which is generally followed by a merely temporary armistice, arranged by some mediating authority....'.[2]

Putting it another way, it was the tension of the struggle between opposing principles, each of which had been developed into a system claiming universal significance and recognition, that constituted the 'natural' state of human thought for Kant. The 'natural', actual, and obvious state of thought, consequently, was just dialectics. Kant was not at all concerned to extirpate it once and for all from the life of reason, i.e. from science understood as a certain developing whole, but only ultimately to find a corresponding 'rational' means of resolving the contradictions, discussions, disputes, conflicts, and antagonisms arising in science. Could reason itself, without the aid of 'authority', overcome the anguish of dissension?

---

[1] Immanuel Kant. *Critique of Pure Reason.* Translated by N. K. Smith (Macmillan, London, 1929) p 601.
[2] *Ibid.*

'The endless disputes of a merely dogmatic reason,' as he put it, 'thus finally constrain us to seek relief in some critique of reason itself, and in a legislation based upon such criticism.'[3]

The state of endless disputes, and hostility between theoreticians, seemed to Kant to be a consequence of the fact that the 'republic of scholars' did not as yet have a single, systematically developed 'legislation' recognised by all, or 'constitution of reason', which would enable it to seek solution of the conflicts not in war 'to the death' but in the sphere of polite, academic discussion, in the form of a 'legal process' or 'action' in which each party would hold to one and the same 'code' of logical substantiation and, recognising the opponent as an equally competent and equally responsible party as himself, would remain not only critical but also self-critical, always ready to recognise his mistakes and transgressions against the logical rules. This ideal of the inter-relations of theoreticians—and it is difficult to raise any objection against it even now—loomed before Kant as the goal of all his investigations.

But thereby, at the centre of his attention, there was above all that field which tradition assigned to the competence of logic. It was quite obvious to Kant, on the other hand, that logic in the form in which it existed could not in any way satisfy the pressing needs of the situation created, or serve as a tool to analyse it. The very term 'logic' was so discredited by then that Hegel was

---

[3] Immanuel Kant. *Op. cit.*, p 604.

fully justified in speaking of the universal and complete scorn for this science that for 'hundreds and thousands of years ... was just as much honoured as it is despised now'.[4] And only the profound reform that it underwent in the work of the classical German philosophers restored respect and dignity to the very name of the science of thought. Kant was the very first to try to pose and resolve the problem of logic specifically by way of a critical analysis of its content and historical fate. For the first time he compared its traditional baggage with the real processes of thinking in natural science and in the sphere of social problems.

Kant above all set himself the goal of bringing out and summing up the undisputed truths which had been formulated within the framework of traditional logic, though also scorned for their banality. In other words he tried to bring out those 'invariants' that had remained unaffected during all the discussions on the nature of thinking stretching over centuries and millennia, the propositions that no one had called in question, neither Descartes nor Berkeley, neither Spinoza nor Leibniz, neither Newton nor Huygens, not one theoretically thinking individual. Having singled this 'residue' out from logic, Kant was satisfied that what remained was not very much, a few quite general propositions formulated in fact by Aristotle and his commentators.

---

[4] *Hegel's Lectures on the History of Philosophy*, Vol. II, p. 210.

From the angle from which Kant surveyed the history of logic it was impossible to draw any other conclusion; for it went without saying that if one sought only those propositions in logic with which everyone equally agreed, both Spinoza and Berkeley, both the rationalist-naturalist and the theologian, and all their disagreements were taken out of the brackets, then nothing else would remain within the brackets, nothing except those completely general *ideas* (notions) about thought that seemed indisputable to all people thinking in the defined tradition. There thus existed a *purely empirical* generalisation, really stating only that not a single one of the theoreticians so far occupying themselves with thought had actually disputed a certain totality of judgments. But you could not tell from these judgments whether they were true in themselves, or were really only common and generally accepted illusions.

For all theoreticians had hitherto thought (or had only tried to think) in accordance with a number of rules. Kant, however, transformed the purely empirical generalisation into a theoretical judgment (i.e. into a universal and necessary one) about the subject matter of logic in general, about the legitimate limits of its subject matter: 'The sphere of logic is quite precisely delimited; its sole concern is to give an exhaustive exposition and a strict proof of the formal rules of all thought. . . .'[5] Here 'formal' means quite independent of how thought precisely is understood, and

---

[5] Immanuel Kant. *Op. cit.,* p 18.

of its origins and objects or goals, its relations to man's other capacities and to the external world, and so on and so forth, i.e. independent of how the problem of the 'external' conditions within which thinking is performed according to the rules is resolved, and of metaphysical, psychological, anthropological, and other considerations. Kant declared these rules to be absolutely true and universally obligatory for thought in general, 'whether it be *a priori* or empirical, whatever be its origin or object, and whatever hindrances, accidental or natural, it may encounter in our minds (*Gemüt*)'.[6]

Having thus drawn the boundaries of logic ('that logic should have been thus successful is an advantage which it owes entirely to its limitations, whereby it is justified in abstracting—indeed, it is under obligation to do so—from all objects of knowledge and their differences....'[7]), Kant painstakingly investigated its fundamental possibilities. Its competence proved to be very narrow. By virtue of the formality mentioned, it of necessity left out of account the differences in the views that clashed in discussion, and remained absolutely neutral not only in, say, the dispute between Leibniz and Hume but also in a dispute between a wise man and a fool, so long as the fool 'correctly' set out whatever ideas came into his head from God knew where, and however absurd and foolish they were. Its rules were such

---

[6] *Ibid.*, p 18.
[7] *Ibid.*

that it must logically justify any absurdity so long as the latter was not self-contradictory. A self-consistent stupidity must pass freely through the filter of general logic.

Kant especially stresses that 'general logic contains, and can contain, no rules for judgment',[8] that is 'the faculty of *subsuming* under the rules; that is, of distinguishing whether something does or does not stand under a given rule (*casus datae legis*)'.[9] The firmest knowledge of the rules in general (including the rules of general logic) is therefore no guarantee of their faultless application. Since 'deficiency in judgment is just what is ordinarily called stupidity', and since 'for such a failing there is no remedy',[10] general logic cannot serve either as an 'organon' (tool, instrument) of real knowledge or even as a 'canon' of it, i.e. as a criterion for testing ready-made knowledge.

For what then, in that case, is it in general needed? Exclusively for checking the correctness of so-called analytical judgments, i.e. ultimately, acts of verbal exposition of ready-made ideas already present in the head, however unsound these ideas are in themselves, Kant stated in full agreement with Berkeley, Descartes, and Leibniz. The contradiction between a concept (i.e. a rigorously defined idea) and experience and the facts (their determinations) is a situation about which general logic has no right to say anything, be-

---

8 Immanuel Kant. *Op. cit.*, p 177.
9 *Ibid.*
10 *Ibid.*

82

cause then it is a ques. on already of an act of subsuming facts un·' r the definition of a concept and
not of disclosures of the sense that was previously
contained in the concept. (For example, if I affirm
that 'all swans are white', then, having seen a
bird identical in all respects except colour with
my idea of a swan, I shall be faced with a difficulty, which general logic cannot help me to resolve in any way. One thing is clear, that this
bird will not be subsumed under my concept
'swan' without contradiction, and I shall be obliged to say: it is not a swan. If, all the same, I
recognise it as a swan, then the contradiction between the concept and the fact will already be
converted into a contradiction between the determinations of the concept, because the subject of
the judgment (swan) will be defined through two
mutually exclusive predicates ('white' and 'not
white'). And that is already inadmissible and
equivalent to recognition that my initial concept
was incorrectly defined, and that it must be altered, in order to eliminate the contradiction.)

So that every time the question arises of whether or not to subsume a given fact under a given
concept, the appearance of a contradiction cannot
be taken at all as an index of the accuracy or
inaccuracy of a judgment. A judgment may prove
to be true simply because the contradiction in the
given case *demolishes* the initial concept, and
reveals its contradictoriness, and hence its falsity.
That is why one cannot apply the criteria of
general logic unthinkingly where it is a matter
of experimental judgments, of the acts of sub-

suming facts under the definition of a concept, of acts of concretising an initial concept through the facts of experience. For in such judgments the initial concept is not simply explained but has new determinations added to it. A synthesis takes place, a uniting of determinations, and not analysis, i.e. the breaking down of already existing determinations into details.

All judgments of experience, without exception, have a synthetic character. The presence of a contradiction in the make-up of such a judgment is consequently a natural and inevitable phenomenon in the process of making a concept more precise in accordance with the facts of experience.

To put it another way, general logic has no right to make recommendations about the capacity of a judgment since this capacity has the right to subsume under the definition of a concept those facts that directly and immediately *contradict* that definition.

Any empirical concept is therefore always in danger of being refuted by experience, by the first fact that strikes the eye. Consequently, a judgment of a purely empirical character, i.e. one in which an empirically given, sensuously contemplated thing or object functions as subject (e.g. our statement about swans), is true and correct only with the obligatory reservation: 'All swans *that have so far come within our field of experience* are white'. Such a statement is indisputable, because it does not claim to apply to any individual things of the same kind that we have not yet been able to see. And further experience has the right to correct our definitions and to alter the predicates of the statement.

Our theoretical knowledge is constantly coming up against such difficulties in fact, and always will.

But if that is so, if science develops only through a constant juxtaposition of concepts and facts, through a constant and never ending process of resolving the conflict that arises here again and again then the problem of the theoretical scientific concept is sharply posed immediately. Does a theoretical scientific generalisation (concept), claiming universality and necessity, differ from any empirical, inductive 'generalisation'? (The complications that arise here were wittily described a century or more later by Bertrand Russell in the form of a fable. Once there was a hen in a hen-coop. Every day the farmer brought it corn to peck, and the hen certainly drew the conclusion that appearance of the farmer was linked with the appearance of corn. But one fine day the farmer appeared not with corn but with a knife, which convincingly proved to the hen that there would have been no harm in having a more exact idea of the path to a scientific generalisation.)

In other words, are such generalisations possible as can, despite being drawn from only fragmentary experience relative to the given object, nevertheless claim to be concepts providing scientific *prediction*, i.e., to be extrapolated with assurance to future experience about the self-same object (taking into consideration, of course, the effect of the diverse conditions in which it may be observed in future)? Are concepts possible that express not only and not simply more or less chance common attributes, which in another place and another time may not be present, but also the 'substance' itself, the *very 'nature' of the given kind of object*, the law of their existence? That is to say, are such determinations possible, in the absence of which the very object of the given concept is absent (impossible and unthinkable), and when there is already another object, which for that very reason is competent neither to confirm nor to refute the definition of the given concept? (As, for example, consideration of a square or a triangle has no bearing on our understanding of the properties of a circle or an ellipse, since the definition of the concept 'circumference of a circle' contains only such predicates as strictly describe the boundaries of the given kind of figure, boundaries that it is impossible to cross without passing into another kind). The concept thus presupposes such 'predicates' as cannot be eliminated (without eliminating the object of the given concept itself) by any future, 'any possible' (in Kant's terminology) experience.

So the Kantian distinction between purely empirical and theoretical scientific generalisations arises. The determinations of concepts must be characterised by universality and necessity, i.e. must be given in such a way that they cannot be refuted by any future experience.

Theoretical scientific judgments and generalisations, unlike purely empirical ones, in any case claim to be universal and necessary (however the metaphysical, psychological, or anthropological foundations of such claims are explained), to be confirmable by the experience of everybody of sound mind, and not refutable by that experience. Otherwise all science would have no more value than the utterances of the fool in the parable who produces sententious statements at every opportune and inopportune moment that are only pertinent and justified in strictly limited circumstances, i.e. thoughtlessly uttering statements applicable only on particular occasions as absolutes and universals, true in any other case, in any conditions of time and place.

The theoretical generalisations of science (and judgments linking two or more) have to indicate not only the definition of the concept but also the whole fullness of the conditions of its applicability, universality, and necessity. But that is the whole difficulty. Can we categorically establish that we have listed the whole series of necessary conditions? Can we be sure that we have included only the really necessary conditions in it? Or have we perhaps included superfluous ones, not absolutely necessary?

Kant remained open on this question, too; and he was right, since there is always the chance of a mistake here. In fact, how many times science has taken the particular for the general. In any case it is clear that 'general', i.e. purely formal, logic has no right here either to formulate a rule making it possible to distinguish the simply general from the *universal*; to distinguish that which has been observed *up to now* from that which will be observed *in the future*, however long our experience goes on for and however broad the field of facts that it embraces. For the rules of general logic judgments of the type of 'all swans are white' are quite indistinguishable from statements of the type of 'all bodies are extended', because the difference in them consists not in the form of the judgment but exclusively in the content and origin of the concept embraced in it. The first is empirical and preserves its full force only in relation to experience already past (in Kant's parlance it is only true *a posteriori*); the second claims to a greater force, to be correct also in relation to the future, and to any possible experience regarding natural bodies (in Kant's parlance it is true *a priori*, i.e. prior to, before being tested by experience). For that reason we are convinced (and science lends our conviction the character of an apodictic affirmation) that however far we travelled in space and however deep we penetrated into matter we would never and nowhere encounter a 'natural body' that refuted our conviction, i.e. 'a body without extension'.

Why? Because there cannot be a body without extension in nature? To answer thus, Kant said, would be impudent. All we can say is the following: if, even in the infinite universe, such remarkable bodies did exist, they could never, in any case, come within our field of vision, within our field of experience. And if they could, then they would be perceived by us as extended, or would not be perceived at all. For such is the structure of our organs of perception that they can only perceive things in the form of space, only as extensions and continuities (in the form of time).

It may be said that they are such 'in themselves' (*an sich*); Kant did not consider it possible to deny that, or to assert it. But 'for us' they are precisely such, and cannot be otherwise, because then they would not in general be part of our experience, would not become objects of experience, and therefore would not serve as the basis for scientific statements and propositions, for mathematics, physics, chemistry, and other disciplines.

The spatial-temporal determinations of things (the modes of describing them mathematically) are thus rescued from danger of refutation by any possible experience, because they are precisely true on condition of that very experience being possible.

All theoretical propositions as such (i.e. all statements linking two or more determinations together) acquire a universal and necessary character and no longer need to be confirmed by experience. That is why Kant defined them as *a priori*, synthetic statements. It is by virtue of this character of theirs that we can be quite confident that two times two are four and not five or six not only on our sinful earth but also on any other planet; that the diagonal of a square will be just as incommensurate with its sides; and that the laws discovered by Galileo, Newton, and Kepler will be the same in any corner of the

Universe as in the part investigated by us. Because only and exclusively *universal* and *necessary* definitions (in the sense explained above), predicates of the concept, are linked together (synthesised) in these propositions. But if the main problem that science comes up against proves not to be analytical judgments but synthetic ones, and general logic is only competent to judge analytical correctness, then we must inevitably conclude that there must be a special logic, apart from general logic, having to do only with theoretical applications of the intellect, with the rules of producing theoretical (in Kant's parlance, *a priori*, synthetic) judgments, i.e. judgments that we are entitled to appraise as universal, necessary, and therefore objective.

'When we have reason to consider a judgment necessarily universal ... we must consider it objective also, that is, that it expresses not merely a reference of our perception to a subject, but a quality of the object. For there would be no reason for the judgments of other men necessarily agreeing with mine, if it were not the unity of the object to which they all refer, and with which they accord; hence they must all agree with one another.'[11]

True, we still do not know anything about the thing in itself, i.e. outside the experience of all people in general; but that, in the experience of all existing and future people organised like our-

---

[11] Immanuel Kant. Prolegomena zu einer jeden künftigen Metaphysik. In: *Sämtliche Werke* (Leipzig, 1938) p 58.

selves, it will necessarily look exactly the same (and therefore anybody will be able to test the correctness of our statement) a theoretical judgment must guarantee.

Hence Kant also drew the conclusion that there must be a logic (or rather a section of logic) that dealt specially with the principles and rules of the theoretical application of thought or the conditions of applying the rules of general logic to the solution of special theoretical problems, to acts of producing universal, necessary, and thus objective judgments. This logic was still not entitled, unlike general logic, to ignore the difference between knowledge (ideas) in content and origin. It could and must serve as an adequate canon (if not as an *organon*) for thinking that laid claim to the universality and necessity of its conclusions, generalisations, and propositions. Kant conferred the title of transcendental logic on it, i.e. the logic of truth.

The centre of attention here naturaliy turned out to be the problem of what Kant called the intellect's synthetic activity, i.e. the activity by which new knowledge was achieved, and not ideas already existing in the head clarified. 'By *synthesis*, in its most general sense,' he said, 'I understand the act of putting different representations together and of grasping what is manifold in them in one (act of) knowledge.'[12] Thus he assigned synthesis the role and 'sense' of the fundamental operation of thinking, preceding any

---

[12] Immanuel Kant. *Critique of Pure Reason*, p 111.

analysis in content and in time. Whereas analysis consisted in act of arranging ready ideas and concepts, synthesis served as an act of *producing* new concepts. And the rules of general logic had a very conditional relation to that act, and so in general to the original, initial forms of the working of thought.

In fact, Kant said, where reason had not previously joined anything together there was nothing for it to divide, and 'before we analyse our representations, the representations must themselves be given, and therefore as regards content no concepts can arise by way of analysis.'[13] So the original, fundamental, logical forms, it transpired, were not the principles of general logic, not the fundamental principles of analytical judgments (i.e. not the law of identity and the principle of contradiction), but only universal forms, schemas, and means of *uniting* various ideas into the body of some new idea, schemas ensuring *unity in diversity*, means of identifying the different and uniting the heterogeneous.

Thus, notwithstanding the formal order of his exposition, and despite it, Kant in essence affirmed that the really universal—initial and fundamental—logical forms were not those at all that were considered such by traditional formal logic, but that these were rather the 'second storey' of logical science, and so derivative, secondary, and true only insofar as they agreed with the more universal and important, with the propositions

---

[13] Immanuel Kant. *Critique of Pure Reason*, p -111.

relating to the *synthesis* of determinations in the composition of a concept and judgment.

It was clearly a complete revolution in views on the subject matter of logic as the science of thought. Not enough attention is usually paid to this point in expounding Kant's theory of thought, although it is here that he proved to be the real progenitor of a fundamentally new dialectical stage in the development of logic as a science. Kant was the first to begin to see the main *logical* forms of thinking in *categories*, thus including everything in the subject matter of logic that all preceding tradition had put into the competence of ontology and metaphysics, and never into that of logic.

'The union of representations in one consciousness is judgment. Thinking therefore is the same as judging, or referring representations to judgments in general. Hence judgments are either merely subjective, when representations are referred to a consciousness in one subject only, and united in it, or objective, when they are united in a consciousness generally, that is, necessarily. The logical functions of all judgments are but various modes of uniting representations in consciousness. But if they serve for concepts, they are concepts of their necessary union in a consciousness, and so principles of objectively valid judgments.'[14]

Categories are also 'principles of objectively valid judgments'. And just because the old logic

_____

14 Immanuel Kant. Prolegomena. *Op. cit.*, p 66.

93

had turned up its nose at investigating these fundamental logical forms of thinking, it could neither help the movement of theoretical, scientific knowledge with advice nor tie up the loose ends in its own theory. 'I have never been able to accept the interpretation which logicians give of judgment in general,' Kant said. 'It is, they declare, the representation of a relation between two concepts. I do not here dispute with them as to what is defective in this interpretation—that in any case it applies only to *categorical*, not to hypothetical and disjunctive judgments (the two latter containing a relation not of concepts but of judgments), an oversight from which many troublesome consequences have followed. I need only point out that the definition does not determine in what the asserted *relation* consists.'[15]

Kant clearly posed the task of understanding categories as logical units, and of disclosing their logical functions in the process of producing and transforming knowledge. True, as we shall see below, he also displayed an almost uncritical attitude to the definitions of the categories borrowed by logic from ontology. But the problem was posed: the definitions of categories were understood as logical (i.e. universal and necessary) schemas or the principles of linking ideas together in 'objective' judgments.

Categories were thus those universal forms (schemas) of the activity of the subject by means of which coherent experience became possible in

---

[15] Immanuel Kant. *Critique of Pure Reason*, p 158.

general, i.e. by which isolated perceptions were fixed in the form of knowledge: '...Since experience is knowledge by means of connected perceptions, the *categories* [my italics.—*EVI*] are conditions of the possibility of experience, and are therefore valid *a priori* for all objects of experience.'[16] Any judgment, therefore, that claimed to universal significance, always—overtly or covertly—included a *category*: 'we cannot think an object save through categories...'.[17]

And if logic claimed to be the science of thinking it must also develop just this doctrine of categories as a coherent system of categorial determinations of thought. Otherwise it simply had no right to call itself the science of thought. Thus it was Kant (and not Hegel, as is often thought and said) who saw the main essence of logic in categorial definitions of knowledge, and began to understand logic primarily as the systematic exposition of categories, universal and necessary concepts characterising an object in general, those very concepts that were traditionally considered the monopoly of metaphysical investigations. At the same time, and this is linked with the very essence of Kant's conception, categories were nothing other than universal forms (schemas) of the cognitive activity of the subject, purely logical forms of thinking understood not as a psychic act of the individual but as the 'generic' activity of man, as the impersonal

---

[16] Immanuel Kant. Prolegomena. *Op. cit.*, p 171.
[17] *Ibid.*, p 173.

process of development of science, as the process of the crystallising out of universal scientific knowledge in the individual consciousness.

Kant, not without grounds, considered Aristotle the founder of this understanding of logic, that same Aristotle on whom, following mediaeval tradition, responsibility had been put for the narrow, formal understanding of the boundaries and competence of logic, though in fact it was not his at all. Kant, however, reproached Aristotle for not having given any 'deduction' of his table of categories, but simply only setting out and summing up those categories that already functioned in the existing consciousness of his time. The Aristotelean list of categories therefore suffered from 'empiricism'. In addition, and on Kant's lips the reproach sounds even more severe, Aristotle, not having been content with explaining the logical function of categories, had also ascribed a 'metaphysical meaning' to them, explaining them not only as logical (i.e. theoretical cognitive) schemes of the activity of the mind but also as universal forms of existence, universal determinations of the world of things in themselves, that is to say he 'hypostatised' the purest logical schemas as metaphysics, as a universal theory of objectivity as such.

Kant thus saw Aristotle's main sin as having taken the forms of thinking for the forms of being or existence, and so having converted logic into metaphysics, into ontology. Hence also the task of having, in order to correct Aristotle's mistake, to convert metaphysics into logic. In other words

Kant still saw the real significance of Aristotle, through the converting prism of his initial precepts, as the 'father of logic' and understood that Aristotle was such in his capacity as author of the *Metaphysics*. So Kant once and for all cut the roots of the mediaeval interpretation both of Aristotle and of logic, which had seen the logical doctrine of the Stagirite only in the texts of the *Organon*. This unnatural separation of logic from metaphysics, which in fact was due not to Aristotle at all but to the Stoics and Scholastics, acquired the force of prejudice in the Middle Ages, but was removed and overcome by Kant.

Kant did not give his system of categories in the *Critique of Pure Reason*, but only posed the task of creating one in general fashion, 'since at present we are concerned not with the completeness of the system, but only with the principles to be followed in its construction...'.[18] He also did not set out the logic, but only the most general principles and outlines of its subject matter in its new understanding, its most general categories (quantity, quality, relation, and modality, each of which was made more concrete in three derivatives). Kant considered that the further development of the system of logic in the spirit of these principles no longer constituted a special work: '...it will be obvious that a full glossary, with all the requisite explanations, is not only a possible, but an easy task.'[19] '...It can easily be carried

---

[18] Immanuel Kant. Prolegomena. *Op. cit.*, p 114.
[19] *Ibid.*, p 115.

out, with the aid of the ontological manuals—
for instance, by placing under the category of
causality the predicables of force, action, pas-
sion; under the category of community the predicables of presence, resistance; under the pre-
dicaments of modality, the predicables of coming
to be, ceasing to be, change, etc.'[20]

Here again, as was the case with general logic,
Kant displayed an absolutely *uncritical* attitude
to the theoretical baggage of the old metaphysics,
and to the determinations of categories developed
in it, since he reduced the business of creating
the new logic to very uncritical rethinking, to a
purely formal transformation of the old metaphysics (ontology) into logic. In practice it some-
times resulted simply in the renaming of
'ontological' concepts as 'logical'. But the very
carrying out of the task posed by Kant very
quickly led to an understanding that it was not
so simple to do, since what was required was not
a formal change but a very serious and far-
reaching, radical transformation of the whole
system of philosophy. Kant himself still did not
clearly and completely realise this fact; he had
only partially detected the dialectical contradictions of the old metaphysics, in the form of the
famous four antinomies of pure reason. A start,
however, had been made.

According to Kant categories were purely
logical forms, schemas of the activity of the intellect linking together the facts of sensuous

---

[20] Immanuel Kant. Prolegomena. *Op. cit.*, p 115.

experience (perceptions) in the form of concepts and theoretical (objective) judgments. In themselves categories were empty, and any attempt to use them as other than logical forms of the generalisation of empirical facts led one way or the other only to balderdash and logomachy. Kant expressed this idea in his own manner, affirming that it was impossible in any case to understand categories as abstract determinations of things in themselves as they existed outside the consciousness of people and outside experience. They characterised, in a universal (abstract-universal) way only the *conceivable* object, i.e. the external world *as and how we of necessity thought of it*, as and how it was represented in consciousness after being refracted through the prism of our sense organs and forms of thinking. Transcendental logic, therefore, the logic of truth, was logic, and *only logic*, only the doctrine of thinking. Its concepts (categories) told us absolutely nothing about how matters stood in the world outside experience, whether, in the world of the 'transcendental' outside the bounds of experience, there was causality, necessity, and chance, quantitative and qualitative differences, a difference in the probability and inevitability of an event occurring, and so on and so forth. That question Kant thought it impossible to answer; but in the world as given to us by experience matters stood exactly as logic pictured them, and science needed nothing more.

Science was therefore always and everywhere obliged to discover causes and laws, to differentiate the probable from the absolutely inevitable, to explain and numerically express the degree of probability of any particular event happening, and so on. In the world with which science was concerned there was no need, even as hypothetically assumed factors, for 'unextended' or 'eternal' factors (i.e. taken outside the power of the categories of space and time), 'incorporeal' forces, absolutely unalterable 'substances', and other accessories of the old metaphysics. The place of the old ontology must now be taken not by some one science, even though new in principle and clarified by criticism, but only the whole aggregate of real experimental sciences—mathematics, mechanics, physics, chemistry, celestial mechanics (i.e., astronomy), geology, anthropology, physiology. Only all the existing sciences (and those that might arise in the future) together, generalising the data of experience by means of the categories of transcendental logic, were in a position to tackle the task that the old ontology had monopolised.

To *tackle* it Kant, however, emphasised, but by no means to *solve* it. They could not solve it; for it was insoluble by the very essence of the matter and not at all because the experience on which such a picture of the world as a whole was built was never complete, and not because science, developing with time, would discover more and more new fields of facts and correct its own propositions, thus never achieving absolute finality in its constructions of the world in concepts. If Kant had argued like that he would have been absolutely right; but with him this quite true thought acquired a rather different form of expression, and was converted into a basic thesis of agnosticism, into an affirmation that it was impossible in general to construct a unified, scientifically substantiated picture of the world even relatively satisfactory for a given moment of time.

The trouble was that any attempt to construct such a picture inevitably collapsed at the very moment of being made, because it was immediately smashed to smithereens by antinomies and immanent contradictions, by the shattering forces of dialectics. The picture sought would inevitably be self-contradictory, which was the equivalent for Kant of its being *false*. Why was that so? The answer is in the chapter of the *Critique of Pure Reason* devoted to analysis of the logical structure of reason as the highest synthetic function of the human intellect.

Another task, it turned out, remained outside the competence of either general or transcendental logic, a task with which scientific understanding was constantly in collision, that of the theoretical synthesis of all the separate 'experimental' statements that made up a single theory developed from a single common principle. Now the job already was not to generalise, i.e. to unite and link together, the sensuously contemplated, empirical facts given in living contemplation, in order to obtain concepts, but the *concepts themselves*. It was no longer a matter of schemas of the synthesis of sensuous facts in reason, but of the unity of reason itself and the products of its activity in the structure of a theory, in the structure of a system of concepts and judgments. Generalising of the factual data by means of a concept, and the generalising of concepts by means of a theory, by means of an 'idea' or general guiding principle, were of course quite different operations. And the rules for them must be different.

There is therefore yet another storey in Kant's logic, a kind of 'metalogic of truth' bringing under its critical control and surveillance not individual acts of rational activity but all reason as a whole: Thinking with a capital 'T', so to say; thinking in its highest synthetic functions and not separate and partial operational schemas of synthesis.

The striving of thought to create a single, integral theory is natural and ineradicable. It cannot be satisfied, and does not wish to be, by simple aggregates, simple piling up of partial generalisations, but is always striving to bring them together, to link them together by means of general principles. It is a legitimate striving, and since it is realised in activity and thus appears as a separate power, Kant called it reason (*Vernunft*) in distinction from understanding. (*Verstand*). Reason is the same as understanding, only it is involved in the solving of a special task, explanation of the absolute unity in diversity, the synthesis of all its schemas and the results of their application in experience. Naturally it also operates there according to the rules of logic, but in resolving this task, thought, though exactly observing all the rules and norms of logic (both general and transcendental) without exception, still inevitably lands in a contradiction, in self-destruction. Kant painstakingly showed that this did not happen as a consequence of slovenliness or negligence in any thinking individuals at all, but precisely because the individuals were absolutely guided by the requirements of logic, true, where its rules and norms were powerless and without authority. In entering the field of reason, thinking invades a country where these laws do not operate. The old metaphysics struggled for whole millenia in hopeless contradictions and strife because it stubbornly tried to do its job with unsuitable tools.

Kant set himself the task of discovering and formulating the special 'rules' that would subordinate the power of thinking (which proved in fact to be its incapacity) to organise all the separate generalisations and judgments of experience into a unity, into the structure of an integral, theoretical schema, i.e. to establish the legislation of reason. Reason, as the highest synthetic function of the intellect, 'endeavours to carry out the synthetic unity, which is thought in the category, up to the completely unconditioned'.[21] In this function thinking strives for a full explanation of all the conditions in which each partial generalisation of understanding (each concept and judgment) can be considered justified without further reservations. For only then would a generalisation be fully insured against refutation

---

[21] Immanuel Kant. Prolegomena. *Op. cit.*, p. 318.

by new experience, i.e. from contradiction with other, just as correct generalisations.

The claim to absolutely complete, unconditional synthesis of the existing determinations of a concept, and so of the conditions within which these determinations are unreservedly true is exactly equivalent to a claim to understand things in themselves. In fact, if I risk asserting that subject A is determined by predicate B in its *absolute totality*, and not just in part that existed or might exist in our field of experience, I remove the very limitation from my assertion (statement) that transcendental logic has established for all experimental judgments; that is to say, I am no longer stating that it is true only in conditions imposed by our own forms of experience, our modes of perception, schemas of generalisation, and so on. I begin to think that the statement ascribing predicate B to subject A is already true not only within the conditions of experience but outside them, that it relates to A not only as the object of any possible experience but also irrespective of that experience, and defines A as an object existing in itself.

That means to remove *all* the limitations governing it from the generalisation, including the conditions imposed by experience. But all the conditions cannot be removed, 'for the conception of the absolute totality of conditions is not applicable in any experience, since no experience is unconditioned'.[22] This illegitimate *demarche* of

_____

[22] Immanuel Kant. Prolegomena. *Op. cit.*, p 318.

thinking Kant called transcendental application of reason, i.e. the attempt to affirm that things in themselves are such as they appear in *scientific* thinking, that the properties and predicates we attribute to them as objects of any possible experience also belong to them when they exist in themselves and are not converted into objects of somebody's experience (perceptions, judgments, and theorising).

Such a transcendental application of understanding entails contradictions and antinomies. A logical contradiction arises within reason itself, disrupting it, breaking up the very form of thinking in general. A logical contradiction is also an index for thought indicating that it has taken on the solution of a problem that is in general beyond its strength. A contradiction reminds thought that it is impossible to grasp the ungraspable (boundless).

Understanding falls into a state of logical contradiction (antinomy) here not only because, and even not so much because, experience is always unfinished, and not because a generalisation justified for experience as a whole has been drawn on the basis of partial experience. That is just what reason can and must do, otherwise no science would be possible. The matter here is quite different; in trying fully to synthesise all the theoretical concepts and judgments drawn from past experience, it is immediately discovered that the *experience already past* was itself internally antinomic if it of course was taken as a whole and not some arbitrarily limited aspect or fragment of it in which, it goes without saying, contradiction may be avoided. And the past experience is already antinomic because it includes generalisations and judgments synthesised according to schemas of categories that are *not only different* but are directly opposite.

In the sphere of understanding (*Verstand*), as transcendental logic showed, there were pairs of mutually opposing categories, i.e. schemas of the action of thinking having diametrically opposite directions. For example, there is not only a category of identity orienting the intellect to discovering the same invariant determinations in various objects, but also its polar category of difference, pointing to exactly the opposite operation, to the discovery of differences and variants in objects seemingly identical. In addition to the concept of necessity there is the concept of chance, and so on. Each category has another, opposite to it and not unitable with it without breaking the principle of contradiction. For clearly, difference is not identity, or is non-identity, while cause is not effect (is non-effect). True, both cause and effect are subsumed purely formally under one and the same category of interaction, but that only means that a higher category embracing both of them is itself subordinated to the law of identity, i.e. ignores the difference between them. And any phenomenon given in experience can always be comprehended by means both of one and of another categorial schema directly opposite to it. If, for example, I look on some fact as an effect, my search is directed to an infinite number of phenomena and circumstances *preceding* the given fact, because behind each fact is the whole history of the Universe. If, on the contrary, however, I wish to understand a given fact as a cause, I shall be forced to go into the chain of phenomena and facts *following* it in time, and to go further and further away from it in time with no hope of encountering it again anywhere. Here are two mutually incompatible lines of search, never coinciding with one another, two paths of investigating one and the same fact. And they will never converge because time is infinite at both ends, and the causal explanation will go further and further away from the search for effects.

Consequently, relative to any thing or object in the Universe, two mutually exclusive points of view can be expressed, and two diverging paths of investigation outlined, and therefore two theories, two conceptions developed, each of which is created in absolute agreement with all the requirements of logic and with all the facts (data of experience) relating to the matter, but which nevertheless, or rather precisely because of this, cannot be linked together within one theory without preserving and without reproducing this same logical contradiction within it. The tragedy of understanding is that it itself, taken as a whole, is immanently contradictory, containing categories each one of which is as legitimate as the other, and whose sphere of applicability *within the framework of experience* is not limited to anything, i.e. is as wide as experience itself. In relation to any object, therefore, two (at least, of course) mutually opposite theories inevitably must always arise and develop, before, now, and henceforth, forevermore, each of which advances a fully logical claim to be universal, to be correct in relation to all experience as a whole.

The antinomies could be eliminated in one way only, by discarding from logic exactly half of its categorial schemas of synthesis, recognising one category in each pair as legitimate and correct, and banning the other from use in the arsenal of science. That is what the old metaphysics did. It, for example, proclaimed chance or fortuity a purely subjective concept, a characteristic of our ignorance of the causes of phenomena, and so converted necessity into the sole objective categorial schema of a judgment, which led to recognition of the fatal inevitability of any fact, however minute and ridiculous.

That is why Hegel somewhat later called this method of thinking *metaphysical*. It was, in fact, characteristic of the old, pre-Kantian metaphysics, delivering itself from internal contradictions simply by ignoring half of all the legitimate categories of thought, half of the schemas of judgments with objective significance; but at the same time the question arises of which category in the polar pair to prefer and keep, and which to discard and declare a 'subjective illusion'. Here, Kant showed, there was not, and could not be, any objective basis for choosing. It was decided by pure arbitrariness, by individual preference. Both metaphysical systems were therefore equally correct (both the one and the other went equally with the universal principle) and equally subjective, since each of them denied the objective principle contrary to it.

The old metaphysics strove to organise the sphere of reason directly on the basis of the law of identity and of the principle of contradiction in determinations. The job was impracticable in principle because, if categories were regarded as the universal predicates necessarily inherent in some subject, then this subject must be the thing in itself; but the categories, considered as the predicates of one and the same subject of a judgment, prove to contradict *one another* and to create a paradoxical situation. And then the statement fell under the principle of contradiction, which Kant formulated thus: '...No predicate contradictory of a thing can belong to it....'[23] So, if I determine a thing in itself through a category, I still have no right, without breaking the principle, to ascribe the determinations of the opposing category to it.

Kant's conclusion was this: quite rigorous analysis of any theory claiming to be an unconditionally full synthesis of all determinations (all the predicates of one and the same thing in itself), claiming the unconditional correctness of its own judgments, will always discover more or less artfully disguised antinomies in the theory.

Understanding, clarified by criticism, i.e. conscious of its legitimate rights and not claiming any

---

[23] Immanuel Kant. Prolegomena. *Op. cit.*, p 190.

sphere of the transcendental banned to it, will always strive for an unconditionally full synthesis as the highest ideal of scientific knowledge, but will never permit itself to assert that it has already achieved such a synthesis, that it has finally determined the thing-in-itself through a full series of its universal and necessary predicates, and so given a full list of the conditions of the truthfulness of its concept. The age-old theoretical opponents should therefore, instead of waging endless war to the death, come to some kind of peaceful co-existence between them, recognising the equal rights of each other to relative truth, to a relatively true synthesis. They should understand that, in relation to the thing-in-itself, they are equally untrue, that each of them, since he does not violate the principle of contradiction, possesses only part of the truth, leaving the other part to his opponent. Conversely, they are both right in the sense that understanding as a whole (i.e. reason) always has not only different interests within it but also opposing ones, equally legitimate and of equal standing. One theory is taken up with the identical characteristics of a certain range of phenomena, and the other with their differences (the scientific determinations, say, of man and animal, man and machine, plant and animal). Each of the theories realises in full the legitimate, *but partial* interest of reason, and therefore neither the one nor the other, taken separately, discloses an objective picture of the thing as it exists outside of and prior to consciousness, and independently of each

110

of these interests. And it is impossible to unite these theories into one without converting the antinomic relation between them into an antinomic relation between the concepts within one theory, without disrupting the deductive-analytical schema of its concepts.

What should 'critique of reason' give to scientific understanding? Not, of course, recipes for eliminating dialectics from knowledge; that is impossible and impracticable because knowledge as a whole is always obtained through polemic, through a struggle of opposing principles and interests. It is therefore necessary that the warring parties in science will be fully self-critical, and that the legitimate striving to apply its principle rigorously in investigating the facts will not be converted into paranoic stubbornness, into dogmatic blindness preventing the rational kernel in the theoretical opponent's statements from being seen. Criticism of the opponent then becomes a means of perfecting one's own theory, and helps stipulate the conditions for the correctness of one's own judgments more rigorously and more clearly, and so on and so forth.

Thus the 'critique of reason' and its inevitable dialectic were converted by Kant into the most important branch of logic, since prescriptions were formulated in it capable of rescuing thought from the bigoted dogmatism into which understanding inevitably fell when it was left to its own devices (i.e. thinking that knew and observed the rules of general and transcendental logic and did not suspect the treacherous pitfalls and traps

111

of dialectics), and also from the natural complement of this dogmatism, scepticism.

After this broadening of the subject matter of logic, after the inclusion in it both of the categorial schemas of thinking and principles of constructing theories (synthesis of all concepts), and after the comprehension of the constructive and regulative role and function of *ideas* in the movement of knowledge, this science acquired the right for the first time to be, and to be called, the *science of thinking*, the science of the universal and necessary forms and patterns of real thought, of the processing of the facts of experience and the facts of contemplation and representation. In addition, *dialectics* was also introduced into the structure of logic, as the most important branch crowning the whole, that same dialectics that had seemed, before Kant, either a 'mistake', only a sick state of the intellect, or the result of the casuistic unscrupulousness and incorrectness of individual persons in the handling of concepts. Kant's analysis showed that dialectics was a necessary form of intellectual activity, characteristic precisely of thinking concerned with solving the highest synthetic problems[24] and with constructing a theory claiming universal significance, and so *objectivity* (in Kant's sense). Kant thus weaned dialectics, as Hegel put it, of its seeming arbitrariness and showed its absolute necessity for theoretical thinking.

---

[24] See V. F. Asmus. *Dialektika Kanta* (Kant's Dialectics) (Moscow, 1930) pp 126-127.

Since it was the supreme synthetic tasks that were pushed to the foreground in the science of that period, the problem of contradiction (the dialectics of determinations of the concept) proved to be the central problem of logic as a science. At the same time, since Kant himself considered the dialectical form of thought a symptom of the futility of scientists' striving to understand (i.e. to express in a rigorous system of scientific concepts) the position of things outside their own Ego, outside the consciousness of man, the problem also rapidly acquired ideological significance. The fact is that at that time the development of science was generating ever tenser conflicts between its theories, ideas, and conceptions. The Kantian 'dialectic' did not in fact indicate any way out, no path for *resolving* conflicts of ideas. It simply stated in general form that conflict of ideas was the natural state of science, and counselled ideological opponents everywhere to seek some form or other of compromise according to the rule of live and let live, to hold to their truth but to respect the truth of the other man, because they would both find themselves ultimately in the grip of subjective interests, and because objective truth common for all was equally inaccessible to both of them.

In spite of this good advice, however, not one of the really militant theories of the time wanted to be reconciled with such a pessimistic conclusion and counsel, and orthodoxy became more and more frantic in all spheres as the revolutionary storm drew nearer. When, in fact, it broke,

Kant's solution ceased to satisfy either the orthodox or the revolutionaries. This change of mood was also reflected in logic in the form of a critical attitude to the inconsistency, reticence, and ambiguity of the Kantian solution.

These moods were expressed most clearly of all in the philosophy of Fichte; through it the 'monistic' strivings of the times to create a single theory, a single sense of law, a single system of all the main concepts on life and the world, also burst into the sphere of logic, into the sphere of understanding of the universal forms and patterns of developing thought.

ESSAY FOUR

The Structural Principle of Logic.
Dualism or Monism

Kant did not accept the improvements that Fichte suggested for his theory of thought, on the grounds that they led directly to a need once more to create that very unified metaphysic that Kant had declared impossible and doomed to death from internal contradictions. Before Fichte, in fact, there loomed the image of a certain, perhaps transcendental (in the Kantian sense), but still single and uncontradictory system of concepts providing the main principles of life for humanity. Dialectics was dialectics, but a true theory appertaining to the most important things in the world should still be the one and only theory: 'The author of this system, for his part, is convinced that there is only one single philosophy, as there is only one single mathematics, and that as soon as this one possible philosophy had been founded and recognised, no new one will arise, and that everything that hitherto had been called philosophy will be counted as an attempt and preparation. . .'.[1]

This single system should still, in spite of Kant's advice, *defeat* any other not agreeing with it. For that it would have to be 'more rational' in every respect, in other words would have to explain and interpret the other system and so become broader than it.

For Fichte the position that Kant pictured as eternally insuperable, i.e. the existence of two equally true, and at the same time equally untrue, theories, was only a temporary, transitional state of spiritual culture that had to be overcome and resolved in a united, single world conception (*Weltanschauung*). The dialectic that Kant recognised on the scale of all scientific knowledge developing through discussion Fichte therefore wished to incorporate into a single scientific system that would include the principle opposing it, interpret it in a certain fashion, and convert it into its own, partial and derivative, principle.

Let the single world conception be transcendental as before, i.e. let it equally say nothing about the world in itself; but for all normally thinking people it should be one and the same, necessarily universal, and in that sense absolutely objective. The dualism that Kant affirmed as a quality of the eternally insuperable state of spiitual culture seemed to revolutionary-minded Fichte only a manifestation of the timidity and

[1] J. G. Fichte. *Sonnenklarer Bericht an das grössere Publikum über das eigentliche Wesen der neuesten Philosophie* (Berlin, 1801) p IV.

inconsistency of thought in realising its own principles. Logic could not justify two mutually exclusive systems at once and if, for all that, it did, then not everything in it was in order. Fichte sought and found the fundamental inconsistency in the Kantian doctrine on thought in the initial concept that Kant consciously proposed as the basis of all his constructions, in the concept of the 'thing-in-itself'. Already, in this concept, and not in the categorial predicates that might be ascribed to things, there was a flagrant contradiction: the supreme fundamental principle of all analytical statements was violated, the principle of contradiction in determinations. This concept was thus inconsistent in a logically developed system-theory. In fact, *in the concept* 'of a thing as it exists before and outside any possible experience' there was included a bit of nonsense not noted by Kant: to say that the Ego was *conscious* of a thing *outside consciousness* was the same as to say that there was money in one's pocket outside one's pocket.

Whether the famous 'thing-in-itself' existed was not the question here; for, Fichte was convinced that its *concept* was logically impossible. It was therefore also impossible to build a *system of concepts* on this foundation because the flaw of contradiction ran right through the very foundation of Kant's theoretical construction.

Fichte's conclusion was irreproachable: to think a thing-in-itself meant to think the unthinkable (from the standpoint of the principle of contradiction, of course), meant to violate the supreme fundamental principle of all analytical statements in the very course of their substantiation. He reproached Kant with having set a bad example of juggling with the rules of logic itself in the course of substantiating his own system of logic.

Fichte posed the problem as follows. Was logic itself, as a science, obliged to follow the same principles that it affirmed as absolutely universal for any correct thinking, or was it entitled to ignore them? Should logic be a science among other sciences, or was it rather to be likened to a wilful princeling who dictated laws obligatory for all other people but not binding in himself? The question, it would seem, was purely rhetorical. But surely, according to Kant, it was right after all that man thought of things given in contemplation (i.e. in the field of all special sciences) by one set of rules (those of the logic of truth) and about the things given in thought by another set (in the spirit of transcendental dialectics). It was not surprising that contradictions and the flaws of antinomies appeared between understanding and reason, and, furthermore, within reason itself.

But in that case the very concept of thinking, of the subject, I, was made senseless from the very beginning, i.e. was made contradictory within itself. All the fundamental categories of logic proved to be concepts that denoted not only different but diametrically opposite objects of thought. So we got the position that there were two different Is in every person, in every thinking individual, in constant polemic with each other. One of them contemplated the world and the other thought. Correspondingly, it was suggested, there were two different worlds, the contemplated and the thought of, although they merged into one in direct experience and in real life.

In general Kant was also inclined to that idea, that the I itself, the subject of thinking, was also a 'thing-in-itself'. And for that reason, when one tried to create a system of all the determinations of this I, i.e. a logic as a system of the logical parameters of thinking, the system proved contradictory through and through, i.e. self-destroying. As a result, if one followed Kant, it was quite impossible to construct a logic as a science. It was impossible, in constructing it, to observe the very rules that it prescribed as universal and necessary for all other sciences. But then there was no thought in general as one and the same capacity in different applications, but two different subjects, two different Is (each of which had to be considered without connection with the other) as two fundamentally heterogeneous objects, yet nevertheless called by one and the same name.

Apart from the fact that this led to a muddle of concepts (Kant himself was forced to call one of the Is phenomenal and the other noumenal), the very idea of logic as a science quite lost sense for, according to Fichte, all the conclusions drawn from considering thinking about *thinking* (as a 'thing-in-itself' or noumenon) would equally have

119

no relation at all to thinking about *things given in contemplation and representation.* So all the propositions of logic (i.e. of thinking about thinking) would have no binding force for thinking about things, i.e. for the thinking of natural scientists.

Hence that central idea of Fichte's philosophy was born, the idea of a general scientific doctrine, a theory that, unlike Kantian logic, would set out principles that were really significant for any application of thought. This science would set out laws and rules equally binding on both thinking about thinking and thinking about things. Thinking about thinking, i.e. logic, must provide a model and example of observation of the principles of thought (the principles of scientific scholarship) for the other sciences in general. These principles must remain *the same* both when thinking was directed to phenomena in mathematics, physics, or anthropology, and when directed to *concepts,* i.e. to itself.

For a concept was just as much an object of scientific study as any other object; the more so that we only knew any other object *scientifically* insofar as it was expressed in concepts, and in no other way. That meant that to determine or define a concept and to determine the object were absolutely identical expressions.

The initial principle of Fichte's science of science (*Wissenschaftslehre*) was therefore not the contrast or opposition of things and consciousness, of the object and its concept, but the opposition within the I itself. From two different, dualistically isolated halves, having no connection at all with each other, you could not create a single, integral system. What was needed was not dualism, but monism, not two initial principles but one only. Because, when there were two different initial principles, there were two different sciences, which never merged into one.

Fichte also interpreted the object and its concept as two different forms of existence of one and the same I, as the result of self-differentiation of the I into itself. What had appeared to Kant as the object or 'thing-in-itself' (object of the concept) was in fact the product of the unconscious, unreflecting activity of the I, since it produced the sensuously contemplated image of the thing by virtue of imagination. A concept was the product of the same activity, but taking place with *consciousness* of the course and meaning of the activities themselves.

The initial identity of concept and object, or rather of the *laws* by which the sensuously contemplated world was constituted and those by which the world thought about, the world of concepts, was built, was therefore already included in the identity of their subject, of their origin. The Ego initially created a certain product, by virtue of imagination, and then began to look on it as something distinct from itself, as the object of the concept, as the non-Ego or not-I. But in fact the Ego, in the form of the not-I, was solely concerned, as before, with itself, and regarded itself as it were from the side, as in a mirror, as an object located outside itself.

121

The job of thought as such thus consisted in understanding its own activity in creating an image of contemplation and representation, in consciously *reproducing* that which it had produced earlier unconsciously, without giving itself a clear account of what it was doing. The laws and rules of discursive thinking (i.e. of thinking that consciously obeyed the rules) were in fact nothing more nor less than the *conscious laws* (expressed in logical schemas) *of intuitive thinking*, i.e., of the creative activity of the subject, the I, creating the world of contemplated images, the world as it is given in contemplation.

Only from that angle did the operation of comparing a concept with its object acquire rational sense. Fichte showed that the opposition, in no way mediated, between the thing-in-itself and its concept (dualism) had also led Kant into the fullest dualism both within the concept itself and within the system of concepts. Fichte quite consistently, from his point of view, showed that denying the principle of the identity of an object and its concept as the initial principle of logic and logical thinking meant, as well, *denying the principle of identity in its general form*, as a logical postulate. In other words, if logic as a science considered the principles of identity and contradiction (the latter was nothing but a negative formulation of the law of identity) as an absolutely indispensable condition of the correctness of any thinking, then it must apply them to the understanding of *thinking* itself, and to determinations of its specific object or subject matter, which was the concept.

In logic, in fact, *the concept was also the object of study*; and logic must dissect the concept of concept. That being so, in logic, of all sciences, the concept and its object were fully synonymous because any other object could only interest logic to the extent that, and insofar as, it had already been converted into a concept, expressed in a concept; for logic was not concerned with sensuously contemplated or intuited things.

There was no place in logic, therefore, as a scientific system of determinations of thought, and could not be, for such expressions as a 'thing-in-itself' or 'the object before its expression in a concept'. Logic had no business in general with such objects, for they were transcendental things for it, that is lying beyond its possibilities of expression, beyond its competence. Beyond those limits began the sphere of super-rational understanding, faith, irrational intuition, and other aptitudes; but they were not competent to operate within science. And Fichte did not want to have anything to do with them, at least within his *Wissenschaftslehre*.

Such, in essence, was Fichte's criticism of Kant's attempt to create a logic, a classically consistent model (from the logical angle) of a 'right-wing' critique of dualism, i.e. from the position of subjective idealism. It is no accident that all modern Neopositivists repeat Fichte word for word, discarding the question of the relation of a concept to the external object in a similar way, and replacing it by the question of its relation to the concept (i.e. of a concept to itself). The latter relation is also naturally defined as an *identity* of 'sign' (the term that takes the place of 'concept') and of the designatum. The law of identity (and correspondingly the principle of contradiction) then boils down to this, that one and the same sign must designate one and the same thing, must have one and the same meaning or sense.

Let us, however, return to Fichte. He, having contemplated building a system of logic and a logical model of the world, naturally came into conflict with the conceptions of his teacher Kant. To Kant his venture immediately seemed unacceptable: '...I declare herewith: that I consider *Fichte's science of knowledge* a completely untenable system. Because a pure science of knowledge is nothing more nor less than a *naked* logic, which, with its principles, does not achieve the material of understanding but abstracts from the content of the latter as *pure logic*, from which it is a vain task to pick out a real object and therefore one never attempted, but which, when transcendental philosophy is at stake, must pass into metaphysics.'[2]

Kant from the outset repudiated the attempt to create a metaphysic; not because it must describe

---

[2] *Johann Gottlieb Fichte's Leben und literarischer Briefwechsel* von seinem Sohne Immanuel Hermann Fichte, Bd. II (Leipzig, 1862) p 161. See also R. Adamson. *Fichte* (London, 1881) pp 50-51.

the world of things in themselves but only because Fichte wanted to create a logic which when applied, would ensure the building of a single system of concepts not cracked by the flaws of antinomies, a system that would synthesise in itself all the most important conclusions and generalisations of science. That, according to Kant, was unrealisable however the system obtained was interpreted, whether objectively (materialistically) or subjectively (transcendentally). One way or the other it was equally impossible. It was quite natural therefore that Kant considered it a groundless reproach that he 'had not created a system' but had only posed the task and equipped science with the important (though not completely and consistently worked out) principles needed for such a construction: 'The presumption, attributing to me the intention, that I wished to provide a propaedeutic to transcendental philosophy and not the system of the philosophy itself, is incomprehensible to me.'3

Fichte began by insisting that Kant's system of philosophical concepts was not a system but only a concatenation of the opinions and principles needed for constructing such and, moreover, very inconsistent ones. The argument therefore passed to a new plane: what was a system? What were the principles and criteria enabling us to differentiate a *system of scientific concepts* from a concatenation of judgments each of which

---

3 *Ibid.*, p 162.

might be true of and by itself, but was not, all the same, linked with the others?

In explaining his concept of 'system', Fichte formulated it as follows: '...My exposition, *as any scientific one must* [my italics—*EUI*], proceeds from the most indefinite, which is again determined before the reader's eyes; therefore, in the course of it, quite other predicates will, of course, be linked to the objects than were originally linked to them; and further this exposition will very often pose and develop propositions which it will afterward refute, and in this way advance through antithesis to synthesis. The finally determined true result obtained from it is only found here in the end. You, of course, only seek this result; and the way that it is found is of no interest to you.'[4] Thus, according to him a *system* proved to be the result of the removal of contradictions. They remained unmediated outside the system, and as such negated each other. Therefore there was no system in Kant, but only propositions unmediated by development that he took over ready-made and vainly tried to link together formally, which was impossible since they had already negated one another. With Fichte the whole arose precisely from bits, through their successive unification.

In counterposing his position to Kant's, Fichte said: 'The generality that I affirm in no way arises through apprehension of plurality under unity, but rather through derivation of endless

---

[4] J. G. Fichte. *Sonnenklarer Bericht*, pp 217-218.

plurality from the unity grasped in a glance.'[5] The initial generality, which was differentiated in the course of its own disintegration into a variety of particulars, also had to be established in scientific system before all else.

But Kant's image of the whole, too, was brought to light through the particulars from which it was built up, as from bits. And now, after Kant, the task could only consist in getting from this whole to the particulars, in testing and re-testing them critically, in purging the system of everything superfluous and fortuitous, and in preserving in it only the diverse definitions that were required of necessity in order to construct the whole. The whole (the generality) then proved to be a criterion for the selection of particulars; it was now necessary to develop the whole system of particulars systematically, step by step, starting from that one, single principle. Then we would get science, a system.

In other words, the logic of analysing Kant's philosophy had immediately concentrated Fichte's attention on the problems that had been brought together in the section of the *Critique of Pure Reason* on transcendental dialectic, on the problems of the absolute synthesis of concepts and judgments into a theory understood as a single system. There also was to be found the 'growing point' of logical science. Fichte proposed calling the new field of investigation of thought 'the science of knowledge' (*Wissenschaftslehre*), i.e.

---

5 *Ibid.*, pp 112-113.

the science of the universal forms and laws of development of a system of scientific determinations. These determinations would, of course, be invariant for any particular science, be it mathematics or physiology, celestial mechanics or anthropology. They must define *any object*, and that meant they must represent a system of universal determinations of every possible object of scientific study, its logical 'parameters'.

Science, consequently, must give itself a clear account of its own activities, achieve self-consciousness, and express its self-consciousness through the same categories through which it comprehended everything else, any other object given in experience. The science of science was in fact a system of determinations outlining any possible object, and at the same time the structure of the subject constructing that object, and the logical forms in turn were the forms realised, abstractly expressed, and built up into a system of rational consciousness in general, i.e. not the empirical consciousness of this or that individual, but only the necessary and universal forms (schemas) of the activity of any possible being possessing thought.

What used to be called 'logic' was only an abstract schema of this universal activity of constructing any possible object in consciousness. Fichte specially investigated and explained his understanding of the relation between his *Wissenschaftslehre* and 'logic'. The latter proved to be only an abstract schema of the same activity as was outlined in the former. Therefore, as he put it, the *Wissenschaftslehre* could not be demonstrated logically, and it was impossible to premise any logical proposition on it, *even the law of contradiction*; on the contrary, any logical thesis and all logic must be deduced from the *Wissenschaftslehre*. Thus logic received its significance from the science of knowledge and not the science of knowledge from logic.

The fact was that theoretical 'schematising' (i.e. operations controlled by logical rules and propositions) by no means lacked necessary and natural premises. Their analysis became vitally important precisely when thinking came up against certain *changes*, which in essence were a uniting of contradictory, opposing determinations.

Here Fichte did not differ with Kant, who well understood that change 'presupposes one and the same subject as existing with two opposite determinations',[6] and that one and the same thing could at *different moments* of time have a certain predicate A, and then lose it and be not-A. If, however, a thing could lose predicate A without ceasing to be itself, and be transformed into something else (into the object of another concept), that meant, according to Kant, that the disappearing predicate did not belong *to the concept* of the given thing, was not one of its universal and necessary determinations. The concept (in contrast to the empirically general representation) expressed only the absolutely unaltered characteristics of the thing. *Theory was not in-*

---

6 Immanuel Kant. *Critique of Pure Reason*, p 218.

terested in change—that old prejudice also trapped Kant. All change was a matter of empirical views and not of theory. Theory, constructed according to the rules of logic, must give a picture of the object withdrawn, as it were, from the power of time. Theory had no right to include in the definitions of a concept those determinations that the passage of time had washed off a thing. A concept therefore always came under the protective cover of the principle of contradiction.

But how did matters stand if the object represented in theory (in the form of a theoretical schema constructed according to the rules of logic) began to be understood not as something absolutely unchanging but as something *coming into being,* if only in consciousness, as with Fichte? How did it stand with the principle of contradiction, if the logical schema had in fact to picture a *process of change,* the beginning or the becoming of a thing in consciousness and by virtue of consciousness? What was to be done if logic itself was understood as an abstract schema of the construction of an object in the eyes of a reader, i.e. as a schema of the consistent enriching of the initial concept with newer and newer predicates, a process whereby there was initially only A, but later B necessarily arose (which in itself was understandably not A or was not-A), and then C, D, E, right down to Z? For even the simple combination of A and B was a combination of A and not-A. Or was B nevertheless A?

Fichte's conclusion was: choose between these two—either the principle of contradiction was absolute (but then no synthesis was possible in general, not uniting of different determinations) or there was ·development and a synthesis of the determinations of concepts (and they did not conform to the absolute requirements of the principle of contradiction).

Fichte followed another, third path. He started from the point that what was impossible to represent in a concept, that is to say the combination or synthesis of mutually exclusive determinations, constantly occurred in *contemplation* or intuition (in activity to construct the image of a thing). Thus, by analysing Zeno's famous paradox and showing that we divide any *finite* length into *infinity*, Fichte concluded: 'From this you see that what is impossible and contradictory in the concept actually happens in the intuition of space.'[7]

If, therefore, you came up against a contradiction in a logical expression, the thing was not to hasten to declare that it could not be, but to return to the intuition (*Anschauung*), the rights of which were higher than those of formal logic; and if analysis of the act of intuition showed you that you were forced *of necessity* to pass from one determination to another, opposing one in order to unite it with the first, if you saw that A was necessarily transformed into not-A, you would then be obliged to sacrifice the requirement of the principle of contradiction. Or rather,

---

[7] J. G. Fichte, *Thatsachen des Bewusstseyns* (Stuttgart and Tübingen, 1817) p 9.

that principle could not then be regarded as the indisputable measure of truth.

Fichte also demonstrated this dialectic from the example of the origin of consciousness, of the 'positing' of the non-Ego (not-I) by the activity of the Ego, the differentiation of the person himself as the thinking being from himself as thought of, as the object of thought. Could a person become aware of himself, of the acts of his own consciousness, of his own constructive activity? Obviously he could. He not only thought, but also thought about his thinking, and converted the very act of thinking into an object; and that exercise was always called logic.

The starting point in this case, as was shown above, could only be I, the Ego (*Ich, das Selbst*) understood as the subject of an activity producing something different from itself, that is to say the product, the recorded result. The Ego was initially equal to itself (I = I) and, considered as something active, creative, creating, already contained in itself the necessity of its own transformation into a non-Ego (not-I). We saw and knew this directly, from self-observation, for consciousness in general was realised only insofar as a representation of something else arose in it, a representation of a non-Ego, a thing, an object. There could not be empty consciousness not filled by anything.

The transformation of the I into the not-I occurred, of course, quite independently of study of the rules of logic, and before their study. It was a matter of natural—'primary'—thought. It

132

was a prototype of logical, reflective thinking that discovered a certain law-governed necessity in itself, in its activity in constructing images of things, and then expressed it in the form of a number of rules, in the form of logic, in order henceforth to follow them consciously (freely) and to submit to them.

All logical rules must therefore be *deduced*, derived by analysis of actual thinking. In other words they had a certain prototype with which they could be compared and contrasted. This approach differed radically from Kant's position, according to which all fundamental logical principles and categories had only to be consistent in themselves so that their predicates did not include contradictions. Kant therefore *postulated* the laws and categories of logic, while Fichte required them to be *deduced*, and their universality and necessity demonstrated.

True, Fichte, like Kant, did not encroach on the actual content of logical forms and laws. On the contrary, he wanted to demonstrate the correctness of all the logical schemas known in pre-Kantian and Kantian logic, by indicating more rigorous conditions for their application. But he thereby also limited them, establishing that the principle of contradiction was only fully authoritative in relation to one determination, and that within a developing system it was constantly being set aside or discarded, since each succeeding determination negated the preceding one both individually and absolutely.

Fichte tried in that way to deduce the whole

system of logical axioms and categories, in order to understand them as the universal schemas, consistently taken into practice, for uniting of empirical data, as degrees or phases of the production of concepts, for concretising the initial, still undivided concept into a number of its universal and necessary predicate-definitions. There is no need here to explain why Fichte did not succeed in his programme of deducing the whole system of logical categories, why he did not succeed in turning logic into an exact science, into a system. In this case it was important to have posed the problem. Let us merely note that the ensuing criticism of his conception was directed precisely at explaining the reasons for his failure, and at analysing the premises that hindered his idea of reforming logic, of deducing its whole content from an investigation of actual thinking, and in that way of uniting within one and the same system categories that stood in a relation of direct negation of one another (formal contradiction), and that had seemed to Kant to be antinomically uncombinable, and not includable within one non-contradictory system.

Schelling, too, occupied himself primarily, from the very start, with the problem of a *system* of knowledge, or rather, with the problem of the antinomies that inevitably arose in attempts to create such a system. The difficulty lay exclusively in representing in a logically systematic way the fact (directly apparent (intuitive) to every thinking being) that the world is one, and that thought, striving for its own systematic presentation, was also one in itself. But the rules of logic and laws of the activity of the intellect were such that the single world, refracted through them, was split into two in the eyes of reason. And each of the halves so formed claimed the role of the sole true, absolute and unconditional, logically systematic representation of the whole world.

Like Kant, Schelling saw the way out not on the plane of logically consistent constructing of determinations but in the practical realisation of the system that presented itself to the human mind as most worthy of it, most acceptable to it, most in accord with its innate strivings. It was impossible to demonstrate anything by formal logic, i.e. to work out a system of uncontradictory proofs that could not be counterposed by its opposite. Such a system simply had to be taken on direct trust and followed unconditionally. The system that Schelling himself chose was expressed in the following principle: 'My *vocation* in criticism is to *strive for unchangeable selfness (Selbstheit), unconditional freedom, unlimited activity.*'[8] This system could never be completed, it must always be 'open-ended' in the future—such was the concept of *activity*. Activity when completed, embodied, 'fixed' in its product, was already not activity.

It is easy to discern Fichte's proud principle in these arguments. It was activity that was the absolute and unconditional that could never and must

8 F. W. J. Schelling. *Frühschriften.* Erster Band (Berlin, 1971) p 152.

never be *completed* by the creation of a system crystallised once and for all; the absolutely universal in which new differences, differentiations, peculiarities, and particulars would ever be arising and accordingly be merged (identified) with what had previously been established, and on *ad infinitum*. This form of criticism, according to Schelling, embraced dogmatism as its own moment, because it confirmed the thesis that the whole edifice of man's spiritual culture must henceforth be built on a clear and categorically established foundation, namely on the understanding that the sole subject of all possible predicates was the Ego, i.e., the infinite creative principle existing in every human being and freely presuming both itself and the whole world of objects that it saw, contemplated (intuited), and thought, and on the understanding that no one result already achieved had the force of an absolute, 'objective' authority for the Ego, i. e. the force of dogma.

And if there were an opposing system that looked upon man as the passive point of application of previously given, externally objective forces, as a speck of dust in the vortex of elemental world forces, or a toy in the hands of God and his representatives on earth, that dogmatic system, though it had been rigorously proved formally and was not self-contradictory, would have to be combated by the supporter of true criticism until final victory.

Like Fichte, Schelling stood for a new, critical, 'enlightened' dogmatism: 'Dogmatism—such is the result of our common inquiry—is irrefutable *in theory* because it itself has quit the theoretical field to complete its system *in practice*. It is thereby *refutable* in practice for us *to realise* a system *in ourselves* absolutely opposed to it.'[9]

Practical activity was the 'third' thing on which all mutually contradictory systems came together as on common soil. It was there, and not in the abstractions of pure reason, that the real battle raged that could and must be won. That was where the proof lay that one party, unswervingly following its principle, defended not only its own, egoistic private interest, but also an interest coinciding with the universal tendencies of the universe, i.e. with absolute and unconditional objectivity.

'Criticism cannot follow dogmatism into the sphere of the Absolute [understood purely theoretically—*EVI*], nor can the latter follow it, because for both there can be only one *assertion* as an absolute assertion that takes on notice of the opposing system, and that determines *nothing* for the opposing system.

'Only now, after both have encountered one another, one of them can no longer ignore the other, and whereas before [i.e. in the purely theoretically logical sphere—*EVI*] they were without any resistance to the position won, now the position must be *won by victory*.'[10]

That is the point that divided Fichte and Schelling from Kant; the intellectual culture of human-

---

[9] F. W. J. Schelling. *Frühschriften.* Erster Band, p 156.
[10] *Ibid.*, pp 131-132.

ity cannot lie eternally like Buridan's ass between two equally logical systems of ideas about the most important things in life. Mankind has, in practice, to act, to live; but it is impossible to act simultaneously in accordance with two opposing systems of recommendations. We are forced to choose one of them and then to act strictly in the spirit of its principles.

Kant himself, it is true, demonstrated in his last works that the arguments of practical reason must all the same tip the scales in favour of one system or the other, although on a purely theoretical plane they are absolutely equal. But with him this theme only broke through as one of the trends of his thinking, while Fichte and Schelling transformed it into the starting point of all their meditations. Hence the slogan about victory, too, in the theoretical sphere. One of the clashing logical conceptions must still prevail over the other, its opposite, and for that it must be reinforced by arguments no longer of a purely logical, rather purely scholastic quality, but armed with practical (moral and aesthetic) advantages as well. Then it was assured of victory, and not simply of the right and the chance of waging an eternal academic dispute.

Like Fichte, Schelling saw the main problem of the theoretical system in synthetic statements and in uniting them: 'It is these riddles that oppress the critical philosopher. His chief question is not how there can be analytical statements, but how there can be synthetic ones... The most comprehensible thing is how we define everything according to the law of identity, and the most enigmatic how we can define anything still outside this law.'[11]

That is aptly formulated. Any elementary act of synthesising determinations in a judgment—be it that A is B—in fact already requires us to go beyond the law of identity, i.e. to infringe the boundaries established by the principle of contradiction in determinations; for, whatever the adjoined statement B, it is in any case not A, is not-A. It is clearly the logical expression of the fact that any new knowledge infringes the strictly acknowledged limits of the old knowledge, refutes it, and revises it.

Any dogmatism that obstinately insisted on the knowledge already attained and mastered would therefore always reject any new knowledge from the outset on the sole grounds that it contradicted the old. And it did in fact formally contradict it because it was not analytically included in the old and could not be 'derived' from it by logical contrivances of any kind. It must be *united* with the old knowledge in spite of the fact that it formally contradicted it.

That meant, according to Schelling, that a genuine synthesis was not realised by purely theoretical ability that strictly adhered to the rules of logic, but by quite another capacity, which was not bound by the strict limitations of the fundamentals of logic, and even had the right to transgress them when it experienced a powerful need

---

[11] F. W. J. Schelling. *Frühschriften,* pp 129, 130.

to do so. 'A *system* of knowledge is necessarily either a trick, a game of ideas. . .—or it must *embrace* reality not through a theoretical ability, but through a practical one, not through a perceptive ability but through a *productive, realising* one, not through *knowledge* but through *action*.'[12]

With Kant this productive ability was called power of imagination (*Einbildungskraft*). Following him Schelling also plunged into analysis of it, which took him along a rather different road than Fichte's, onto the rails of an objective idealism that was not only reconciled to the thesis of the real existence of the external world but also built a theory of understanding it, although with Schelling himself this theory proved to be something quite different from *logic* and tended rather to a kind of aesthetics, to a theory of the artistic, aesthetic comprehension of the mysteries of the universe. For the men of science Schelling retained, as a working tool, the same old logic that he himself, following Fichte, declared to be a completely unsatisfactory instrument for understanding and to be justified solely as a canon of the outward systematisation and classification of material obtained by quite other, illogical, and even alogical, means.

Whereas Fichte had provided a classical model of criticism of Kant and his logic from the right, from the standpoint of a consistently constructed subjective idealism, another motif began to be

_____
[12] F. W. J. Schelling. *Frühschriften.* pp 126-127.

clearly seen in the reformatory strivings of the young Schelling, in tendencies leading him to materialism.

In the circles in which he moved, and where his thinking matured, quite other moods prevailed than those induced by Fichte's philosophy. All Fichte's thought had been concentrated on the social and psychic revolution stimulated in minds by the events of 1789-93. The flight of his imagination was also linked with the events and problems of those years; as the revolutionary wave subsided his philosophy folded its wings, and he could not find a new source of inspiration. For Schelling the fervour born of the revolution was only a certain stage that he reached as a sympathiser and even a disciple of Fichte; but, just as the forces of rude reality forced the most zealous Jacobins to reckon with them, so too it became clear to Schelling that to insist on one infinite creative power, the Ego, and on the strength of its moral fervour, in face of the persistent external world meant to bang one's head against the wall of incomprehension, as had actually happened in the end to Fichte.

Being closely linked with the circle of Goethe and the romantic writers, Schelling was much more interested than Fichte in nature (read: natural science) on the one hand, and in the inherited, traditional (in the parlance of Kant and Fichte, objective) forms of social life on the other hand. From the very beginning natural science and art constituted the medium that shaped his mind and his aspirations as an inquirer.

Schelling, it is true, began in the same way as Fichte; he too treated the opposition between subject and object as an opposition within human consciousness, as an opposition between the images of the external world that a person produced 'freely', and the images of the same world that he produced not freely but unconsciously, in obedience to a compelling force of necessity unknown to him. Like Fichte, Schelling warred with dogmatism (in the idea of which, for him, there were merged both religious orthodoxy, which ascribed necessity to an external God, and philosophical materialism, which ascribed it to external things, to 'pure objects'). For Schelling criticism was a synonym for the standpoint that the objective (universal and necessary) determinations of the human psyche were initially innate in the psyche itself and discovered in it in the course of its active self-discovery.

In that way Schelling, following Fichte, tried to overcome the dualism of Kant's conception; but with Fichte the dualism had still been preserved and even reproduced in ever sharper form within his conception. All the Kantian antinomies had in fact been merged by him in a single antinomy, in the contradiction between two halves of one and the same Ego. One of them unconsciously created the objective world of images by the laws of causality, space, and time, while the other reconstructed it in the spirit of the requirements of the transcendental ideal, in accordance with the requirements of 'morality'.

It was presupposed, as before, that there were

two different Egos in every person, but it was not known how and why they were connected together; and although Fichte united them in the concept *activity*, the opposition was reproduced again within the Ego in the form of two different principles of activity. And as before it remained an open question what was the inner necessary relation between the two halves of the human Ego. Did they have a common root, a common source, a common 'substance', through the splitting of which the two halves of necessity arose?

Fichte did not find the solution, in spite of his concept of activity. The world of necessary ideas was formed within all Egos quite independently of the activity of the 'better' I, before it awoke in man. The 'better' I already, during its awakening, found the existing world in itself. In turn it (the pure form of practical reason or the ideal) came into the world of necessarily produced ideas, as it were, from outside, like a judge who emerged from somewhere unknown and who brought with him the criteria for evaluating and re-evaluating what existed, i.e. the fruits of the Ego's past labour.

The human Ego was again converted into a field of endless battle between two originally heterogeneous principles. The absolute Ego must take the world of existing ideas, incomplete and unconnected, even mutually contradictory, in accordance with itself and one another. But that again was only attainable in infinity. 'Full agreement of man with himself, and—so that he can agree with himself—agreement of all things outside him with his necessary practical concepts of them—concepts that determine how they must be. . . .' (as Fichte formulated the essence of the problem[13]), proved unattainable in the existing world.

Fichte freed himself from the Kantian form of antinomies but reproduced them all intact in the form of contradictions within the very concept of 'activity'. The problem was simply transferred to the sphere of the individual psyche and so made completely insoluble. Schelling reached the same conclusion and began to seek a way out along a new path with the young Hegel. Gradually, in the course of criticising Fichte, the main outlines of a new conception began to appear.

Schelling and Hegel were more and more dissatisfied with the following 'points' in the position of Kant and Fichte:

(1) the posing of all the concrete burning issues of the day in a subjective, psychological form;

(2) the feeble appealing to 'conscience' and 'duty' that stemmed from that, which put the philosopher into the pose of a preacher of fine and noble but impracticable phrases and slogans;

(3) the interpretation of the whole sensuous empirical world, if not as hostile, at least as a passive obstacle to the dictates of 'duty' and the 'ideal';

(4) the absolute indifference to everything except pure morality (including the history of humanity

---

[13] J. G. Fichte. *Über den Gelehrten* (Berlin, 1956) p 45.

and of nature), and to natural science (which underlay Fichteanism);

(5) the powerlessness of the categorical imperative (ideal) in the struggle against the 'egoistic', 'immoral', 'irrational' motives of man's behaviour in society, the indifference of real earthly men to the preachers of the higher morality (how light all the means of paradise developed by the Church and supported by the fullest scholastic explanations were in the scales when the passions and forces of circumstance, upbringing, example, and government were thrown into the other pan; the whole history of religion from the beginning of the Christian era went to prove that Christianity could only make people good when they were already good, the young Hegel said, having in mind by the 'scholastic explanations' any philosophy oriented on morality, including that of Kant and Fichte);

(6) the difference, insuperable in principle, between the real and the proper, between necessary and free activity, between the world of phenomena and the active essence of man, etc., etc.

All that led to one thing, namely, to comprehending that it was ultimately necessary to find the 'common root' itself of the two halves of human being from which they both stemmed and could be understood. Only then would the human personality appear before us not as the passive point of application of external forces (be they nature or God), i.e. not as an object, but as something acting independently (*das Selbst*), as *subject*.

From that was born the idea of the philosophy

of identity. Like any *idea* it existed originally only in the form of an hypothesis, in the form of a principle not yet realised in detail, in the spirit of which the whole mass of existing theoretical material, and in particular the conception of Kant and Fichte, had to be critically revised.

Originally the young Schelling only affirmed that the two halves of the human being, which had been depicted by Kant and Fichte as originally heterogeneous in essence and origin (in spite of their efforts to link them), had something in common after all, i.e. that somewhere in the depths, in the initial essence of matter, they had been merged in one image before being torn apart and separated in dispute, discussion, and antinomy. Schelling's thesis stated that both forms of the Ego's activity (the unconscious and the consciously free) had really to be understood as two branches growing from one and the same trunk, and that it was necessary to discover that trunk first and then trace its growth before it forked.

Schelling had not yet affirmed anything more concrete and definite besides that such identity *must be* and *was*. He had said nothing about where exactly this initial identity was to be seen. His description was, in essence, negative; it was *not* consciousness, but it was also *not* matter; it was *not* spirit, but it was also *not* substance; it was *not* ideal, but it was also *not* real. What then was it?

Here, in Heine's witty comment 'philosophy ends with Herr Schelling and poetry—I mean folly—begins.' 'But Herr Schelling has now left

146

the philosophical path and is seeking through an act of mystical intuition to achieve contemplation of the absolute itself; he is seeking to intuit it at its centre, in its essence, where there is nothing ideal and nothing real, neither idea nor extension, neither subject nor object, neither mind nor matter, but there was who knows what!'[14]

Why did Schelling nevertheless turn from the path of philosophy here, from the path of thinking in rigorously defined determinations, to the path of poetry, to the path of metaphors and a kind of aesthetic intuition? Only because the logic that he knew and recognised did not permit the uniting of opposing contradictory predicates in concepts of one and the same subject. He, like Kant, held it sacred that the law of identity and the principle of contradiction were absolutely unbreakable laws for conceptual thinking, and that breaking them was tantamount to breaking the laws of thought in general, the forms of scientism. Here, he thought, in agreement with Fichte, that everything that was impossible in a concept (because of contradiction) became possible in contemplation or intuition.

Schelling supposed that all the acts performed consciously by man in accordance with the rules of logic had been quite fully and exactly described in the transcendental philosophy of Kant and Fichte. That part of philosophy seemed to

---

[14] Heinrich Heine. Zur Geschichte der Religion und Philosophie in Deutschland. In: *Werke und Briefe*, Bd. 5 (Aufbau-Verlag, Berlin, 1961) p 299.

him to have been created once and for all. He did not intend to reform it at all; he only wanted to broaden the scope, the sphere of action, of its principles, wanted them to embrace the fields that had fallen outside Fichte's field of vision, in particular natural science.

The turn to natural science here was not fortuitous. The fact was that the attempt to investigate the sphere of *unconscious activity* in more detail led directly to it, that is to say the attempt to investigate the mode of vital activity that man had followed before and irrespective of how he began a special reflection, converted himself into an object of special investigation, and began to reflect specifically on what originated within himself, and how it did so. But all his activity at this stage (which also followed from Kant's point of view), being subordinated to the conditions of space, time, and causality, came within the competence of the natural sciences. In other words, the forms and modes of unconscious activity were scientifically described precisely through the concepts of physics, chemistry, physiology, psychology, and so on.

For unconscious activity was nothing else than *life*, the mode of existence of *organic nature*, of the organism. But in the life of the organism (of any biological individual) mechanical, chemical, and electrical motions were joined together, and the organism could therefore be studied by mechanics, chemistry, physics, and optics. In the living organism, Nature had concentrated all her secrets and determinations, and had synthesised them. After the organism had been broken down into its constituents, however, the chief thing of all remained uncomprehended, namely, why were they linked together that way and not in some other way? Why in fact was a living organism obtained and not a pile of its components?

With a purely mechanical approach the organism proved to be something quite incomprehensible, because the principle of a mechanism was the uniting (consistent synthesis) of ready-made, previously given parts; the living organism, however, did not originate through the *building up of parts into a whole* but, on the contrary through the beginning or origin, the *generation of parts* (organs) from an originally undifferentiated whole. Here the whole preceded its own parts, and functioned in relation to them as the purpose they all served. Here each part could only be understood through its role and function in the whole, outside of which it simply did not exist, or not, in any case, as such.

The problem of understanding organic life was analysed by Kant in his *Critique of the Power of Judgment (Kritik der Urteilskraft)* as the problem of the purposefulness of the structure and function of the living organism. But the standpoint of transcendental idealism forced him to affirm that, although we and our reason could not cognise the organism other than by means of the concept of a goal, nevertheless it was impossible to attribute any goal to the organism in itself, because a goal presupposed consciousness (and that meant the whole apparatus of transcendental apperception) and the animal and vegetable did not possess such.

The problems of life also proved to be the stumbling block that forced Schelling to stop and critically re-examine certain concepts of the philosophy of transcendental idealism. Like Kant, he categorically objected to introducing supernatural causes into the framework of the thinking of the natural sciences On those grounds he resolutely rejected vitalism, the idea that, in inorganic nature (i.e. the world of mechanics, physics, and chemistry), a certain 'higher principle' descended from somewhere outside and organised the physical, chemical particles in the living body. There was no such principle *outside consciousness*, Schelling affirmed, following Kant. The naturalist must seek in nature itself the causes of the origin of the organism from inorganic nature. Life must be fully explained by way of natural science, without implicating any kind of extranatural or supernatural force in it. 'There is an older delusion, which is that organisation and life are inexplicable by the principles of Nature.—With it only so much can be said: the first source of organic nature is physically inscrutable; so this unproved statement serves no purpose other than to sap the courage of the investigator. . . . It would be at least one step toward that explanation if one could show that the succession of all organic beings had come about through the gradual evolution of one and the same organisation.'[15]

---

[15] F. W. J. Schelling. *Von der Weltseele* (Hamburg, 1809) pp vi-vii.

Man and his peculiar organisation stood at the logic apex of the pyramid of living creatures. And in that case we had every grounds and right to ascribe to nature itself, if not purpose in the transcendental sense, at least that objective characteristic which is reproduced in our reason (by virtue of its specifically transcendental structure) as a purpose, 'in the form of a goal'.

What was that characteristic Schelling did not consider it possible to say. In any case it was a matter of the capacity involved in nature itself to engender a succession of more and more complex and highly organised living creatures, up to and including man, in whom a 'soul', consciousness, was awakened and transcendental mechanisms arose, i.e. a capacity consciously (freely) to reproduce everything that occurred in nature unconsciously, without a goal or purpose.

But then it was necessary to think of nature not as naturalists had so far done (the mathematician plus the physicist, plus the chemist, plus the anatomist, each of them occupying himself with only his own private field and not even trying to link the results of his investigations with those of his neighbour). It must be considered as some kind of *primordial whole* in which the subject matter of the special sciences was *differentiated*. We must therefore not build up the picture of the whole like a mosaic, from the special sciences, but must endeavour, on the contrary, to understand them as consecutive stages in the development of one and the same whole, initially undivided. The idea of nature as a whole, quite characteristic of the classical Greeks and of Spinoza, Schelling also advanced as the main principle by which alone the antinomy between mechanism and organism could be scientifically resolved (without appeal to supernatural factors). 'As soon as our investigation ascends to the idea of Nature as an entity the opposition between mechanism and organism disappears immediately, an opposition that has long hampered the progress of natural science and that will long continue to block our enterprise's success in the eyes of quite a few....'[16]

Schelling sought the way out by developing the concepts of mechanics and organic life from one and the same truly universal principle, which led him to the idea of representing nature as a whole, as a *dynamic process* in the course of which each successive stage or phase negated the preceding one, i.e. included a *new* characteristic. The purely formal (analytical) determination of a higher phase of the process could therefore not be deduced from the determination of a lower one; that was done simply by making a synthesis, by adding on a new determination. It was not surprising that, when the higher phase of a dynamic process was put directly alongside a lower phase of the same process, they were thought to be two simultaneously co-existing 'objects' (which is precisely how they look in empirical intuition),

---

[16] F. W. J. Schelling. *Von der Weltseele*, pp vii-viii.

and proved to be mutually directly *contradictory*.

The basic task of the philosophy of nature, consequently, consisted just in tracing and showing how, in the course of a dynamic process, determinations *arose that were directly opposed* to the initial one. In other words, we thought of a dynamic process only as one of the gradual engendering of oppositions, of determinations of *one and the same thing*, i.e. of nature as a whole, that mutually negated one another.

Schelling saw in that the universal law of the natural whole, operating identically in the field of mechanics, and of chemistry, and of electromagnetism, and of organic life. Such was the truly universal (i.e. identical for all the phenomena of nature) law of bifurcation, of the polarisation of the initial state. The attraction and repulsion of masses in mechanics, the north and south poles in magnetism, positive and negative electricity, acids and alkalis in chemical reactions—such were the examples flooding in on Schelling from all sides, and supplied again and again by the discoveries of Volta and Faraday, Lavoisier and Kielmeyer. The most diverse scientific discoveries were seen as fulfilment of Schelling's predictions, and his fame grew. His disciples were to be found among doctors, geologists, physicists, and biologists; and that not by chance. Schelling's philosophy proposed a form of thinking, the need for which was already imminent in the womb of theoretical natural science. Exhilarated by success, Schelling continued to work the lode he had discovered for all it was worth.

But the transition of mutual opposites described appeared most marked and unsullied precisely on the boundary where natural and transcendental philosophy met, which was where the Ego arose from the sphere of the unconscious dynamic process (from the non-Ego), i.e. the transcendental, spiritual organisation of man, or, on the contrary, where objective knowledge of the not-I was born from the conscious activity of the I. This mutual, reciprocal passage of the determination of the Ego into a determination of the non-Ego demonstrated the action of the universal law of the dynamic process in its purest and most general form, i.e. the act of the transformation of A into not-A, of the bifurcation or splitting into two, of the 'dualisation' of the initial, originally undifferentiated state.

But how was the initial absolute state, identical in itself, to be thought of, from the polarisation of which there arose the main 'dualism' of the natural whole, i.e. the Ego and the non-Ego, the I and the not-I, the freely conscious creativity of the subject and the whole vast sphere of the 'dead', congealed, fossilised creative activity, the world of objects?

That was where the specifically Schelling philosophising began. It turned out that it was impossible to think of the initial identity, i.e. to express it in the form of a rigorously delimited concept. On being expressed in a *concept* it immediately came forward as an antinomic bifurcation. Identity was realised in the concept (in science) precisely through its absence, through

154

contrasts that had nothing formally in common between them.

We have reached a very important point. That Schelling called his system the philosophy of identity was not at all because it represented a system of determinations or definitions common to the I and the not-I. Rather the contrary. Schelling denied the possibility of such a *system of concepts* in principle. His philosophy was put forward in the form of two formally unjoined systems of concepts, formally opposed in all their determinations yet nevertheless mutually presupposing each other. One was the system of determinations of the Ego as such (transcendental philosophy); the other was the system of assembled universal determinations of the object, of the non-Ego (natural philosophy).

The first disclosed and described in the shape of formally non-contradictory constructions the specifically subjective forms of man's activity that it was impossible to ascribe to nature existing outside of and before human consciousness. The second, on the contrary, strove to disclose pure objectivity, carefully purged of everything introduced into it by man's *conscious, volitional* activity, and to depict the object as it existed 'before it entered consciousness'.

Within the confines of natural philosophy (theoretical natural science) the theoretical scientist 'fears nothing more than interference of the subjective in this kind of knowledge'. Within the limits of transcendental philosophy (logic and epistemology), on the contrary, he was 'most of all afraid that something objective has been implicated in the purely subjective principle of knowledge.'[17]

To sum up: if transcendental philosophy were constructed just as correctly as natural philosophy, there would be nothing of the other in the structure of each and there could not be a single concept or theoretical determination between them; for such a determination would directly infringe the two supreme principles of logic, the law of identity and the principle of contradiction. It would simultaneously express both the objective and the subjective, and would contain directly *identified opposites*. The two given sciences could not therefore be formally united into one. It was impossible to develop two series of scientific (formally correct) determinations from one and the same *concept* because it would be formally incorrect and inadmissible from the standpoint of the rules of logic.

Therefore philosophy on the whole was impossible as one science. From that Schelling concluded that the whole system of philosophy would 'find consummation in two fundamental sciences, which, mutually opposed in principle and direction, seek each other out and complement each other'.[18] There was not, and could not be, some 'third' science in which would be discovered whatever there was in common between the world in consciousness and the world outside consciousness,

---

[17] F. W. J. Schelling. *System des transzendentalen Idealismus* (Hamburg, 1957) p 11.

[18] *Ibid.*, p 10.

and which would be a system of laws and rules obligatory in the same way for the one world and the other. It was impossible in principle to present such laws and rules *in the form of a science* because it would then be built from the outset on an infringement of the law of identity.

But there were, all the same, laws common to the world and knowledge, otherwise it would be senseless in general to speak of knowledge, of agreement of the objective and the subjective, and the very concept of *truth* as the coincidence of knowledge with its object would be nonsense. *General* laws consequently did operate, but not as rigidly binding rules, but rather as reasons not strictly formulated, related to the aspirations of the poet-artist who directly experienced his blood relationship and unity with the cognised object and with nature. The artist of genius and nature operated by the same laws.

The identity of the laws of the subjective and objective worlds could only be realised in the act of creation. But creativity did not submit to formal schematising, dying and becoming fossilised in it. Thus it came about that 'an absolute Simple, Identical, cannot be comprehended or communicated through description, and not at all through conception. It can only be intuited.'[19] Here intuition was all powerful, the inspired intuition of creative insight, intellectual and aesthetic intuition. Thus it was, therefore, that Schelling's sys-

---

[19] F. W. J. Schelling. *System des transzendentalen Idealismus*, p 294.

tem culminated in and was completed by a philosophy of art.

Thus the primary identity was a fact but was not expressible in a *concept,* was the initial premise of any concept, but was not determined through a concept. Identity was, as it were, made up of two always diverging trends of investigation, namely demonstration of how the objective was transformed into the subjective (which was the competence of theoretical natural science, spinning its thread from mechanics through chemistry to biology and anthropology, i.e. to man), and demonstration of how the subjective was transformed into the objective (which was the competence of transcendental philosophy, starting from knowledge and its forms *as from fact,* and demonstrating the objectivity, i.e. the universality and necessity, of knowledge).

The problem consequently began to appear as follows: two diametrically opposite spheres stood facing one another contrasted in all their characteristics. Their identity (the fact of their agreement was truth) was realised precisely through the transition that transformed the one into the other. But the transition, the moment of the transition itself, was *irrational* and could not be expressed by a *non-contradictory concept,* because it was at that very moment that the transition from A into not-A took place, i.e. their coincidence, their *identity.* To express it in a *concept* meant to smash the form of the concept.

Here Schelling came directly up against the narrowness of the Kantian logic, which attributed to the law of identity and the principle of contradiction the character of the absolute premises of the very possibility of thinking in concepts. For there was *no room* within these rules for the moment of the *transition of opposite*s into one another, and it broke them. Schelling, while agreeing that there was self-destruction of the form of thinking here, was forced in fact to conclude that real truth could not be caught and expressed *through* a concept. In his eyes therefore art and not science represented the highest form of mental activity.

If the rules of general logic were absolute, then the passage of consciousness into nature and vice versa, by which the time-honoured identity of the subjective and the objective was realised, remained inexpressible in concepts; and the act of knowing was forced again and again to make a leap, a jump, an act of irrational intuition, of poetic seizing of the absolute idea, of truth.

In other words, Schelling, beginning with a quite justified statement of the fact that logic in its Kantian conception actually put an insurmountable barrier in the way of attempts to understand, that is to *express, the fact of the transformation of opposites into one another in concepts,* i.e. in rigorously defined determinations, took the step toward rejection of *logic in general.* It did not even occur to him to reform *logic itself* in order to make it a means of expressing what appeared in intuition (contemplation) as a self-evident fact. Instead he began to make up for and compensate the limitedness and insufficiency of the existing

159

logic (mistaken by him as the inferiority of thought as such), by the force of intellectual and aesthetic intuition, an absolutely irrational capacity that it was impossible either to study or to teach. This magic force also had to unite everything that reason (thought in general) was not in a position to join together but was only capable of ripping to bits, separating, and choking to death.

In his own constructions, in spite of a mass of bold guesses and ideas, some even of genius, that influenced the development of nineteenth century science, and which in essence had a clearly marked dialectical character, Schelling kept adopting the pose of a God-inspired prophet and genius, uniting without fear or doubt concepts that seemed to contemporary scientists to be fundamentally ununitable. And whereas he himself, in his youth, had had sufficient tact and competence in the field of the natural sciences, and had often hit the nail on the head by intuition, his pupils and successors, who adopted the empty schema from him but did not possess his erudition in science or his talent, reduced his method and manner of philosophising to the caricature that Hegel later jeered at so caustically.

Schelling, however, exposed the rigidity of Kant's logic. And though he did not set himself the task of reforming it radically, he prepared the ground very thoroughly for Hegel.

Logic as such remained only an episode in Schelling's system of ideas, an insignificant section of the transcendental philosophy, a scholastic description of rules of a purely formal order in accordance with which it was necessary only *to formalise*, i.e. to classify and schematise, knowledge obtained in quite another way and by quite other abilities. For Schelling logic, consequently, was by no means a *schema for producing knowledge*, but served as a means of describing it verbally, terminologically 'for others', of expressing it through a system of rigorously defined and non-contradictorily determined terms (Schelling himself called them 'concepts'). Ultimately its recommendations seemed only external, verbally explicated forms of knowledge, and nothing more.

The process of producing knowledge was itself, in fact, done by the power of imagination, which Schelling analysed very closely and circumstantially in the form of various 'intuitions'. And here, in the field of intuition and imagination he also discovered *dialectics* as the true schema of the productive, actively subjective capacity of man to understand and alter the world of the images and concepts of science.

So Schelling confirmed dialectics as the genuine theory of scientific knowledge, but then broke all its links with logic. His position returned logic once more to the pitiable condition in which it had been before the attempts of Kant and Fichte to reform it in accordance with the needs of the times.

After Schelling the problem consisted in *uniting dialectics* as the true schema of developing knowledge *and logic* as the system of rules of thinking in general. What was the relation of the rules of logic to the real schemas (laws) of the development of understanding? Were they different, mutually unconnected 'things'? Or was logic simply the conscious and deliberately applied schema of the real development of science? If it was, it was all the more inadmissible to leave it in its old, so primitive form. At this point the torch was taken up by Hegel.

Dialectics as Logic

Hegel's solution of the problem of the subject matter of logic has played a special role in the history of this science. In order to understand the Hegelian logic it is not enough just to clarify the direct sense of its propositions. It is more important and difficult to consider the real subject matter through the fanciful turns of Hegel's style. It is about this that we shall now speak, which will also give us a chance to understand Hegel critically, and to restore for ourselves an image of the original from its distorted presentation. Learning to read Hegel in a materialist way, as Lenin read him and advised reading him, means learning to compare his representation of the object critically with the *object itself,* at every step tracing the divergence between the copy and the original.

It would be an easy task if the reader had the two objects of this comparison—the copy and the original—ready-made before him. The copy exists. But where is the original? We cannot take the existing logical consciousness of the scientist as the original, for this consciousness itself must be tested for its logicality, and itself presupposes a

11•   163

critical analysis of existing logical forms from the standpoint of their correspondence with the real requirements of the development of science. And for an understanding of the real forms and laws of theoretical cognition Hegel's *Science of Logic*, despite all its faults associated with idealism, can offer more than the 'logic of science'.

The true logic of science is not given to us directly; it still has to be dug out and understood, and then converted into a consciously applied instrument for working with concepts, into a logical method of resolving problems that do not admit of solution by traditional logical methods. That being so, critical study of the *Science of Logic* cannot be reduced to a simple comparison of its propositions with those of the logic by which scientists are consciously guided, accepting it as irreproachable and admitting of no doubts.

So comparing the copy (the science of logic) with the original (with the actual forms and laws of theoretical understanding) proves to be quite a difficult matter. The difficulty is that Hegel's presentation of the subject matter (in this case thought) has to be compared critically not with a ready-made, previously known prototype of it, but with an object whose outlines are only beginning to be traced out for the first time in the course of a critical surmounting of the idealist constructions. This reconstruction is feasible if the structure of the optics through which Hegel examined the object of his investigation is clearly understood. This distorting lens, while a magnifying one (the system of the fundamental principles of

Hegelian logic) enabled him to see exactly, although in an idealistically distorted form, the *dialectic* of thought, which is the logic that remains invisible to the eye not philosophically equipped, and to simple common sense.

It is important, first of all, to understand clearly what the *real object* was that Hegel investigated and described in his *Science of Logic*, so as to find the critical range immediately in regard to his presentation. 'That the subject matter of logic is thought, with that everyone agrees,' Hegel stressed in his *Lesser Logic*.[1] Later, quite naturally, logic as a science received the definition of *thinking about thought* or thought thinking about itself.

In that definition and the conceptions expressed by it there is still nothing either of the specifically Hegelian or of the specifically idealist. It is simply the traditional ideas of the subject matter of logic as a science, quite clearly and succinctly expressed. In logic the object of scientific comprehension proves to be thought itself, while any other science is thinking about something else. In defining logic as thinking about thought, Hegel quite accurately indicated its sole difference from any other science.

The next question, however, arises from that and requires a no less clear answer. *But what is*

---

[1] G. W. F. Hegel. System der Philosophie. Erster Teil, Die Logik. In: *Sämtliche Werke*, Vol. 8 (Stuttgart, 1929) p 69. (In other works it is known by its original title *Encyclopaedie der philosophischen Wissenschaften im Grundrisse.—Tr.*)

thought? It goes without saying, Hegel replied (and one again has to agree with him), that the sole satisfactory answer can only be an exposition of the heart of the matter, i.e. a concretely developed theory, a *science of thought*, a 'science of logic', and not an ordinary definition. (Compare Engels' view in *Anti-Dühring*: 'Our definition of life is naturally very inadequate.... All definitions are of little value. In order to gain an exhaustive knowledge of what life is, we should have to go through all the forms in which it appears, from the lowest to the highest.'[2] And later: 'To science definitions are worthless because always inadequate. The only real definition is the development of the thing itself, but this is no longer a definition.'[3]

In any science, however, and therefore in logic too, one has to mark everything out in advance and outline its contours, if only the most general boundaries of the object of investigation, i.e. to indicate the field of the facts to which the given science must devote its attention. Otherwise the criterion for their selection will be unclear and its role will be tyrannous and arbitrary, taking only those facts into consideration that confirm its generalisations, and ignoring everything else as allegedly having no relation to the matter or to the competence of the science concerned. Hegel gave such a *preliminary* explanation, not concealing from the reader exactly what he understood by the word 'thought'.

[2] Frederick Engels. *Anti-Dühring*, p 98.
[3] *Ibid.*, p 391.

This is a very important point, and everything else hangs on proper understanding of it. It is no accident that the main objections to Hegel, both justified and unjustified, have hitherto been directed precisely at it. Neopositivists, for example, unanimously reproach Hegel with having inadmissibly broadened the subject matter of logic by his conception of thought, including in the sphere of examination a mass of 'things' that one cannot call thought in the usual and strict sense; above all the concepts traditionally referred to metaphysics, and to 'ontology', i.e. to the science of things themselves, the system of *categories* (the universal definitions of reality outside consciousness, outside subjective thinking understood as the psychic capability of man).

If thinking were to be so understood, the Neopositivist reproach must really be considered reasonable. Hegel actually understood as thought something at first glance enigmatic, even mystical, when he spoke of it as taking place outside man and apart from man, independently of his head, and of 'thought as such', of 'pure thought', and when he considered the object of logic to be precisely that 'absolute' superhuman thought. Logic in his definition must be understood even as having a content that *'shows forth God as he is in his eternal essence before the creation of Nature and of a Finite Spirit'.*[4]

---

[4] *Hegel's Science of Logic.* Translated by W. H. Johnston and L. G. Struthers, Vol. I (Allen and Unwin, London, 1929) p 60.

Such definitions are capable of confusing and disorienting at the very start. But of course there is no such 'thought' as some superhuman force creating nature, and history, and man himself and his consciousness from itself somewhere in the Universe. But is Hegel's logic then the presentation of a non-existent subject? Of an invented, purely fantastic object? In that case, how are we to rethink his constructions critically? With what, with what real object, must we compare and contrast his strings of theoretical determinations in order to distinguish the truth in them from the fallacy? With the real thinking of man? But Hegel would reply that in his *Science of Logic* it is a matter of quite *another* object, and that if empirically observed human thought is not like it, that is no argument against *his* logic, for criticism of a theory only makes sense when the theory is compared with the same object as it represents, and not with another one; and it is impossible to compare logic with the acts of thinking actually taking place in people's heads because people think very *illogically* at every step, even elementarily illogically, let alone according to a logic of a much higher order, of the kind that Hegel had in mind.

When you point out to a logician, therefore, that man's real thinking does not occur as it is depicted in his theory, he could reasonably reply that it was so much the worse *for this thinking* and that the theory did not need to be adapted to the empirical but that real thought must be made logical and brought into harmony with logical principles.

For logic as a science, however, a fundamental difficulty arises here. If it were only permissible to compare logical principles with logical thought, did that then not wipe out any possibility whatsoever of checking whether or not they were *correct*? It is quite understandable that these principles would always be in agreement with thoughts that had previously been made to agree with them. After all, it only meant that logical principles agreed with themselves, with their own embodiment in empirical acts of thought. In that case, a very ticklish situation was created for theory. Logic had in mind only logically immaculate thinking, and logically incorrect thinking was not an argument against its schemas. But it consented to consider only such thinking as logically immaculate as exactly confirmed its own ideas about thought, and evaluated any deviation from its rules as a fact falling outside its subject matter and therefore to be considered solely as a 'mistake' needing to be 'corrected'.

In any other science such a claim would evoke consternation. What kind of a theory was it that consented to take into account only such facts as confirmed it, and did not wish to consider contradictory facts, although there must be millions and billions such? But surely that was exactly the traditional position of logic, which was presented by its devotees as standing to reason, and which made logic absolutely unself-critical on the one hand and incapable of development on the other.

That, incidentally, was where Kant's illusion

originated, the illusion that logic as a theory had long ago acquired a fully closed, completed character and not only was not in need of development of its propositions but could not be by its very nature. Schelling also understood Kant's logic as an absolutely precise presentation of the principles and rules of thinking in concepts.

Hegel had doubts about the fact that it was the rules of logic that prevented understanding of the process of the passage of the concept into the object and vice versa, of the subjective into the objective (and in general of opposites into one another). He saw in it not evidence of the organic deficiency of thought but only the limitations of Kant's ideas about it. Kantian logic was only a limitedly true theory of thought. Real thought, the real subject matter of logic as a science, as a matter of fact was something else; therefore it was necessary to bring the theory of thought into agreement with its real subject matter.

Hegel saw the need for a critical reconsideration of traditional logic primarily in the extreme, glaring discrepancy between the principles and rules that Kant considered absolutely universal forms of thought and the real results that had been achieved by human civilisation in the course of its development. 'A comparison of the forms to which Spirit has risen in the worlds of Practice and Religion, and of Science in every department of knowledge Positive and Speculative—a comparison of these with the form which Logic—that is, Spirit's knowledge of its own pure essence—has attained, shows such a glaring discrepancy that it cannot fail to strike the most superficial observer that the latter is inadequate to the lofty development of the former, and unworthy of it.'[5]

Thus the existing logical theories did not correspond to the real *practice of thought,* and *thinking about thought* (i.e. logic) consequently lagged behind *thinking about everything else,* behind the thinking that was realised as the science of the external world, as consciousness fixed in the form of knowledge and things created by the power of knowledge, in the form of the whole organism of civilisation. In functioning as *thinking about the world,* thought had achieved such success that beside it *thinking about thought* proved to be something quite incommensurable, wretched, deficient, and poor. To take it on faith that human thought had really been and was guided by the rules, laws, and principles that in the aggregate constituted traditional logic was to make all the progress of science and practice simply inexplicable.

Hence there arose the paradox that the human intellect, which had created modern culture, had come to a standstill in amazement before its own creation. Schelling had also expressed this amazement of the 'spirit', and it was just at this point that Hegel began to differ with him.

Hegel considered that the rules by which the 'spirit' was actually guided, contrary to the illusions that it had created on its own account (in

5 *Ibid.,* p 62.

the person of professional logicians) and had set out in the form of textbooks of logic, could and must be brought out and set forth in the *form of a concept*, quite rationally, without shifting everything hitherto not comprehended onto 'intuition', i.e. onto an ability that was from the very outset something quite different from thought. Hegel's posing of the matter played a special role because it, for the first time, subjected all the main concepts of logical science, above all the concept of *thought*, to careful analysis.

At first glance (and people usually proceed from such a 'first glance', adopting it absolutely uncritically from everyday usage), thought represented one of man's subjective psychic abilities along with others like intuition, sensation, memory, will, and so on and so forth. By thinking was also understood a special kind of *activity* directed, unlike practice, at altering ideas, at reorganising the images that were in the individual's *consciousness*, and directly at the verbal shaping of these ideas in speech; ideas, when expressed in speech (words, terms) were called concepts. When man altered real things outside his head, and not ideas, that was no longer considered thinking, but at best only activities *in accordance with thought*, according to the laws and rules dictated by it.

Thought was thus identified with *reflection*, i.e. with psychic activity in the course of which a person gave himself an account of what he was doing, and how, and became aware of all the schemas and rules by which he acted. The sole job of logic then proved, quite understandably, to be simply the ordering and classifying of the corresponding schemas and rules. Every individual could discover them for himself in his own *consciousness* because, even without any study of logic, he was guided by them (only not, perhaps, systematically). As Hegel justly put it, 'such logic had no other business than could be done through the activity of simple formal thought, and so it certainly produced nothing that one could not otherwise have done just as well'.[6]

Everything we have said also applied fully to Kant, which is why Hegel said that 'the Kantian philosophy could not have any effect on the treatment of the sciences. *It left the categories and methods of ordinary knowledge quite undisturbed'.*[7] It only introduced order into the schemas of existing consciousness, only built them into a system (in so doing, true, it came up against the facts of a mutual contradiction between the various schemas). So the Kantian logic appeared as a kind of honest confession of existing consciousness, of its systematically expounded self-consciousness, and nothing more; or rather, of its *conceits*—an exposition of what existing thought thought of itself. But just as it was a blunder to judge a person according to what and how he thought of himself, so it was impossible to judge thinking by its self-opinion; it was much more useful to examine what it was really doing, and

---

6 G. W. F. Hegel. *Sämtliche Werke*, Vol. 8, p 70.
7 *Ibid.*, p 159.

how, possibly even without giving itself a proper evaluation of it.

Having thus posed the problem Hegel proved to be the first professional logician who resolutely and consciously threw aside the old prejudice that thought was presented to the investigator only in the form of speech (external or internal, oral or written). The prejudice was not accidental; thought could only look at itself from the side, as it were, as an object different from itself, only insofar as it had expressed itself, embodied itself in some external form. And the completely conscious thought that all the old logic had in view really assumed language, speech, the word, as its outward form of expression. In other words thought achieved *awareness* of the schemas of its own activity precisely through and in language. (This circumstance had in fact been recorded in the very name of logic, which is derived from the Greek *logos,* word.) Not only Hegel and the Hegelians, incidentally, spoke of this, but also some of their opponents in principle, like Trendelenburg, who noted that traditional (formal) 'logic becomes conscious of itself in speech and so in many respects is a grammar absorbed with itself'.[8]

Let us note in passing that all schools of logic, without exception, having ignored Hegel's criticism of the old logic have shared this old prejudice to this day as though nothing had happened. It is most outspokenly professed by Neopositiv-

---

[8] Adolf Trendelenburg. *Logische Untersuchungen* (Berlin, 1840) p 16.

ists, who directly identify thought with linguistic activity and logic with the analysis of language. The most striking thing about this is the self-conceit with which they project this archaic prejudice as the latest discovery of twentieth century logical thinking, as the manifestation to the world at long last of the principle of the scientific development of logic, as an axiom of the 'logic of science'.

Language (speech) is, nevertheless, not the *sole* empirically observed form in which human thought manifests itself. Does man really not discover himself as a *thinking* being in his actions, in the course of actually shaping the world around him, in the making of things? Does he really only function as a thinking being when talking? The question is surely purely rhetorical. The thought of which Hegel spoke discloses itself in human *affairs* every bit as obviously as in words, in chains of terms, in the lacework of word combinations. Furthermore, in real affairs man demonstrates the real modes of his thinking more adequately than in his narrations of them.

But, that being so, man's *actions*, and so too the results of his actions, the things created by them, not only could, but must, be considered *manifestations of his thought,* as acts of the objectifying of his ideas, thoughts, plans, and conscious intentions. Hegel demanded from the very start that thought should be investigated *in all the forms* in which it was realised, and above all in human affairs, in the creation of things and events. Thought revealed its force and real power not solely in talking but also in the whole grandiose process of creating culture and the whole objective body of civilisation, the whole 'inorganic body of man' (Marx), including in that tools and statues, workshops and temples, factories and chancelleries, political organisations and systems of legislation.

It was on that basis that Hegel also acquired the right to consider in logic the objective determinations of things outside consciousness, *outside the psyche of the human individual*, in all their independence, moreover, from that psyche. There was nothing mystical nor idealist in that; it meant the forms ('determinations') of things created by the activity of the thinking individual. In other words, the forms of his thought embodied in natural materials, 'invested' in it by human activity. Thus a house appeared as the architect's conception embodied in stone, a machine as the embodiment of the engineer's ideas in metal, and so on; and the whole immense objective body of civilisation as thought in its 'otherness' (*das Idee in der Form des Anderssein*), in its sensual objective embodiment. The whole history of humanity was correspondingly also to be considered a process of the 'outward revelation' of the power of thought, as a process of the realisation of man's ideas, concepts, notions, plans, intentions, and purposes, *as a process of the embodying of logic*, i.e. of the schemas to which men's purposive activity was subordinated.

The understanding and careful analysis of thought in this aspect (investigation of the 'active

side' as Marx called it in his first thesis on Feuerbach) was still not idealism. Logic, furthermore,
by following such a path, thus took the decisive
step toward genuine ('intelligent') materialism,
toward understanding of the fact that all logical
forms without exception were universal forms of
the development of reality outside thought,
reflected in human consciousness and tested in the
course of millennia of practice. In considering
thought in the course of its materialisation as well
as in its verbal revelation Hegel did not go beyond
the bounds of the analysis of *thought* at all,
beyond the limits of the subject matter of *logic* as
a special science. He simply brought into the field
of view of logic that real phase of the process of
development of thought without understanding
which logic could not and never would be able to
become a real science.

From Hegel's standpoint the real basis for the
forms and laws of thought proved to be only the
aggregate historical process of the *intellectual development of humanity* understood in its universal and necessary aspects. The subject matter of
logic was no longer the abstract identical schemas
that could be found in each individual consciousness, and common to each of them, but the *history
of science and technique* collectively created by
people, a process quite independent of the will
and consciousness of the separate individual
although realised at each of its stages precisely
in the conscious activity of individuals. This process, according to Hegel, also included, as a phase,
the act of realising thought in object activity, and

through activity in the forms of things and events outside consciousness. In that, in Lenin's words, he 'came *very close* to materialism'.[9]

In considering thought as a real productive process expressing itself not only in the movement of words but also in the changing of things, Hegel was able, for the first time in the history of logic, to pose the problem of a special analysis of thought-forms, or the analysis of thought from the aspect of form. Before him such an aim had not arisen in logic, and even could not have. 'It is hardly surprising that economists, wholly under the influence of material interests, have overlooked the formal side of the relative expression of value, when professional logicians, before Hegel, even overlooked the formal aspect of the propositions and conclusions they used as examples.'[10]

Logicians before Hegel had recorded only the external schemas in which logical actions, judgments and inferences functioned *in speech*, i.e. as schemas of the joining together of *terms* signifying general ideas, but the logical form expressed in these figures, i.e. the category, remained outside their sphere of investigation, and the conception of it was simply borrowed from metaphysics and ontology. So it had been even with Kant, despite the fact that he had nevertheless seen categories precisely as the *principles of judgments* (with objective significance, in his sense).

---

[9] V. I. Lenin. Philosophical Notebooks. In: *Collected Works*, Vol. 38 (Progress Publishers, Moscow, 1963) p 278.

[10] See Karl Marx. *Das Kapital*, Vol. I (Hamburg, 1867) p 21.

And since logical form, about which Marx spoke in the first edition of *Das Kapital*, was understood as a form of activity realised equally well in the movement of verbal terms and in the movement of the things involved in the work of the thinking being, there then for the first time only, arose the possibility of analysing it specially *as such*, of abstracting it from the special features of its expression in some partial material or other (including those which were linked with the specific features of its realisation in the fabric of language).

In *logos*, in reason, *Sage und Sache*[11], i.e. myth and fact, or rather legend and true story, were equally expressed in the logical aspect (in contrast to the psychological-phenomenological). (Incidentally, play on words, for example, was very characteristic of Hegel, puns however that threw light on the genetic relationship of the ideas expressed by the words. *Sage* is legend, myth, hence 'saga', a legend of high deeds (cf. *bylina*, the form of Russian epic); *Sache* is a broad capacious word signifying not so much a single, sensuously perceived thing, as the essence of the matter, situation, the point, the actual state of affairs (or things), i.e. everything that is or was in the matter itself (cf. Russian *byl'*, meaning a true story, fact, what really happened). This etymology is used in the *Science of Logic* to express very important shades of meaning, which sound as follows in

---

[11] See G. W. F. Hegel. *Jenaer Realphilosophie* (Berlin, 1969) p 183.

Lenin's translation and materialist interpretation: ' "With this introduction of Content into logical consideration", the subject becomes not *Dinge* but *die Sache, der Begriff der Dinge* [i.e. not things, but the essence, the concept of things— *Ed.*], not things but the laws of their movement, materialistically.'[12]

Considered as the activity of the thinking being in its universal form, thought was also fixed in those of its schemas and moments as remained *invariant* in whatever special material the relevant activity was performed and whatever product it put out at any one instant. In the Hegelian view it was quite irrelevant how, precisely, the action of thinking took place or takes place, whether in articulated vibrations of the ambient air and their identifying signs or in some other natural, physical substance. 'In all human contemplation there is thought, just as thought is the general in all conceptions, recollections, and on the whole any mental activity, in all wishes, desires, etc. All these are only further specifications of thought. While we so conceive thought, it itself appears in another aspect than when we only speak; we have intellectual power over and above any other abilities, like contemplation, imagination, will and the like.'[13]

All the universal schemas being depicted in the activity of the thinking being, including that directed toward immediately intuited or repre-

---

[12] V. I. Lenin, *Op. cit.*, p 94.
[13] G. W. F. Hegel. *Sämtliche Werke*, Vol. 8, pp 84-85.

sented material, must therefore be considered not less as *logical* parameters of thought than the schemas of its expression in language, or in the form of the figures known in the old logic. Thought in the broadest sense of the word, as activity altering images of the external world in general expressed in words (and not the words in themselves), the thought that really 'effects everything human and makes humanity human',[14] as a capacity that creates knowledge in any forms, including that of the contemplated images, and 'penetrates' into them, and hence not simply the subjective, psychic act of using or treating words, was the subject matter of logic, the science of thought.

Thought, in fact, included the human '*determination* of sensation, intuition, images, ideas, aims, obligations, etc., and also thoughts and concepts'[15] ('thoughts and concepts' here have the meaning of the old, purely formal logic). Thought in general thus '*appears* at first not in the form of thought but as feeling, intuition, imagination—*forms* that are to be distinguished from thought as form'.[16] The thought-form as such appears to us only in the *course of thinking about thought itself*, i.e. only in logic.

But before man began to think about *thought*, he had already *to think*, though still not realising the logical schemas and categories within which

---

14 *Ibid.*, p 42.
15 *Ibid.*, p 44.
16 *Ibid.*, p 42.

this thinking took place, but already embodying them in the form of the concrete statements and concepts of science, engineering, morals, and so on. Thought was thus realised at first as activity in all the diversity of its outward manifestations. The thought-form here was 'sunk' into the material of concrete thoughts, sense images, and ideas, was 'sublated' in them, and was therefore counterposed to conscious thinking as the form of external reality. In other words, thought and the thought-form did not appear at first to the thinking being as forms of his own activity at all (of his 'self'—*das Selbst*), creating a certain product, but as forms of the *product itself*, i.e. of concrete knowledge, images and concepts, intuition and representation, as the forms of tools, machines, states, etc., etc., and as the forms of realised aims, wishes, desires, and so on.

Thought could not 'see' itself otherwise than in the mirror of its own creations, in the mirror of the external world, *which we knew through thought-activity*. Thought, as it appeared in logic, was thus the same thought as had been realised in the form of knowledge of the world, in the form of science, engineering, art, and morality. But it was far from the same thing *in form*, because 'there is a difference between having sensations and ideas, determined and *penetrated by thought*, and having *thoughts about them*'.[17]

Neglect of this very important distinction led the old logic into a dual error. On the one hand it

---

[17] G. W. F. Hegel. *Sämtliche Werke*, Vol. 8, p 43.

only defined thought as 'a subjective, psychic capability of the individual' and therefore counterposed to thought so understood the whole sphere of 'intuition, ideas, and will' as something existing outside thought and having nothing in common with it, as the object of reflection existing outside thought. On the other hand, in not distinguishing *in form* between the relative strength of the two revelations of thought mentioned above, it could also not say how the *thought-form* as such ('in and for itself') was differentiated from the form of intuition and representation, in the shape of which it had originally appeared and was hidden, and consequently confused the one with the other, taking the form of the concept for the form of intuition, and vice versa.

Hence, too, it came about that, under the form of *concept*, the old logic considered every kind of *idea* or *notion* whatsoever, insofar as it was expressed in speech or in a term, that is to say, the image of intuition or contemplation held in consciousness by means of speech, which recorded it. As a result, too, the old logic embraced the concept itself only from the aspect from which it was really not distinguished in any way from any notion or intuitive image expressed in speech, from the aspect of the abstract and general, which was really just as common to the concept as to the notion. Thus it came about that it took the form of *abstract identity* or *abstract universality* for the specific form of the concept, and could therefore only raise the law of identity and the principle of contradiction in determinations to the rank of absolute, fundamental criteria of the thought-form in general.

Kant also took that stand, understanding by concept *any general notion* insofar as it was fixed by a term. Hence his definition: 'The concept is ... a general image or representation of that which is common to many objects, consequently a general idea, *provided that it can be included in several objects.*'[18]

Hegel himself required a more profound solution of the *problem of the concept and of thinking in concepts* from logic. For him a concept was primarily a synonym for real *understanding* of the essence of the matter and not simply an expression of something general, of some identity of the objects of intuition. A concept disclosed the real nature of a thing and not its similarity with other things; and not only should it express the abstract generality of its object (that was only one of the moments of a concept, relating it to notion), but also the *special nature* or peculiarity of the object. That was why the form of the concept proved to be a dialectical unity of universality and particularity, a unity that was also *revealed* through manifold forms of judgment and inference, and came out into the open in judgments. It was not surprising that any judgment destroyed the form of abstract identity and represented its self-evident *negation*. Its form was: A is B (i.e. not-A).

Hegel distinguished clearly between universality, which dialectically contained the whole rich-

---

[18] Immanuel Kant. *Logik* (Leipzig) p 98.

ness of the particular and the singular within it-self and in its determinations, and the simple abstract generality, identicalness, of all the single objects of a given kind. The universal *concept* expressed in itself the *actual law* of the origin, development, and fading or disappearance of single things. And that was already quite another angle on the concept, much truer and deeper, because, as Hegel demonstrated with a mass of examples, the real law (the immanent nature of the single thing) did not always appear on the surface of phenomena in the form of a simple identicalness, of a common sign or attribute, or in the form of identity. If that were so there would be no need for any theoretical science. The job of thought was not limited to empirically register-ing common attributes. The central concept of Hegel's logic was therefore the *concrete-univers-al*: he brilliantly illustrated its distinction from the simple, abstract universality of the sphere of notions in his famous pamphlet *Wer denkt ab-strakt? (Who Thinks Abstractly?)*. To think abstractly meant to be enslaved by the force of current catchphrases and cliches, of one-sided, empty definitions; meant to see in real, sensuously intuited things only an insignificant part of their real content, only such determinations of them as were already 'jelled' in consciousness and func-tioned there as ready-made stereotypes. Hence the 'magic force' of current catchphrases and ex-pressions, which fence reality off from the thinking person instead of serving as the form of its ex-pression.

In this last interpretation logic finally became a real logic of the understanding of *unity in variety*, and not a scheme for manipulating ready-made ideas and notions; a logic of critical and self-critical thought and not a means of the uncritical classification and pedantic, schematic presentation of existing ideas.

From premises of that kind Hegel concluded that real thought in fact took other forms and was governed by other laws than those that current logic considered the sole determinations of thinking. Thought had obviously to be investigated as collective, co-operative activity in the course of which the individual, with his schemas of conscious thinking, performed only partial functions. In fulfilling them, however, he was constantly forced at the same time to perform actions that were not fit in, in any way, with the schemas of ordinary logic. In really taking part in common work he was all the time subordinating himself to the laws and forms of *universal thought*, though not conscious of them as such. Hence the 'topsy-turvy' situation arose in which the real forms and laws of thought were expressed and understood as some kind of *external necessity*, as an *extra-logical* determination of the action; and on the sole ground that they were still not revealed and realised by logic, not acknowledged as logical interpretations.

As can easily be seen, Hegel criticised traditional logic, and the thinking appropriate to it, by the same 'immanent procedure' that was one of his main conquests, namely, he counterposed to the assertions, rules, and basic propositions of logic not some kind of opposing assertions, rules and basic propositions but the process of the practical realisation of its own principles in real thought. He showed it its own image, pointing out those of its features that it preferred not to notice and not to recognise. Hegel required only one thing of thinking in accordance with logic, namely uncompromising consistency in applying the principles adduced. And he showed that it was the consistent application of these principles (and not departure from them) that in fact led inevitably, with inexorable force, to *negation* of the principles themselves as one-sided, incomplete, and abstract.

That was the very critique of reason, from the standpoint of reason itself, that Kant had begun; and this critique (self-criticism) of reason and its circumscribing logic led to the conclusion that 'the nature of thought is itself dialectics, that as understanding it must fall into the negative of itself, into contradiction. . .'.[19] Kant had actually reached a similar conclusion; and whereas before him logic could be unself-critical *out of ignorance,* now it could maintain its precarious position only if it quite consciously rejected facts unacceptable to it, only by becoming *consciously unself-critical.*

The historically unavoidable defect of Kantian logic was that it pedantically schematised and described a mode of thought that led to a bringing out and sharp formulation of the contradic-

---

[19] G. W. F. Hegel. *Sämtliche Werke,* Vol. 8, p 55.

tions contained in any concept but did not show how they could and should be resolved *logically* without shifting this difficult task onto 'practical reason', onto 'moral postulates', and other factors and abilities lying outside logic. Hegel, however, saw the main job facing logic after the work of Kant, Fichte, and Schelling, as precisely in finding, bringing out, and indicating to thought, the means of intelligently and concretely resolving the contradictions into which it inevitably fell when consciously guided by the traditional, purely formal logic. That, too, was the real distinction between Hegel's conception of thought and logic and all preceding ones.

The old logic, coming up against the logical contradiction that it itself brought to light just because it rigorously followed its own principles, always balked at it, retreated to analysis of the preceding movement of thought, and always strove to find an error or mistake in it leading to the contradiction. For formal logical thinking contradictions thus became an insurmountable barrier to the forward movement of thought, an obstacle in the way of concrete analysis of the essence of the matter. It therefore also came about that 'thought, despairing of managing *by itself* to resolve the contradiction into which it had got itself, turns back to the solutions and reliefs that were the spirit's lot in its other modes and forms'.[20] It could not be otherwise, since the contradiction did not develop through a mistake. No

---

[20] G. W. F. Hegel. *Sämtliche Werke*, Vol. 8, p 56.

mistake, it ultimately proved, had been made in the preceding thinking. It was necessary to go even further back, to uncomprehended contemplation, sense perception, aesthetic intuition, i.e. to the realm of lower forms of consciousness (lower, that is, in relation to conceptual thinking), where there was really no contradiction for the simple reason that it had still not been disclosed and clearly expressed. (It never hurts, of course, to go back and analyse the preceding course of argument and check whether there has not been a formal mistake, for that also happens not infrequently; and here the recommendations of formal logic have a quite rational sense and value. It may turn out, as a result of checking, that a given logical contradiction is really nothing but the result of committing an error or mistake somewhere. Hegel, of course, never dreamed of denying such a case. He, like Kant, had in mind only those antinomies that developed in thought as a result of the most formally 'correct' and faultless argumentation.)

Hegel also suggested that a contradiction should be resolved as well as disclosed, and resolved by the same logical thinking as had brought it out when a definite concept was being developed.

He treated both the origin and the mode of resolution of logical contradictions differently. Like Kant he understood that they did not arise at all through the negligence or carelessness of individual thinking persons but unlike Kant he understood that they could and must be resolved and must not always be preserved as antinomies. But so that it could resolve them thought must fix them sharply and clearly in advance, precisely as antinomies, as *logical* contradictions, as *real*, and not imaginary, contradictions in determinations.

Dialectics, according to Hegel, was the form (or method or schema) of thought that included the process both of elucidating contradictions and of concretely resolving them in the corpus of a higher and more profound stage of rational understanding of the same object, on the way toward further investigation of the essence of the matter, i.e. in the course of developing science, engineering, and 'morality', and all the spheres he called the 'objective spirit'.

This conception immediately brought about constructive shifts in the whole system of logic. Whereas Kant's 'dialectic' was only the final, third part of logic (the doctrine on the forms of understanding and reason), where it was a matter actually of the statement of the logically unresolvable antinomies of theoretical cognition, with Hegel it appeared quite another matter. With him the sphere of the logical was divided into three main sections or aspects, i.e. three main directions were distinguished in it, as follows:

(1) the abstract or rational;

(2) the dialectical or negatively reasonable;

(3) the speculative or positively reasonable.

Hegel specially stressed that 'these three aspects in no case constitute three *parts* of logic, but are only *moments of any logically real na-*

ture, that is of any concept or of any truth in general'.[21]

In the empirical history of thought (as in any given, historically achieved state of it) these three aspects appeared either as three consecutive 'formations' or as three different but closely related systems of logic. Hence we got the illusion that they could be depicted as three different sections (or 'parts') of logic, following one after the other.

Logic as a whole, however, could not be obtained by a simple uniting of these three aspects, each of which was taken in the form in which it had been developed in the history of thought. That called for critical treatment of all three aspects from the standpoint of higher principles, those historically last achieved. Hegel characterised the three 'moments' of logical thought that should constitute Logic as follows. (1) 'Thought as *understanding* remains stuck in firm determination and does not get beyond differentiation of the latter; such a limited abstraction applies to it as existing and being for itself.'[22] The separate (isolated) historical embodiment of this 'moment' in thought appeared as *dogmatism,* and its logical, theoretical self-awareness as 'general', i.e. purely formal logic.

(2) 'The *dialectical* moment is the own self-abolition of such ultimate determinations and their transition into their opposites.'[23] Historically

---

21 G. W. F. Hegel. *Sämtliche Werke,* Vol. 8, pp 184-185.
22 *Ibid.,* p 185.
23 *Ibid.,* p 189.

this moment appears as *scepticism,* i.e. as the state in which thought, feeling bewildered among opposing, equally 'logical' and mutually provoking dogmatic systems, is powerless to choose and prefer one of them. Logical self-awareness, corresponding to the stage of scepticism, was distinguished in the Kantian conception of dialectics as a state of the insolubility of the antinomies between dogmatic systems. Scepticism (Kant's type of 'negative dialectic') was higher than dogmatism both historically and in content because the dialectic included in reason or understanding was already *realised,* and existed not only 'in itself' but 'for itself'.

(3) *'The speculative or positively reasonable* conceives the unity of determinations in their opposition, the *affirmation* that is contained in their resolution and their transition.'[24] Hegel also saw systematic treatment of this last 'moment' (and correspondingly critical rethinking of the first two from the angle of the third) as the historically pressing task in logic, and therefore his own mission and the aim of his work.

When critically rethought in the light of the principles only now elicited, the 'moments' considered ceased to be independent parts of logic and were transformed into three abstract aspects of one and the same logical system. Then a logic was created such that, when thinking was guided by it, thought became fully self-critical and was in no danger of falling into either the dullness of

---

[24] G. W. F. Hegel. *Sämtliche Werke,* Vol. 8, p 195.

dogmatism or into the sterility of sceptical neutrality.

Hence, too, there followed the external, formal division of logic into (1) the doctrine of being, (2) the doctrine of essence, and (3) the doctrine of the notion (concept, idea).

The division of logic into the objective (the first two sections) and the subjective coincided at first glance with the old division of philosophy into ontology and logic proper; but Hegel stressed that such a division would be very inexact and arbitrary because, in logic, the opposition between the subjective and the objective (in their ordinary meaning) disappeared'.[25]

His position on this question calls besides for a thorough commentary since superficial criticism of his conception of logic and its subject matter has so far been primarily that his position *ignored* the opposition (contrast) between the subjective and the objective (between thinking and being) and therefore casuistically produced specifically logical schemas of thought for the ontological determination of things outside thought and, on the contrary, universal definitions of the reality outside thought for schemas of the logical process, thus committing two sins: (a) hypostatising logical forms, and (b) logicalising reality.

If the original sin of Hegelianism had really been a simple, naive blindness in relation to the contrast between thought and reality, between the concept and its object, then Kant's dualism would

---

[25] *Ibid.*, p 84.

have been the apex of philosophical wisdom. In fact, however, Hegel's 'error' was not so simple, and was not in the least characterised by the evaluation cited above. Hegel saw the difference and, what is more important, the contradiction (opposition) between the world of things outside consciousness and the world of thought (the world in thought, in science, in *concepts*), and was much more acutely aware of it than his naive critics among the Kantians; and in any case he ascribed much greater significance for logic to this opposition than, say, positivists do (who, especially in logic, directly identify the concept and the object of the concept).

The point is quite another one; and another understanding of it follows from the specifically Hegelian conception of *thought*, and thus also from Hegel's solution of the problem of the relation of thought and the world of things.

That is why, when Hegel formulated a programme for the critical transformation of logic as a science, he posed the task of bringing it (i.e. thought's awareness of the universal schemas of its own work) into correspondence with its real object, i.e. with real thought, with its real universal forms and laws.

The last-named do not exist in thought simply or even so much as schemas and rules of *conscious* thinking, but rather as universal schemas of *objective* thinking that are realised not so much as a subjective psychic act as the productive process that created science, technique and morality.

In defending the objectivity of logical forms

so understood, Hegel of course was right in many respects; and his critique of the subjective idealist interpretation of the logical (Hume, Kant, Fichte) is topical in the struggle against many of their present-day successors, in particular Neopositivists. As social formations science and technique ('the materialised power of knowledge' as Marx defined it) exist and develop of course outside the individual's consciousness. But, according to Hegel, there was no other consciousness than that of the individual, never had been, and never would be; and the logical forms of development of science and technique really stood in opposition to the consciousness and will of the individual as quite objective limits to his individually performed actions, even as limits *dictated* to him *from outside.* 'According to these determinations, thoughts can be called objective, and they can also be taken to include the forms that are considered for the present in ordinary logic and are looked upon only as forms of *conscious* thought. *Logic* here coincides with *Metaphysics,* with the science of *things* conceived in thought. . . .'[26]

In this conception of the objectivity of thought-forms there was as yet, of course, no facet of the specifically Hegelian, i.e. *objective,* idealism. One cannot reproach Hegel with having allegedly extended the boundaries of the subject matter of logic impermissibly so that it began to embrace not only thought but things. Hegel (and Kant,

---

[26] G. W. F. Hegel. *Sämtliche Werke,* Vol. 8, p 83.

too) did not in general speak just about *things as such;* he had in mind exclusively things *comprehended in thoughts.* It was in that sense that he asserted that 'in logic thoughts are so conceived that they have no other content than that belonging to the thought itself and produced through it'.[27] In other words logic had in mind not things but those of *their determinations* as were posited by the action of thought, i.e. *scientific* determinations.

Thus, what Hegel affirmed within the limits of consideration of pure thought was much more rigorous and consistent than the logic before him; and he justly reproached it precisely for not having been able to confine itself rigorously within the bounds of its own subject matter, and for having imported into it material not assimilated by thought and not reproduced by thought-activity.

His requirement of including all the categories (the subject matter of the old metaphysics and ontology) in logic in no way meant going beyond the limits of thought. It was equivalent to a demand for a critical analysis to be made of the *thought-activity* that had engendered the determinations of the old metaphysics, and for those thought-forms to be brought out that both logic and metaphysics had applied quite uncritically and unconsciously, without clearly realising what they consisted of. Hegel had no doubt that 'thought-forms must not be used without having

---

[27] G. W. F. Hegel. *Sämtliche Werke*, Vol. 8, p 87.

been subjected to investigation' and that 'we must make the thought-forms themselves the object of cognition'.[28] But such an investigation was already thought, and the activity taking place in those very forms was the act of applying them. If we looked on logic as investigation (cognition) of thought-forms, he wrote, this investigation 'must also unite the activity of thought-forms and their critique in cognition. The thought-forms must be taken in and for themselves; they are the object and the activity of the object itself; they themselves inquire into themselves, must determine their limits and demonstrate their defects themselves. That will then be that activity of thought that will soon be given separate consideration as *dialectics.* . . .'.[29]

The subject matter of logic then proved to be those really *universal* forms and patterns within which the collective consciousness of humanity was realised. The course of its development, empirically realised as the history of science and technique, was also seen as that 'whole' to the interests of which all the individual's separate logical acts were subordinated.

And inasmuch as the individual was involved in the common cause, in the work of *universal* thought, he was continually forced to perform actions dictated 'by the interests of the whole' and not confined to the schemas of 'general' logic. He would naturally not realise his actions in

---

28 *Ibid.*, p 125.
29 *Ibid.*

logical concepts, although these acts were performed by *his own thinking*. The schemas (forms and laws) of universal thought would be realised *unconsciously* through his psyche. (Not 'unconsciously' in general, but without *logical* consciousness of them, without their expression in logical concepts and categories.)

In this connection Hegel introduced one of his most important distinctions between thought 'in itself' *(an sich)*, which also constituted the subject matter, the object of investigation, in logic, and thought 'for itself' *(für sich selbst)*, i.e. thought that had already become aware of the schemas, principles, forms, and laws of its own work and had already worked quite consciously in accordance with them, fully and clearly realising what it was doing, and how it was doing it. Logic was also consciousness, the expression through concepts and categories of those laws and forms in accordance with which the process of thinking 'in itself' *(an sich)* took place. In logic it also became the *object for itself.*

In logic thought had consequently to become the same 'for itself' as it had earlier been only 'in itself'.

Hegel therefore also formulated the task of bringing logic into line with its *real subject matter*, with *real thought*, with the really universal forms and laws of development of science, technique, and morality.

In other words he wanted to make the subjective consciousness of thought about itself *identical* with its object, with the real universal and necessary (objective) forms and laws of universal (and not individual) thought. That also meant that the principle of the *identity of the subjective and the objective* must be introduced into logic as the highest principle, i.e. the principle that the real forms and laws of thought must be delineated in logic exactly, adequately, and correctly. The principle of the identity of subject and object signified nothing more, and did not signify any 'hypostatisation' of the forms of subjective thought, because *one and the same thought* was both object and subject in logic, and it was a matter of the agreement, coincidence, and identity of this thought (as a consciously performed activity) with itself as unconsciously performed productive activity, or as activity hitherto taking place with a false consciousness of its own actions.

In defending the *objectivity* of logical forms, Hegel of course stood head and shoulders above (and closer to materialism) than all those who up to the present have reproached him with having 'hypostatised' logical forms in order to defend their version of the identity of thought and object as a purely conventional principle, as the principle of the identity of sign and thing designated, of the concept and that which is thought in it. Hegel was 100 per cent right in his critique of the subjective idealist version of the logical and of its objectivity (as merely the agreement of all thinking individuals, as merely the identity— read *equality*—of all the schemas by which each Ego taken separately operated). His critique not only hit at Kant, Fichte, and Schelling, but also strikes all today's Neopositivists.

(Marx, incidentally, also defined the categories of political economy as 'objective thought-forms': 'They are the socially valid, and therefore objective thought-forms. . . .'[30])

Thus the statement that there was no difference for logic between the subjective and the objective did not mean anything else on Hegel's lips than an affirmation that logic must consider, within itself, within its own theory, and link together in one system, literally *all* the logical schemas of thought activity, beginning with the categories and finishing up with the figures of judgments and conclusions. And within it there must be room both for those schemas that prior to Kant were considered simply determinations of things outside consciousness and for those that were usually considered to be 'specific' to consciousness and had allegedly *no* relation to things outside the mind.

Hegel did not dream of repudiating the differences between the categorial schemas given in the determinations of categories and the figures of formal logic, of course; but he did require them to be explained and disclosed within logic itself and not to be presumed in advance, uncritically borrowed from the old metaphysic and its corresponding logic. He required the one and the other to be included in logic in critically rethought form.

---

[30] Karl Marx. *Capital*, Vol. I. Translated by Eden and Cedar Paul (International Publishers, New York, 1929) p 50.

'The relation of such forms as concept, judgment, and conclusion to other forms like causality, etc., can only be discovered within logic itself.'[31]

Hegel thus did not include the determinations of things as they existed outside the mind or in everyday consciousness in logic at all, but solely those determinations that appeared to the mind in *science*, and in theoretical consciousness, that were 'posited' or formulated by *thought itself*. And since science was the realised force (faculty) of thought, materialised mental, theoretical labour, he also saw primarily 'objectified' *determinations of thought* in the determinations of things.

The requirement of including all *categories* in logic was therefore equivalent to requiring a critical analysis to be made of those *activities of thought* that were materialised or objectified in the concepts of the old metaphysic, and to requiring disclosure of the *logic of thought* that was earlier realised in the form of various schemas of the universe, and so to requiring a critical understanding of all the categories that the old logic had taken over quite uncritically from ontological systems.

Hegel thus did not go outside the framework of the subject matter of logic at all but only beyond the limits of the notions of earlier logicians about these limits. While remaining within the boundaries of the investigation of thought, and only of thought, he nevertheless saw more within those boundaries than previous logicians,

---

[31] G. W. F. Hegel. *Sämtliche Werke*, Vol. 8, p 83.

and saw those logical (universal) schemas of developing thought that the old logic had not considered universal at all and had therefore not included in the theory. Logic thus proved to be pinned to discovery and investigation of the *objective* laws governing the subjective activity of individuals, and those forms in which, whether or not the individuals so wished it, or whether or not they realised it, they were forced, insofar in general as they thought, to express the results of their subjective efforts.

That is in what Hegel saw the true difference between the real *laws* of thought and the rules that the old logic had promoted to the rank of laws. Man can break rules, unlike laws, and does so at every step, thus demonstrating that they are not laws. Because laws cannot be broken, they constitute the determinateness of the object, which cannot be omitted without the object itself, in this case *thought*, ceasing to exist.

And if man thinks, then his activities are subordinated to law and cannot overstep its bounds, although he may at the same time break the rules in the most flagrant way. A law can be 'broken' in one way only, by ceasing to think, i.e. by escaping from the realm that is governed by the laws of thought and where they operate as inexorably as the law of gravitation in the world of spatially determined bodies. But for man such a 'way out' is equivalent to overstepping the bounds of human existence in general.

Hegel also showed that the real development of determinations, i.e. the real forward movement of thought, even in the simplest cases, not to mention the process of development of science, technique, and morality, took place precisely through breach (or removal) of all the rules that had been established for thought by the old logic, through their dialectical negation. But the constant *negation* of the rules established by conscious thought for itself got out of control, was not aware of itself, and proved to be a fact *outside thought,* although it took place within the latter. Thought had this fact 'in itself' but not *'for itself'.*

But as soon as this fact was recognised as a universal and necessary—logical—thought-form, it was also transformed into a *fact of consciousness,* a fact of conscious thought, and the latter became *consciously* dialectical. Previously it had only been so 'in itself', i.e. despite its own consciousness of itself. But now it became 'for itself' precisely what it had previously been only 'in itself'.

The subject matter of logic consequently could not merely be the forms that had already been realised or apprehended, and had already been included in existing consciousness (in textbooks of logic and metaphysics). It was impossible to grasp them *ready-made,* or to classify them. They had to be brought out in the very course of reasoning about them, in the course of actual thinking about thought.

And when Kant considered the forms of thought as some ready-made object, already depicted (realised, comprehended), his logic represented only an uncritical classification of existing notions about thought.

But if logic was to be a science, it must be a critical, systematic investigation that did not accept a single determination on faith, and unproved by thought, i.e. without being reproduced by it quite consciously. In this investigation *criticism* of the thought-forms known to cultivated thinking was only possible and thinkable as *self-criticism*. The schemas, rules, forms, principles, and laws of this thought were here subjected to criticism not by comparing them with some object lying outside them, but solely by bringing out the dialectic they included in themselves and which was discovered immediately as soon as we began in general to think, rigorously and fully realising what we were doing and how we were doing it.

In that way, too, the very identity of the forms of cultivated thought with the forms of the unconsciously performed actions of the intellect must be carried out, actions to which thought had had to submit during the historical process of its realisation in the form of science, technique, art and morality. Logic was nothing else (or rather should be nothing else) than the proper apprehension of those forms and laws within which the real thinking of people took place. The identity of thought and the conceivable, as the principle of the logical development and construction of logic, signified nothing more.

It was merely a matter of this, that the schemas of *cultivated thought* (i.e. of the processes taking place in the consciousness of the individual) should coincide with those of the structure of the science in the movement of which the individual was involved, i.e. with the 'logic' dictated by its content. If the schema of the activity of a theoretician coincided with that of the development of his science, and the science was thus developed through his activity, Hegel would attest the *logicality* of his activity, i.e. the *identity* of his thinking with that impersonal, universal process which we also call the development of science. Logic recognised the activities of such a theoretician as logical also when they were even formally not quite irreproachable from the standpoint of the canons of the old logic.

Hegel therefore began to consider all the categories (of quality, quantity, measure, causality, probability, necessity, the general and the particular, and so on and so forth) in quite a new way. For him they were not at all the most general determinations of the things given in intuition or contemplation or in direct experience to each individual, not transcendental schemas of synthesis directly inherent (i.e. inborn) in each individual consciousness (as Kant, Fichte, and Schelling had in fact treated them). It was impossible to discover these thought-forms in the separate consciousness taken in isolation, within the individual Ego. They were there at best only 'in themselves', only in the form of unrealised tendencies and so not brought to awareness. Categories were only discovered and demonstrated their determinations through the historically developing scientific, technical, and moral 'perfecting' of the human race, because only in it, and not in the experience of the isolated individual, did thought become 'for itself' what it had been 'in itself'.

Categories manifested themselves in the individual's own experience (were revealed in action, in processing of the data of perception) not in the whole fullness and dialectical complexity of their composition and connections but only in abstract, one-sided aspects. It was therefore impossible to derive them from analysis of the experience of the isolated individual. They were only discovered through the very complex process of the interaction of a mass of single minds mutually correcting each other in discussion, debate, and confrontations, i.e. through a frankly dialectical process that, like a huge centrifuge, ultimately separated the purely objective schemas of thought from the purely subjective (in the sense of individual, arbitrary) schemas of activity, and as a result crystallised out logic, a system of determinations of purely universal, impersonal, and featureless thought in general.

Categories were therefore also universal forms of the origin of any object in *thought,* gradually depicted in the aggregate scientific consciousness of humanity. They were universal determinations of the object *as and how* it appeared in the eyes of science, in the ether of 'universal thought'. Hegel consented to call determinations of things only those determinations that had been developed by science, by active thought. They were, therefore, none other than thought-forms realised in concrete material, determinations of thought embodied in the object, i.e. in the scientific concept of the external thing. Hegel, therefore, and only therefore, also spoke of the identity of thought and object and defined the object as a concept realised in sensuous, physical material.

The determinations of categories, naturally, could also function as determinations of things in the contemplation (experience) of the individual; not of every individual, however, but only of those who in the course of their education had mastered the historical experience of humanity, and 'reproduced' in their individual consciousness the path taken by human thought (of course, only in its main, decisive features and schemas). Categories were the forms of organisation of this experience (described by Hegel in his *Phenomenology of Mind*).

Categories were thus universal forms of the reconstruction, reproduction, in the *consciousness of the individual* of those objects that had been created before him by the collective efforts of past generations of thinking beings, by the power of their collective, impersonal thought. In individually repeating the experience of humanity, which had created the world of spiritual and material culture surrounding him from the cradle, this individual also repeated that which had been done before him and for him by the 'universal spirit', and so acted according to the same laws and in the same forms as the impersonal 'universal spirit' of humanity. That means that categories appeared at once as universal schemas of the scientific formation of the individual consciousness, rising gradually from the zero level of its erudition to the highest stages of spiritual culture at the given moment, and as schemas of the individual mastery (reproduction) of the whole world of images created by the thought of preceding generations and standing opposed to the individual as a quite objective world of spiritual and material culture, the world of the concepts of science, technique, and morality.

This world was the materialised thought of humanity, realised in the product, was alienated thought in general; and the individual had to de-objectify, and arrogate to himself, the modes of activity that were realised in it, and it was in that the process of his education properly consisted. In the trained mind categories actually functioned as active forms of thought-activity, forms of processing the material of sense impressions into the form of a concept. When the individual had them in his experience, and made them forms of his own activity, he also possessed them, and knew and realised them, *as thought-forms*. Otherwise they remained only *general forms of the things* given in contemplation and representation, and counterposed to thought as a reality existing outside it and independently of it.

With this was linked the naive fetishism that directly accepted the *available* concepts and notions of science about things, the norms of morals and justice, the forms of the state and political

208

system and the similar products of the thinking of people who had objectified their own conscious activity in them, for purely objective determinations of things in themselves. It accepted them as such only because it *did not know* that they had not been created without the involvement of thought, and did not know *how*, moreover, they were produced by thought. It could not reproduce or repeat the process of thought that had brought them into being and therefore, naturally, considered them eternal and unalterable determinations of things in themselves, and the expression of their essence. It believed quite uncritically, on trust, everything that it was told about these things in the name of science, the state, and God. It believed not only that these things *appeared* so today in the eyes of the thinking man but also that they were really so.

Hegel's conception of thought (in the context of logic as a science) thus of necessity also included the process of the 'objectification of thought' (*Vergegenständlichung oder Entäusserung des Denkens*), i.e. its sense-object, practical realisation through action, in sensuous-physical material, in the world of sensuously contemplated (intuited) things. Practice, the process of activity on sense objects that altered things in accordance with a concept, in accordance with plans matured in the womb of subjective thought, began to be considered here as just as important a level in the development of thought and understanding, as the subjective-mental act of reasoning (according to the rules) expressed in speech.

Hegel thus directly introduced practice into logic, and made a fundamental advance in the understanding of thought and in the science of thought.

Since thought outwardly expressed itself *(sich entäussert, sich entfremdet,* i.e. 'alienates itself', 'makes itself something outside itself') not only in the form of speech but also in real actions and in people's deeds, it could be judged much better 'by its fruits' than by the notions that it created about itself. Thought, therefore, that was realised in men's actual actions also proved to be the true criterion of the correctness of those subjective-mental acts that were outwardly expressed only in words, in speeches, and in books.

ESSAY SIX

Once More about the Principle
of Constructing a Logic.
Idealism or Materialism?

So far we have spoken almost exclusively about Hegel's positive gains, which constituted an epoch in logic as a science. Let us now touch on the historically inevitable 'costs of production' connected with the idealism of Hegel's conception of thought, and on the defects in his logic that do not permit us to adopt his conception *in toto,* and that can only be surmounted by developing materialist philosophy.

Historically things developed in such a way that Feuerbach was the first person in Germany to speak about the 'costs of production' of Hegelian idealism.

Like every materialist Feuerbach fought the dualist opposing of thought to being as the initial principle of philosophy. In the course of his reasoning, therefore, he naturally reproduced Spinoza's decisive arguments against Cartesian dualism. This line of polemic, it is true, has to be deduced by analysis, since Feuerbach had in mind not only dualism in the pure form in which it was expressed by Kant, but also the philosophy of Fichte, Schelling, and Hegel, i.e. the attempts systematically made to overcome dualism 'from the right', in the form of idealistic monism. Feuerbach strove, however, to show that the surmounting of dualism in this case inevitably remained fictitious, formal, and verbal, and that idealism in general did not, and could not, encroach on the fundamental premises of the Kantian system. In Schelling and Hegel, therefore, he primarily considered the unsurmounted Kant. 'The Hegelian philosophy is the abolition of the contradiction of thought and being as *Kant* in particular expressed it, but, mark you, only its abolition ... within *one* element, *within* thought.'[1]

As a matter of fact, the so-called philosophy of absolute identity was a philosophy of the *identity of thinking in itself*; as before there was an unfilled gap between thought and being outside thought. The problem seemed to be resolved only because conceivable being, i.e. being in the form in which it had already been expressed in thought, had been put everywhere in the place of real being. Under the grandiose, profoundly thought-out construction of the Hegelian philosophy, therefore, there was hidden as a matter of fact an empty tautology; we thought the surrounding world as and how we thought it.

So the philosophy of Schelling and Hegel had not, in fact, established any identity of thought

---

[1] Ludwig Feuerbach. Vorläufige Thesen zur Reform der Philosophie. In: *Kleinere Schriften II (1839-1846)* (Berlin, 1970) p 257.

and being and not just an 'absolute' one, because 'being as such'—free, independent, self-sufficient being existing outside and independently of thought—had simply not been taken into account in it, and remained something wholly immaterial and undetermined.

The fundamental principle of Kantian dualism thus remained untouched. The thinking mind was considered from the very outset as something absolutely opposed to everything sensuous, corporeal, and material, as a special immaterial being, organised in itself and formed by immanent logical laws and schemas as something independent and self-sufficient. Hegel's *Logic* also represented thought as the activity of such a supernatural and extraphysical subject, which was then forced to enter into special relations of 'mediation' from outside with nature and man so as to shape them in its own image and likeness.

Such a presentation of the thinking mind of necessity presupposed, in addition, that nature and man, as the 'opposites' of the mind, or spirit, as the object and material of its moulding activity, were represented as something passive and amorphous in themselves. Only as a result of the moulding activity of the thinking spirit did nature and man become what they were and acquire all their well-known, concrete forms. Moreover, nothing other was represented in fact, as the product of the activity of the spirit, than the empirically obvious state of affairs in the real world; and the whole complicated magic of mediation once more merely served, in the guise of a 'gift of God', to return the same determinations to man and nature that had been previously taken from them by the act of abstraction. Without this preliminary 'robbery' of man and nature the spiritualistic philosophy could not have attributed a single one of its very impoverished determinations to the thinking spirit.

In this interpretation of the problem of the relation of thought and being, Feuerbach above all saw a scholastically refurbished, 'rationalised' theology. The absolute thinking spirit of spiritualism, like the Biblical God, was a fantastic creature, constructed out of determinations alienated from man by an act of abstraction. The thinking about which Hegelian logic was concerned was, in fact, human thought, but abstracted from man and counterposed to him as the activity of a special being existing outside him.

Proceeding from that quite correct understanding (in general and on the whole) of the root errors of Hegelian idealism (and thereby of idealism in general, since the Hegelian system was the most consistent expression of the idealist point of view), Feuerbach rethought the very posing of the problem of the relation of thought to being. It was impossible, he showed, to ask how 'thought in general' was related to 'being in general', since that already presupposed that thought (in its form alienated from man) was looked upon as something independent, contrasted with being from outside. But being, however, understood not in Hegel's way, i.e. not as an abstract, logical category, not as being in thought, but as the real, sensuously objective world of nature and man, already included thought. Being included not only stones, trees, and stars, but also the thinking body of man.

Thus, to represent being as something deprived of thought meant to represent it incorrectly, to exclude man, capable of thinking, from it in advance; and that meant to deprive being of one of its most important 'predicates', to think of it 'imperfectly'. The argument given here repeated the course of Spinoza's thought, was its developed interpretation, its translation into the language of a more modern philosophical terminology.

The whole problem thus boiled down to resolving whether thought could, in general, be distinguished from man as a material, sensuously objective creature, and to fixing it and considering it from the very beginning as something independent, in contrast to everything corporeal, sensuous, and material; or whether thought should be understood as a property ('predicate') inseparable from man. Feuerbach considered the decisive argument in favour of materialism to be the arguments of natural science, medicine, and physiology. Materialism, relying on medicine, was also 'Archimedes' fulcrum in the dispute between materialism and spiritualism, for it was a matter here, in the final count, not of the divisibility or nondivisibility of matter, but of the divisibility or nondivisibility of man, not of the being or not-being of God but of the being or not-being of man, not of the eternity or temporality of matter but of the eternity or temporality of man, not of matter scattered and extended outside man in heaven and earth but of matter concentrated in the human skull. In short, it is a matter, in this dispute, so long as it is not conducted in mad confusion, only of the head of man. It alone is both the source and the goal and end of this dispute'.[2]

Feuerbach considered that the basic problem of philosophy was thus, and only thus, put on a firm footing of fact, and so, naturally, resolved in favour of materialism.

Thought was the real function of the living brain, and was inseparable from the matter of the brain. If we had brain matter in mind, then it was quite ridiculous in general to ask how thought was 'linked' with it, how the one was connected with the other and 'mediated' it, because there simply was no 'one' and 'the other' here, but only one and the same thing; *the real being of the living brain was also thought, and real thought was the being of the living brain.*

That fact, expressed in philosophical categories, revealed 'the *immediate* unity of soul and body, which admits of nothing in the middle between them, and leaves no room for distinction or even contrast between material and immaterial being, is consequently the point where matter thinks and the body is mind, and conversely the mind is body and thought is matter'.[3] The 'identity' of thought and being, so understood, must

---

[2] Ludwig Feuerbach. Über Spiritualismus und Materialismus. In: *Kleinere Schriften IV* (Berlin, 1972) p 125.

[3] *Ibid.*, pp 152-153.

also (according to Feuerbach) constitute an axiom of true philosophy, i.e. a fact not requiring scholastic proof and 'mediation'.

Feuerbach did not reproach Schelling and Hegel at all for having recognised in general the unity ('identity') of thought and being in the *thinking man*, but only for having tried to depict it as the *final* unity of opposites, as the *product* of the joining together of an insubstantial thinking spirit and unthinking flesh. He reproached them with thus having tried to stick together a picture of the real fact from two equally false abstractions, of proceeding from illusion to fact and from abstraction to reality.

The materialist, Feuerbach affirmed, must proceed in the opposite way, taking as his starting point the directly given fact, in order to explain the origin of those false abstractions that idealists uncritically accepted as facts.

Schelling and Hegel started from the thesis of the initial opposition of incorporeal thought and of flesh without thought in order ultimately to reach the unity of the opposites. That was false path of spiritualism. The materialist must proceed from the factual direct unity (indivisibility) of the human individual in order to understand and show how and why the illusion of an imaginary opposition of thinking and corporeal being arose in the head of this individual.

The illusion of the opposition of the thinking spirit and the flesh in general was consequently a purely subjective fact, i.e. a fact existing only in the head of the human individual, a purely psychological fact. It arose for a quite natural reason, precisely because the thinking brain was the same sort of material, sensuous organ as all of man's other organs.

The position was the same as with the eye, the organ of vision. If I saw stars by means of the eye, then quite understandably I could not at the same time see the eye itself; and conversely, if I wanted to examine the eye, even in a mirror, I would have to turn my gaze away from the stars. Vision would be impossible in general if I were to see all the detail of the structure of the eye itself at the same time as the object, i.e. all the inner material conditions by means of which this vision was effected. In the same way, too, 'the brain could not think if, in thinking, the organic foundation and conditions of thought became objects of its consciousness',[4] i.e. the material structures and processes themselves by means of which thinking took place in the body of the brain. As structures they became objects only for physiology and anatomy. As the organ of thought the brain was structurally and functionally adapted exactly so as to perform activity directed toward external objects, so as to think *not about itself but about the other, about the objective.* And it was quite natural that 'the organ gets lost, and forgets and disavows itself in the *opus fervet* (the work heat) of its own activity, the activity in its objects'.[5] Hence, too, arose the illusion of

---

[4] L. Feuerbach. *Kle inere Schriften IV*, p 123.
[5] *Ibid.*, p 124.

the complete independence of everything corporeal, material, and sensuous, including the brain, from thought.

But the illusion is understandably no argument in favour of idealism. Of itself, in spite of the inevitable illusions, thought always remained the material activity of a material organ, a material process. 'What *for me*, or *subjectively*, is a purely mental, immaterial, unsensuous act, *in itself* or *objectively* is a material, sensuous act.'[6] 'In the brain-act, as the highest act, arbitrary, subjective, mental activity, and involuntary, objective material activity are identical and indistinguishable.'[7]

Thus the logic of the struggle against dualism and spiritualism directly forced Feuerbach, in essence, to express a dialectical proposition to recognise that the living, thinking brain was an 'object' in which there proved to be directly identical oppositions, namely, thought and sensuously objective being, thinking and what was thought, the ideal and the real, the spiritual and the material, the subjective and the objective. The thinking brain was the special 'object' that could be properly expressed in philosophical categories only through directly identifying mutually exclusive determinations, through a thesis that embraced a direct unity, i.e. identity, of opposing categories.

---

6 Ludwig Feuerbach. Wider den Dualismus von Leib und Seele, Fleisch und Geist. In: *Kleinere Schriften III* (Berlin, 1971) p 125.
7 *Ibid.*

Not having mastered dialectics in its general form, Feuerbach, it is true, often wavered, constantly admitting determinations that he was then forced to correct, supplement, and make specific; as a result his exposition was made rather nebulous and ambiguous, but the essence remained the same.

It was just because thinking was a material process, the material activity of a material organ directed to material objects, that the products of that activity (thoughts) could be correlated, compared, and collated with 'things in themselves', with things outside thought, which everybody did at every step without the aid of the mediating activity of God or an absolute spirit. Concepts and images existed in the same space and in the same time as real things; and *one and the same subject* thought about and sensuously perceived the surrounding world, and that subject was precisely the human individual, the same individual who really lived and existed as a sensuously objective creature. The unity (indivisibility) of the object, of the surrounding, sensuously objective world, corresponded to the unity (indivisibility) of this subject. Just as a thinking and sensuously contemplating person was one and the same person and not two different beings coordinating their inter-relations with the help of God or the absolute spirit; so the world thought of, on the one hand, and sensuously contemplated, on the other hand, were again *one and the same world* (namely the real one), and not two different worlds between which one had to look for a special passage or bridge, or mediation, resorting to the aid of a divine principle.

That was why determinations of the world in thought (logical determinations) were directly and spontaneously determinations of the sensuously contemplated or intuited world. And it was absurd to ask what was the special relation of the system of logical determinations to the sensuously given world, to the world in intuition and representation. A logical system was nothing else than the expression of the determinateness of the sensuously contemplated or intuited world. The question of the relation of logical and metaphysics was also an illusory and sham question. There was no such *relation*, because logic and metaphysics were spontaneously and directly *one and the same*. The universal determinations of the world in thought (logical determinations, categories) were nothing else than the expression of the abstract, universal determinateness of things given in intuition, because both thought and intuition (contemplation) had to do with one and the same real world.

And if by logic was understood not a collection of rules for the expression of thought in speech, but the science of the laws of development of real thinking, then, similarly, by logical forms must be understood not the abstract forms of sentences and expressions, but the abstract, universal forms of the real content of thought, i.e. of the real world sensuously given to man. 'The so-called *logical* forms of judgments and conclusions are therefore not *active* thought-forms, not *causal* conditions of reason. They *presuppose* the metaphysical concepts of universality, singularity, and particularity, the whole and the parts, necessity, foundation and consequence; they are given only through these concepts; they are consequently arbitrary, derived, not original thought-forms. Only metaphysical conditions or relations are logical ones—only metaphysics as the science of categories is the true *esoteric* logic—that was Hegel's profound thought. The so-called logical forms are only *abstract, elementary speech-forms*; but speech is not thought, otherwise the greatest chatter-box would be the greatest thinker.'[8]

Thus Feuerbach agreed completely with Hegel on logical forms and laws being absolutely identical with metaphysical ones, although he understood the reason and the grounds for that circumstance quite differently from the idealist Hegel. Here we have a clearly expressed materialist interpretation of the principle of the identity of the laws and forms of thought and being. From the materialist point of view it states that *logical* forms and patterns are nothing else than the *realised universal forms and patterns of being,* of the real world sensuously given to man.

That is the reason why Neokantians like Bernstein called consistent materialism spiritualism inside out. Nevertheless Feuerbach's interpretation of the identity of thought and being remains true and indisputable for any materialist, includ-

[8] Ludwig Feuerbach. *Zur Kritik der Hegelschen Philosophie* (Berlin, 1955) p 35.

ing the Marxist, but only, of course, in the most general form, so long as we are concerned with the fundamentals of logic and the theory of knowledge, and not with the details of the knowledge built up on that foundation. Since Feuerbach later began a specifically anthropological concretisation of general materialist truths, arguments developed in his exposition that were obviously weak not only in comparison with the Marxist-Leninist solution of the problem, but even in comparison with Spinoza's conception; and they subsequently gave vulgar materialists, positivists, and even Neokantians occasion to consider him their predecessor and their—though not completely consistent—ally.

A rather more detailed analysis of the features of Feuerbach's treatment of the identity of thinking and being is not without interest for two reasons: (1) because it was materialism; and (2) because it was materialism without dialectics.

The materialism consisted in this case in an unqualified recognition of the fact that thought was the mode of the real existence of the material body, the activity of the thinking body in real space and time. The materialism appeared, furthermore, in recognition of the identity of the mentally comprehended and sensuously perceived world. Feuerbach's materialism, finally, was expressed in man's being recognised as the subject of thought, that same man who lived in the real world, and not a special being hovering outside the world, contemplating and comprehending it 'from outside'. All those are fundamental tenets of materialism in general, and consequently also of dialectical materialism.

What then were the weaknesses of Feuerbach's position? In general, and on the whole, they were the same as those of all pre-Marxian materalism, and primarily incomprehension of the role of practical activity as activity altering nature. For even Spinoza had in mind only the movement of the thinking body along the given contours of natural bodies and lost sight of this moment, a point that Fichte made against him (and so in general against the whole form of materialism represented by him), namely that man (the thinking body) did not move along ready-made forms and contours presented by nature but actively created new forms, not inherent in nature, and moved along them, overcoming the 'resistance' of the external world.

'The chief defect of all materialism up to now (including Feuerbach's) is that the object, reality, what we apprehend through our senses, is understood only in the form of the *subject or contemplation**; but not as *sensuous human activity*, as *practice*, not subjectively. Hence in opposition to materialism the *active* side was developed abstractly by idealism—which of course does not know real sensuous activity as such. Feuerbach wants sensuous objects, really distinguished from

---

* Note by R. Pascal (*Ibid.*, p 207): '*Anschauung*. I have used "contemplation" for this term. This, the normal translation, is somewhat ambiguous, and should be understood as "sense-perception" in strong contrast to its meaning of "meditation".'

the objects of thought: but he does not understand human activity itself as *objective* activity.*9

Hence it followed that man (the subject of
cognition) was considered the passive side of the
object-subject relation, as the determined member of this inter-relation. Furthermore, man was
abstracted here from the combination of social
relations and transformed into an isolated individual. The man-environment relations were therefore interpreted as the relations of the individual to all the rest, to everything that lay *outside
the individual brain* and existed *independently
of it.* But outside the individual, and independently of his will and consciousness, there existed
not only nature but also the social historical
environment, the world of things created by
man's labour, and the system of relations between
man and man, developed in the labour process.
In other words, not only did nature by itself ('in
itself') lie outside the individual but also humanised nature, altered by labour. For Feuerbach
the surrounding world or environment given in
intuition or contemplation was taken as the starting point, and its premises were not investigated.

When, therefore, he faced the problem of
where and how man (the thinking body) was in
immediate union (contact) with the environment,
he answered: in intuition, *in the individual's con-*

---

9 Karl Marx. *Theses on Feuerbach.* Translated by Roy
Pascal. In: Karl Marx and Frederick Engels. *The German
Ideology* (Lawrence & Wishart, London, 1938), p 197.

* Second note by R. Pascal: 'Activity through objects.'

templation, since it was the individual that he always had in mind. That was the root of all his weaknesses, because in contemplation there was given to the individual the product of the activity of other individuals interacting among themselves in the process of producing material life, and those properties and forms of nature that had already been transformed into the properties and forms of the activity of man, its object and its product. The 'nature as such' that Feuerbach wished to 'contemplate' did not, as a matter of fact, lie within his field of view, because this 'nature, the nature that preceded human activity, is not by any means the nature in which Feuerbach lives, nor the nature which to-day no longer exists anywhere (except perhaps on a few Australian coral-islands of recent origin) and which, therefore, does not exist for Feuerbach'.[10]

Feuerbach's attention was also diverted from the real complexities of the social relations between theory and practice, from the division of labour that 'alienated' thought (in the form of science) from the majority of individuals and converted it into a force existing independently of them and outside them. He therefore saw nothing in the thought idolised by Hegel (i.e. science) than a certain modification of religious illusions.

---

[10] Karl Marx and Frederick Engels. *The German Ideology*, p 37.

PART TWO

CERTAIN PROBLEMS
OF THE MARXIST-LENINIST THEORY
OF DIALECTICS

ESSAY SEVEN

A Contribution to the Problem
of a Dialectical Materialistic Critique
of Objective Idealism

In order to overcome the weaknesses, or rather defects, of any philosophical system, it is necessary to understand them. Marx demonstrated this sort of 'understanding' in relation to Hegel, and thereby went much further in matters of logic than either Hegel or his materialist antipode Feuerbach.

Marx, Engels, and Lenin showed both the historical contribution of Hegel and the historically conditioned limitations of his scientific advances, the clearly drawn boundary across which the Hegelian dialectic could not step, and the illusions, whose power it was incapable of overcoming despite all the strength of its creator's mind. Hegel's greatness, like his limitations, was due on the whole to his having exhausted the possibilities of developing dialectics on the basis of idealism, within the limits of the premises that idealism imposed on scientific thinking. Irrespective of his intentions, Hegel showed, with exceptional clarity, that idealism led thinking up a blind alley and doomed even dialectically enlightened thought to hopeless circling within itself, to an endless procedure of 'self-expression' and 'self-consciousness'. For Hegel (precisely because he was a most consistent and unhypocritical idealist, who thereby disclosed the secret of every other, inconsistent and incomplete idealism) 'being', i.e. the world of nature and history existing outside thought and independently of it, was inevitably transformed into a mere pretext for demonstrating the logical art, into an inexhaustible reservoir of 'examples' confirming over and over again the same schemas and categories of logic. As the young Marx remarked, 'the matter of logic' (*die Sache der Logik*) fenced the 'logic of the matter' (*die Logik der Sache*)[1] off from Hegel, and therefore both the Prussian monarch and the louse on the monarch's head could equally well serve the idealist dialectician as 'examples' illustrating the category 'real individuality in and for itself'.

With such an approach both a boiling tea-kettle and the Great French Revolution were only 'examples' illustrating the relation of the categories of quality and quantity; but any empirical reality impinging on the eye, however fortuitous it might be in itself, was thereby converted into an external embodiment of absolute reason, into

---

[1] See Karl Marx. Contribution to the Critique of Hegel's Philosophy of Law. *Op. cit.*, p 18.

one of the necessary dialectical stages of its self-differentiation.

The profound flaws in the Hegelian dialectic were directly linked with idealism, due to which the dialectic was readily transformed into ingenious, logically subtle apologies for everything that existed. It is therefore necessary to look into all these circumstances more closely.

Hegel actually counterposed man and his real thought to impersonal, featureless—'absolute'—thought as some force existing for ages, in accordance with which the act of 'divine creation of the world and man' had occurred. He also understood logic as 'absolute form', in relation to which the real world and real human thought proved to be something essentially derivative, secondary and created.

In that, too, the idealism of Hegel's conception of thinking was revealed; and it was the specifically Hegelian objective idealism that converted thought into some new god, into some supernatural force existing outside man and dominating him. This specifically Hegelian illusion, however, did not at all express an idea simply taken uncritically by Hegel from religion, or a simple atavism of religious consciousness, as Feuerbach suggested, but a much more profound and serious circumstance.

The fact is that the Hegelian conception of thought represented an uncritical description of the real position of things formed on the soil of a narrowly professional form of the division of social labour, that is to say, on the division of mental work from physical labour, from immediately practical, sensuously objective activity.

Under the spontaneously developing division of social labour there arose of necessity a peculiar inversion of the real relations between human individuals and their collective forces and collectively developed faculties, i.e. the universal (social) means of the activity, an inversion known in philosophy as *estrangement* or *alienation*. Here, in social reality, and not at all simply in the fantasies of religiously minded people and idealist philosophers, universal (collectively realised) modes of action were organised as special social institutions, established in the form of trades and professions, and of a kind of caste with its own special rituals, language, traditions, and other 'immanent' structures of a quite impersonal and featureless character.

As a result, the separate human individual did not prove to be the bearer, i.e. to be the subject, of this or that universal faculty (active power), but, on the contrary, this active power, which was becoming more and more estranged from him, appeared as the subject, dictating the means and forms of his occupation to each individual from outside. The individual as such was thus transformed into a kind of slave, into a 'speaking tool' of alienated universally human forces and faculties, means of activity personified as money and capital, and further as the state, law, religion, and so on.

The same fate also befell *thought*. It, too, became a *special occupation*, the lot for life of professional scholars, of professionals in mental, theoretical work. *Science is thought transformed in certain conditions into a special profession.* Given universal alienation, thought achieved the heights and levels of development needed for society as a whole only in the sphere of science (i.e. within the community of scholars), and in that form was really *opposed* to the majority of human beings and not simply opposed to them but also dictating to them what they must do from the standpoint of science, and how they must do it, and what and how they must think, etc., etc. The scientist, the professional theoretician, lays down the law to them not in his own name, personally, but in the name of Science, in the name of the Concept, in the name of an absolutely universal, collective, impersonal power, appearing before other people as its trusted representative and plenipotentiary.

On that soil, too, there arose all the specific illusions of the professionals of mental, theoretical work, illusions that acquired their most conscious expression precisely in the philosophy of objective idealism, i.e. of the self-consciousness of alienated thought.

It will readily be noted that Hegel, in his logic, quite exactly expressed, in scholastically disguised form, the fundamental features of human life activity: man's faculty (as a thinking creature) to look at himself 'from outside' as it were, as something 'other', as a special object; or in other words to transform *the schemas of his own activity into its own object.* (That is the very special feature of man which the young Marx recognised as follows, and that in the course of a critique of Hegel: 'The animal is immediately one with its life activity. It does not distinguish itself from it. It is *its life activity*. Man makes his life activity itself the object of his will and of his consciousness. He has conscious life activity. It is not a determination with which he directly merges.'[2])

Since Hegel looked upon this feature of human life activity exclusively through the *eyes of logic*, he registered it solely to the extent that it was already transformed into a scheme of thought, into a logical schema, into a rule in accordance with which man more or less consciously built this or that specific activity (be it in the material of language or something else). He therefore registered things, and the position of things (acts) located outside the individual's consciousness and beyond his will (*Dinge und Sache*), exclusively as moments, as metamorphoses of thought (subjective activity), realised and realisable in natural, physical material, including in that also the organic body of man himself. The special feature of human life activity described above in Marx's words also appeared in the Hegelian representation as a *scheme of thought* realised by man, as a logical figure.

The real picture of human life activity obtained here is a topsy-turvy, upside-down representa-

---

[2] Karl Marx. Economic and Philosophic Manuscripts of 1844. *Op. cit.*, p 277.

tion. In reality man thinks because that is his real life activity. Hegel said the contrary, that real human life activity was such because man thought in accordance with a definite schema. All determinations of human life activity, naturally, and through it the position of things outside man's head, were only fixed here insofar as they were 'posited by thought', and appeared *as the result* of thought.

This is only natural because the logician who specially studied thought was no longer interested in things (or the position of things) as such, as a reality existing before, outside of, and independently of man and his activity (the logician did not look on reality at all as the physicist or biologist, economist or astronomer did), but in things as, and as what, they appeared as a result of the activity of a thinking being, of the subject, as the *product* of thought understood as an activity, the specific product of which was the *concept*.

So Hegel was 'guilty' of remaining a 'pure' logician just there where the standpoint of logic was inadequate. This peculiar professional blindness of the *logician* showed up primarily in the fact that he looked upon practice, i.e. the real, sensuously objective activity of man, *solely* as a criterion of truth, *solely* as the verifying authority for thought, for the mental, theoretical work completed before and independently of practice, or rather for the results of that work.

Practice there was thus also understood abstractly, was only illuminated from that aspect, and in those characteristics, which it owed in fact to thought, because it was the act of realising a certain intention, plan, idea, concept, or some aim selected in advance, was absolutely not analysed as such in a determination of its own, not dependent on some thought. All the results of people's practical activity—things made by human labour, and historical events and their consequences—were correspondingly only taken into account insofar as they embodied or objectified some idea or another. In a conception of the historical process as a whole such a point of view was understandably the purest ('absolute') idealism. As regards logic, however, the science of thought, it was not only justified but was the sole rational position.

In fact, can we reproach the *logician* for abstracting everything in the most rigorous fashion that had nothing to do with the subject matter of his investigation, and for paying attention to any fact only insofar as it could be understood as the consequence, as the form of disclosure, of his *subject matter*, of the subject matter of *his science*, i.e. of thought? To reproach the professional logician for the fact that the 'matter of logic' concerned him more than the 'logic of the matter', (i.e. the logic of any other concrete sphere of human activity) would be as stupid as to reproach the chemist for excessive attention to the 'matter of chemistry'. But Marx's words above, directed at Hegel, concealed quite another meaning.

The fault of the narrow professional was not at all his rigorous limitation of thought to the framework of the subject matter of his science, but his incapacity to see clearly the boundaries of the competence of his science associated with this limitation of his view of things.

The same applied to Hegel, the typical professional logician. As a logician he was right to look upon a statement or a fact exclusively from the standpoint of the abstract schemas of thought revealed in it, when the logic of any matter interested him only insofar as it was revealed in it in general. The mysticism of Hegel's logic, and at the same time its insidious feature, which Marx called his 'false positivism',[3] began where the special standpoint of the logician *ex professo* was adopted and distinguished from the sole *scientific* standpoint from the heights of which only the 'ultimate', most profound, most cherished, and most important truth accessible in general to man and to humanity was allegedly discovered.

As a logician Hegel was quite right in looking on any phenomenon in the development of human culture as an act disclosing the power of thought. But it was the work of a moment, by adding a little something to that view (admissible and natural in logic), namely that the *essence of the phenomena in themselves* from which the special, logical abstractions were drawn was expressed just in those abstractions, for the truth to be transformed into a lie. The exact results of a chemical investigation of the composition of the

---

[3] Karl Marx. Economic and Philosophic Manuscripts of 1844. *Op. cit.*, p 339.

colours used to paint the Sistine Madonna would be converted into such a lie the moment the chemist looked on them as the sole scientific explanation of the unique 'synthesis' created by Raphael's brush.

Abstractions that quite precisely expressed (described) the forms and schemas of the flow of thought in all forms of its concrete realisation were immediately and directly passed off as schemas of the process that had *created* the whole diversity of human culture, in which they were discovered. As a result the whole mystique of Hegel's conception of thought was concentrated in a single point. In considering all the manifold forms of human culture as a result of manifestation of the faculty to think that functions in man, he lost any chance of understanding from where in general this unique faculty, and its schemas and rules, appeared in man. By raising thought to the rank of a divine power and force impelling man to historical creation from within, Hegel simply passed off the absence of a reply to this reasonable question as the only possible answer to it.

The sensuously objective activity of the millions of people who by their labour created the body of culture, the self-consciousness of which is scientific thought, remained outside Hegel's field of view, seemed to him the 'prehistory' of thought. The external world therefore appeared as the initial material for producing the concept, as something that had to be processed by means of existing concepts in order to concretise them.

Thought was thus transformed into the only active and creative force, and the external world into its field of application. Naturally, if the sensuously objective activity (practice) of social man was represented *as the consequence*, as the *external objectification of ideas*, plans, and concepts created by thought (i.e. by persons occupied in mental work), it became in principle impossible to say either what was the source of thought in the head of theoreticians or how it arose.

Thought *was*, Hegel replied; and to ask about its *origin* from something else was to ask a futile question. It *was*, it *operated* in man, and gradually arrived at awareness of its own activities, and of their schemas and laws. Logic was self-consciousness of this creative principle, of this infinite creative power, of this absolute form, which had never arisen from anywhere. In man this creative force was only revealed, objectified, and estranged so as then in logic to cognise itself as such, as the universal creative force.

That was the whole secret of Hegel's objective idealism. In logic, consequently, objective idealism means the absence of any answer whatsoever to the question from whence thought originates. In the form of logic, defined as a system of eternal and absolute schemas of every kind of creative activity, Hegel deified real human thought and its logical forms and patterns.

That was at once the strength and the weakness of his conception of thought and logic. Its strength was that he idolised (i.e. defined as given outside time, as absolute) the nevertheless *real logical forms and laws of human thought* discovered by him through study of human spiritual and material culture. Its weakness was that, for all that, he *idolised* the logical forms and laws of human thought, i.e. declared them absolute, without even allowing the problem of their *origin* to be posed.

The fact was that idealism, i.e. the view of thought as a universal faculty that was only *'aroused'* to self-consciousness in man and did not *arise* in the exact and strict sense from the soil of definite conditions formed outside him and independently of him, led to a number of absolutely unresolvable problems in logic itself.

While making an exceptionally important advance in understanding of the logical forms of thought, Hegel stopped halfway, and even turned back, as soon as he was faced with the question of the inter-relation of sensuously perceived forms of the embodiment of the mind's activity (thought), in which the mind (or spirit) became the object of consideration for itself. Thus he refused to recognise the word (speech, language) as the sole form of the 'effective being of the spirit', of the external disclosure of the creative power of thought. Nevertheless, he continued to consider it the principal, most adequate form, the form in which thought was counterposed to itself.

'In the beginning was the Word'—in respect of human thought (the thinking mind of man) Hegel maintained the Biblical position unsullied, accepting it as something self-evident and making it the basic principle of all subsequent construction, or rather reconstruction, of the development of the thinking spirit to self-consciousness.

The thinking mind of man was first aroused (i.e. counterposed itself to everything else) precisely *in the word* and through the word, as the faculty of 'naming', and therefore took shape primarily as the 'kingdom of names' and titles. The *word* also functioned as the first 'objective reality of thought activity', both in essence and in time, as the initial and *immediate* form of being of the spirit for itself.

This appeared clearly as follows: one 'finite spirit' (the thought of the individual) made itself the subject matter (object) of another, also 'finite', spirit in the word and through the word. Having arisen from the 'mind' as a definitely articulated sound, the word on being heard was again converted into 'spirit', into the state of the thinking mind of another person. The vibrations of the ambient air (the audible word) also proved to be only the pure *mediator* between the two states of the spirit, the mode of the relation of spirit to spirit, or, expressing it in Hegelian language, of the spirit *to itself.*

The word (speech) functioned here as the first tool of the external objectification of thought, which the thinking spirit created 'from itself' in order to become the object for itself (in the image of another thinking spirit). The real tool— the stone axe or cutting tool, scraper or wooden plough—began to appear as the second and secondary, derived tool of the same process of objectification as the sensuously objective *meta-morphosis of thought.*

Thus Hegel saw in the word the form of the actual being of the thinking spirit in which the latter manifested its own creative force (faculty) before everything, before and independently of the real moulding of nature by labour. Labour only realised what the thinking spirit had found in itself in the course of *utterance*, in the course of its dialogue with itself. But in this interpretation the *dialogue* proved to be only a *monologue* of the thinking spirit, only its mode of 'manifestation'.

In the *Phenomenology of Mind* all history therefore began with an analysis of the contradiction that arose between thought (insofar as it *expressed itself in the words* 'here' and 'now') and all its other content *not yet expressed in words.* The *Science of Logic* also suggested this schema, and contained the same, though implicit premise at its very beginning. Thought, it was suggested there, had realised and was realising itself primarily in and through the word. So it was no accident that the consummation of all the 'phenomenological' and 'logical' history of the thinking spirit consisted in returning to the starting point: the thinking spirit achieved its absolutely exact and perfect representation, naturally in the printed word—in a treatise on logic, in the *Science of Logic.*

Hegel therefore also maintained the following in logic: 'It is in human Language that the Forms of Thought are manifested and laid down in the first instance. In our day it cannot be too often recalled, that what distinguishes man from the beasts is the *faculty of Thought*. Language has penetrated into whatever becomes for man *something inner*—becomes, that is, an idea, something which he makes his very own;—and what man transforms to Language contains concealed, or mixed up with other things, or worked out to clearness—a Category....'[4]

That was the deepest root of Hegel's idealism. By that step thought as an activity taking place in the head in the form, precisely, of inner speech, was converted into the starting point for understanding all the phenomena of culture, both spiritual and material, including all historical events, social, economic, and political structures, and so on and so forth. The whole world of the products of human labour, and all history, then began to be interpreted as a process taking place 'from the head', 'from the power of thought'. The whole grandiose conception of the history of the estrangement (objectification) of the creative energy of thought and its inverse mastering of the fruits of its labour (disobjectification), which began with the word and completed its cycle in the word, was just the history outlined in the *Science of Logic*.

The clue to Hegel's conception is not so very complicated. The idea that man *thought initially,* and then only really *acted* served as the foundation of his schema. Hence also the schema 'word—

---

[4] *Hegel's Science of Logic*, Vol. I, pp 39-40.

act—thing made by the act—again word' (this time a verbally expressed report on what had been done). And further, there was a new cycle according to the same schema, but on a new basis, owing to which the movement had the form not of a circle but of a spiral, each turn of which, however, both began and ended at one and the same point, in a word.

The rational kernel and at the same time the mystifying feature of the schema described here are most easily considered by analogy (although it is more than a simple analogy) with the metamorphoses that political economy brings out when analysing commodity-money circulation. Just as accumulated labour concentrated in machines, in the instruments and products of labour, functions in the form of *capital,* in the form of 'self-expanding value', for which the individual capitalist functions as 'executor', so too scientific knowledge, i.e. the *accumulated mental labour* of society functions in the form of Science, i.e. the same sort of impersonal and featureless anonymous force. The individual professional theoretician functions *as the representative* of the self-developing power of knowledge. His social function boils down to being the individual embodiment of the *universal* spiritual wealth accumulated over centuries and millenia of mental labour. He functions as the animated tool of a process that is completed independently of his individual consciousness and his individual will, the process of the increase of knowledge. He does not think here *as such*— Knowledge, which has taken root in his head during his education, 'thinks'. He does not control the concept; rather the Concept controls him, determining both the direction of his research and the modes and forms of his activity.

There is the same *turning upside down* as in the sphere of material production based on exchange value, the same real mystification of the relations between the universal and the particular in which the abstract universal is not an aspect or property of the sensuously concrete (in this case living man) but rather the contrary, the sensuously concrete, individual man proves to be only an abstract, one-sided 'embodiment' of of the universal (in this case Knowledge, Concept, Science). This is not simply an analogy with what happens in the world of relations founded on value, but the same social process, only in the sphere of mental rather than material production. 'This inversion, by which the sensibly concrete is regarded as a form of manifestation of the abstract and general, instead of the abstract and general being regarded on the contrary as a property of the concrete, is characteristic of the expression of value. At the same time, it makes the expression of value difficult to understand. If I say: Roman law and German law are both law, that is self-evident. If, on the other hand, I say: *the* law, which is an abstraction, *is realised as such* in Roman law and in German law, which are concrete laws, the connection between the abstract and the concrete becomes mystical.'[5]

---

[5] Karl Marx. *Das Kapital,* Vol. I, p 771.

So Hegel's idealism was not in the least the fruit of religious fantasy or of a religiously oriented imagination. It was only an uncritical description of the real state of things, on the soil of which the professional theoretician, the narrow specialist of mental labour, operated (thought). The forms of his philosophy were the practically inevitable illusions (even practically useful) that he inevitably created in his own work, illusions that were fed by the objective position of that work in society, and reflected its position. It was the knowledge acquired by him as concepts immediately in the course of his education, i.e. in the form of verbal-sign expressions, which was *for him* the beginning (starting point) of his specific activity, and the end, its specific *goal*, its real 'entelechy'.

But the analogy we have used enables us also to understand another circumstance, i.e. the mechanism itself of the 'inversion' or 'turning upside down' described above. The pattern of commodity-money circulation is, as we know, expressed by the formula C—M—C. The commodity (C) appears in it as both the *beginning* and the *end* of the cycle, and money (M) as its *mediating link*, as the 'metamorphosis of the commodity'. But at a certain point in the self-closing cyclical movement C—M—C—M—C—M... and so on, money ceases to be a simple 'intermediary', the means of circulation of the mass of commodities and suddenly discloses an enigmatic faculty for 'self-expansion'. Schematically this phenomenon is expressed in the formula as follows: M—C—M′. The Commodity, the *real starting point* of the process as a whole, acquires the former role of money, the role of *intermediary* and *means* of the transient *metamorphosis of money*, in which the latter is embodied in order to complete the act of 'self-expansion'. Money, having acquired so mysterious a property, is also *capital*, and in the form of the latter acquires 'the occult quality of being able to add value to itself'[6] and 'suddenly presents itself as substance endowed with an independent motion of its own, a substance of which commodities and money are themselves merely forms'.[7] In the formula M—C—M′ value appears as an 'automatically operating subject', as the 'substance-subject' of the whole cyclic movement, constantly returning to its starting point; 'value is here the active factor in a process in which, while continually assuming by turns the form of money and the form of commodities, it at the same time changes in magnitude, gives birth to surplus value, so that the original value spontaneously expands'[8] and this happens 'in itself'.

In his *Science of Logic* Hegel recorded the same situation, only not in regard to value but to knowledge (understanding, truth). In fact he dealt with the process of accumulation of knowledge, because the concept is also *accumulated knowledge*, the 'constant capital', so to say, of thought,

---

6 Karl Marx. *Capital*, Vol. I, p 140.

7 *Ibid.*, p 140.

8 *Ibid.*, pp 139-140.

which always appears in science in the form of the word. Hence, too, the idea of knowledge, analogous to the idea of *value*, as a self-expanding substance, as a subject-substance.

Thus we are dealing not with the abstract fantasies of an idealist but with the same uncritical description of the real process of the production and accumulation of knowledge as the theory of political economy, which takes as the starting point of its explanation an exactly recorded but not understood fact. The fact is that money, appearing as the form of movement of capital, as the starting point and goal of the whole cyclical process of coming back 'to itself', discloses a mysterious, occult faculty for self-expansion and self-development. This fact, left unexplained, becomes mysterious and occult; and a property is ascribed to it that in fact belongs to quite another process that is *expressed* ('reflected') in its form.

In disclosing the secret of the self-expansion of value, i.e. the secret of the production and accumulation of surplus value, in *Capital* Marx employed (and not by chance, but deliberately and consciously) the whole terminology of Hegelian logic given above, and of Hegel's conception of thought. The fact is that the idealist illusion created by Hegel the logician had the same nature as the practically necessary ('practically true') illusions that entrap the mind of man caught up in the process of the creation and accumulation of surplus value, which is not understood by him and takes place independently of his consciousness and will. The logical and socio-historical patterns of the origin of these illusions were objectively and subjectively the same.

For the capitalist a certain sum of money (a certain value *indispensably expressed in money form*) is the starting point of all his further activity as a capitalist, and therefore the *formal goal* of his special activity. From where this sum of money arose, originally, with its occult properties, and how, may have no special interest for him.

Something analogous also happens with the professional theoretician, with the person who represents 'personified' knowledge, science, the concept. For him, the knowledge accumulated by humanity, and recorded moreover in verbal, sign form, also appears simultaneously as the *starting point* and as the *goal* of his special work.

From his point of view, naturally, the concept makes itself out to be a 'self-developing substance', 'an automatically operating subject', 'the subject substance of all its changes', and of all its metamorphoses.

Hence, from the real form of the life activity of the professional theoretician there also grow all the practically necessary illusions about thought and concept that were systematically expressed in Hegel's *Science of Logic*. The Hegelian logic described the system of the objective forms of thought within the limits of which revolved the process of *extended reproduction of the concept*, which never began, in its developed forms, 'from the very beginning', but took place as the *perfecting of already existing* concepts, as the transformation of *already accumulated* theoretical knowledge, as its 'increment'. The concept was always already *presupposed* here in the form of a jumping-off point for new conquests, since it was a matter of *extending* the sphere of the cognised, and in that the initial concepts played a most active role.

If the separate forms of the manifestation that expanding, growing knowledge drew by turns into its living circulation were recorded, the following definitions would be obtained: science (accumulated knowledge) is words (the 'language of science'); science is the things created on the basis of knowledge, i.e. the objectified, materialised force of knowledge. Knowledge becomes the subject of a certain process in which, here, while constantly changing its verbal form into an objective material one it alters its magnitude and its scale, throws off as surplus (added) knowledge from itself as the initial knowledge, and *'self-develops'*. For the movement in which knowledge unites new knowledge to itself is its own movement, and its expansion is consequently *self-expansion*, self-intensification, self-development. It has acquired the occult faculty of creating knowledge by virtue of the fact that it is itself knowledge.

By analogy with the production and accumulation of surplus value, *logical forms* (the real forms of the production of knowledge) began therefore to appear here as forms of the *'self-development'* of knowledge, and so were *mystified*. The mystification consisted in the pattern or scheme that expressed the features of the activity of the professional theoretician, being accepted and passed off as the pattern of development of knowledge in general.

So, we see, it was the same mystification as in political economy, in analysing which Marx stressed that his investigation did not begin with an analysis of value, but with analysis of a commodity.

From the logical standpoint that is most important in principle, because it was the analysis of a commodity that bared the secret of the birth and origin of value, and then also the secret of its manifestation in money, in money form. In the contrary case, the secret of the birth of value was unresolvable in principle.

The same thing took place with the concept of thought in the Hegelian scheme. Hegel recorded those features that were actually realised in the process of thought in its developed form, in the form of science, as a special (isolated) sphere of the division of social labour, and the formula that there quite accurately reflected the surface of the process appeared as follows: word—act—word (W—A—W), in which by 'word', is understood verbally recorded knowledge, knowledge in its universal form, in the form of the 'language of science', in the form of formulae, diagrams, symbols, models of all kinds, blueprints, etc., etc.

A really critical mastering of Hegel's logic, carefully preserving all its positive features and purging it of mystic worship of 'pure thought' and the 'divine concept', proved only to be within the power of Marx and Engels. No other philosophical system since Hegel has been able to handle it as a 'tool of criticism', since not one of them has adopted the standpoint of a revolutionary, critical attitude to the objective conditions that feed the illusions of idealism, i.e. to the situation of the estrangement (alienation) of the real, active faculties of man from the majority of individuals, the situation in which all the universal (social) forces, i.e. the active faculties of social man, appear as forces independent of the majority of individuals and dominating them as external necessity, as forces monopolised by more or less narrow groups, strata, and classes of society.

The sole path to a real, critical mastering of Hegel's conception of thought lay through a revolutionary, critical attitude to the world of alienation, i.e. to the world of commodity-capitalist relations. Only along that path could the objective-idealist illusions of Hegel's conception be really *explained*, and not simply attacked by such biting epithets (that equally explained nothing) as 'mystical nonsense', 'theological atavism', and others of that kind.

The Materialist Conception
of Thought as the Subject Matter
of Logic

After what Hegel had done it was only possible to advance in a single direction, along the road to materialism, to a clear understanding of the fact that all the dialectical schemas and categories revealed in thought by Hegel were universal forms and laws, reflected in the collective consciousness of man, of the development of the external real world existing outside of and independently of thought. Marx and Engels had already begun a materialist rethinking of the Hegelian dialectic at the beginning of the 1840s, and the materialistically rethought dialectic fulfilled the role, for them, of the logic of the development of the materialist world outlook.

This movement was seen as a direct continuation of Feuerbach's argumentation; and when it was expressed in the terms of his philosophy it appeared approximately as follows. The Ego did not think, nor Reason, nor even the brain. *Man thought* by means of his brain and, moreover, in unity and contact with nature. Abstracted from that unity he no longer thought. That was where Feuerbach left it.

But, continued Marx, man, too, did not think in immediate unity with nature. Man only thought when he was in unity with society, with the social and historical collective that produced his material and spiritual life. Abstracted from the nexus of the social relations within and through which he effected his human contact with nature (i.e. found himself in human unity with it), he thought as little as a brain isolated from the human body.

Thus it was along the path of development of logic that the problem of the nature of human thought, the problem of the *ideal*, reached its full stature.

The ideal is the subjective image of objective reality, i.e. reflection of the external world in the forms of man's activity, in the forms of his consciousness and will. The ideal is not an individual, psychological fact, much less a physiological fact, but a socio-historical one, the product and form of mental production. It exists in a variety of forms of man's social consciousness and will as the subject of the social production of material and spiritual life. In Marx's description, 'the ideal is nothing other than the material when it has been transposed and translated inside the human head'.[1]

All the diverse forms of resolving the problem of the ideal in the history of philosophy are at-

---

[1] Karl Marx. *Capital*, Vol. I, p 873.

tracted to two poles—the materialist and the idealist. Pre-Marxian materialism, while justly rejecting spiritualist and dualist ideas of the ideal as a special substance counterposed to the material world, considered the ideal as an image, as the reflection of a material body in another material body, i.e. as an attribute, a function, of specially organised matter. This general materialist conception of the nature of the ideal, which constituted the essence of the line of Democritus-Spinoza-Diderot-Feuerbach, irrespective of the variants of its concretisation by individual materialists, also served as the starting point for the Marxist-Leninist solution of the problem.

The weak sides of the pre-Marxian materialism, which appeared as a trend among the French materialists (especially in Cabanis and La Mettrie) and later in Feuerbach, and acquired independent form in the middle of the nineteenth century as so-called vulgar materialism (Büchner, Vogt, Moleschott, and others), were linked with an unhistorical, anthropological, naturalistic conception of the nature of man and led to a rapprochement and ultimately to direct *identification of the ideal with the material, neurophysiological structures of the brain and their functions.* The old materialism set out from a conception of man as part of nature but, not bringing materialism as far as history, it could not understand man in all his peculiarities as a product of labour transforming both the external world and man himself. By virtue of that the ideal could not be understood as the result and active function of labour, of the sensuously objective activity of social man, as the image of the external world arising in the thinking body not in the form of the result of passive contemplation but as the product and form of active transformation of nature by the labour of generations succeeding one another in the course of historical development. The main transformation that Marx and Engels effected in the materialist conception of the nature of the ideal therefore related primarily to the active aspect of the relation of thinking man to nature, i.e the aspect that had been mainly developed, as Lenin put it, by 'clever' idealism, by the line of Plato-Fichte-Hegel, and was emphasised by them in an abstract, one-sided, idealist way.

The main fact on which the classic systems of objective idealism had grown up was the independence of the aggregate social culture and its forms of organisation from the individual, and more broadly the conversion in general of the universal products of social production (both material and spiritual) into a special social force opposed to individuals and dominating their wills and minds. It was for that reason that 'the social power, i.e. the multiplied productive force, which arises through the co-operation of different individuals as it is determined within the division of labour, appears to these individuals, since their co-operation is not voluntary but natural, not as their own united power but as an alien force existing outside them, of the origin and end of which they are ignorant, which they thus cannot control, which on the contrary passes through a peculiar series of phases and stages independent of the will and the action of man, nay even being the prime governor of these'.[2] The power of the social whole over individuals was directly disclosed and functioned in the form of the state and the political system of society, in the form of a system of moral, ethical, and legal limitations and norms of social behaviour, and further, of aesthetic, logical and other standards and criteria. The individual was forced from childhood to reckon much more seriously with the requirements and limitations expressed and socially sanctioned in them than with the immediately perceived external appearance of single things and situations, or the organically inherent desires, inclinations, and needs of his own body. The social whole was also mystified in the 'fundamental' principles of objective idealism.

Exposing the earthly basis of idealist illusions, Marx and Engels wrote: 'This sum of productive forces, forms of capital and social forms of intercourse, which every individual and generation finds in existence as something given, is the real basis of what the philosophers have conceived as "substance" and "essence of man", and what they have deified and attacked....'[3]

---

[2] Karl Marx and Frederick Engels. *The German Ideology*, p 24.
[3] *Ibid.*, p 29.

All general images, however, without exception, neither sprang from universal schemas of the work of thought nor arose from an act of passive contemplation of nature unsullied by man, but took shape in the course of its practical, objective transformation by man, by society. They arose and functioned as forms of the *social-man determination of the purposive will of the individual*, i.e. as forms of real activity. General images, moreover, were crystallised in the body of spiritual culture quite unintentionally, and independently of the will and consciousness of individuals, although through their activities. In intuition they appeared precisely as the forms of things created by human activity, or as 'stamps' ('imprints') laid on natural, physical material by man's activities, as forms of purposive will alienated in external substance.

People were only concerned with nature as such to the extent that it was involved in one way or another in the process of social labour, was transformed into material, into a means, a condition of active human practice. Even the starry heavens, in which human labour still could not really alter anything, became the object of man's attention and contemplation when they were transformed by society into a means of orientation in time and space, into a 'tool' of the life activity of the organism of social man, into an 'organ' of his body, into his natural clock, compass, and calendar. The universal forms and patterns of natural material really showed through and were realised just to the extent to which this material had already been transformed into building material of the 'inorganic body of man', of the objective body of civilisation and so the universal forms of 'things in themselves' appeared to man immediately as active forms of the functioning of his 'inorganic body'.

The ideal existed immediately only as the form (mode, image) of the *activity* of social man (i.e. of a quite objective, material being), directed to the external world. When, therefore, we spoke of the material system, of which the ideal was the function and mode of existence, that system was only social man in unity with the objective world through which he exercised his specifically human life activity. The ideal thus did not boil down to the state of matter found in the cranium of the individual, i.e. the brain. It was the *special function of man as the subject of social labour activity*, accomplished in forms created by preceding development.

Between contemplating and thinking man and nature in itself there existed a very important mediating link through which nature was transformed into thought, and thought into the body of nature. That was practice, labour, production. It was production (in the broadest sense of the word) that transformed the object of nature into the object of contemplation and thought. 'Even the objects of the simplest "sensuous certainty" are only given to him [i.e. to man—*EUI*] through social development, industry and commercial intercourse.'[4]

Therefore, Marx said, Feuerbach also stopped at the standpoint of *contemplation* (intuition) of nature and 'never manages to conceive the sensuous world as the total living sensuous *activity* of the individuals composing it',[5] did not see that the object of his contemplation was the product of joint human labour. And in order to single out the image of nature in itself it was necessary to expand rather more labour and effort than the simple efforts of 'disinterested', aesthetically developed contemplation.

In immediate contemplation (intuition) the objective features of 'nature in itself' were bound up with the features and forms that had been stamped on it by the transforming activity of man, and all the purely objective characteristics of natural material, moreover, were given to contemplation through the image that the natural material had acquired in the course of, and as a result of, the subjective activities of social man. Contemplation was immediately concerned not with the object but with objective activity (i.e. activity on objects), transforming it, and with the results of this subjective (practical) activity.

A purely objective picture of nature was therefore disclosed to man not in contemplation but

---

[4] Karl Marx and Frederick Engels. *The German Ideology*, p 35.
[5] *Ibid.*, p 37.

only through activity and in the activity of man socially producing his own life, of society. Thought, setting itself the aim of depicting the image of nature in itself, had to take that circumstance fully into account, because only the same activity as transformed (altered and occasionally distorted) the 'true image' of nature, could indicate what it was like before and without 'subjective distortions'.

Only practice, consequently, was capable of resolving which features of the object given in contemplation belonged to the object of nature itself, and which had been introduced into it by man's transforming activity, i.e. by the subject.

Therefore 'the question whether objective truth is an attribute of human thought—is not a theoretical but a *practical* question. Man must prove the truth, i.e. the reality and power, the "this-sidedness" of his thinking in practice', Marx wrote in his second thesis on Feuerbach. 'The dispute over the reality or non-reality of thinking that is isolated from practice is a purely *scholastic* question.'[6]

That, too, constitutes the solution of many of the difficulties that have faced and still face philosophers.

In analysing the relation of production to consumption, i.e. a problem of political economy, and hence not a psychological one, Marx formulated the question as follows: 'If it is clear that production offers consumption its external

---

[6] *Ibid.*, p. 197.

object, it is therefore equally clear that consumption *ideally posits* the object of production as an internal image, as a need, as a drive and as purpose.'[7] But consumption, as Marx showed, is only an inner moment of production, or production itself, since it creates not only the external object but also the subject capable of producing and reproducing this object, and then of consuming it in the appropriate manner. In other words, production creates the form itself of man's active practice, or the faculty of creating an object of certain form and using it for its purpose, i.e. in its role and function in the social organism. In the form of an active, real faculty of man as the agent of social production, the object exists ideally as a product of production, i.e. as an inner image, requirement, and an urge and goal of human activity.

The ideal is therefore nothing else than the form of things, but existing outside things, namely in man, in the form of his active practice, i.e. it is *the socially determined form of the human being's activity.* In nature itself, including the nature of man as a biological creature, the ideal does not exist. As regards the natural, material organisation of the human body it has the same external character as it does in regard to the material in which it is realised and objectified in the form of a sensuously perceived thing. Thus the form of a jar growing under the hands

---

[7] Karl Marx. *Grundrisse*. Translated by Martin Nicolaus (Penguin Books, London, 1973) pp 91-92.

of a potter does not form part either of the piece of clay or of the inborn, anatomical, physiological organisation of the body of the individual functioning as potter. Only insofar as man trains and exercises the organs of his body on objects created by man for man does he become the bearer of the active forms of social man's activity that create the corresponding objects.

It is clear that the ideal, i.e. the active form of social man's activity, is immediately embodied, or as it is now fashionable to say, is 'coded', in the form of the neuro-cerebral structures of the cortex of the brain, i.e. quite materially. But the *material* being of the ideal is not itself ideal but only the *form of its expression in the organic body of the individual*. In itself the ideal is the socially determined form of man's life activity corresponding to the form of its object and product. To try and explain the ideal from the anatomical and physiological properties of the body of the brain is the same unfruitful whim as to try and explain the money form of the product of labour by the physico-chemical features of gold. Materialism in this case does not consist at all in identifying the ideal with the material processes taking place in the head. Materialism is expressed here in understanding that the ideal, as a socially determined form of the activity of man creating an object in one form or another, is engendered and exists not in the head but with the help of the head in the real objective activity (activity on things) of man as the active agent of social production.

Scientific determinations of the ideal are therefore obtained by way of a materialist analysis of the 'anatomy and physiology' of the social production of the material and spiritual life of society, and in no case of the anatomy and physiology of the brain as an organ of the individual's body. It is the world of the products of human labour in the constantly renewed act of its reproduction that is, as Marx said, 'the perceptibly existing human psychology'; and any psychology to which this 'open book' of human psychology remains unknown, cannot be a real science.[8] When Marx defined the ideal as the material 'transposed and translated inside the human head', he did not understand this 'head' naturalistically, in terms of natural science. He had in mind the socially developed head of man, all of whose forms of activity, beginning with the forms of language and its word stock and syntactical system and ending with logical categories, are products and forms of social development. Only when expressed in these forms is the external, the material, transformed into social fact, into the property of social man, i.e. into the ideal.

At first hand, transformation of the material into the ideal consists in the external fact being expressed in language, which 'is the immediate actuality of thought' (Marx). But language of itself is as little ideal as the neuro-physiological

    [8] See Karl Marx. Economic and Philosophic Manuscripts of 1844. *Op. cit.*, pp 302-303.

structure of the brain. It is only the *form of expression* of the ideal, its material-objective being. Neopositivists, who identify thought (i.e. the ideal) with language, with a system of terms and expressions, therefore make the same naturalistic mistake as scientists who identify the ideal with the structures and functions of brain tissue. Here, too, the form only of its material expression is taken for the ideal. The material is really 'transplanted' *into the human head,* and not simply into the brain as an organ of the individual's body, (1) only when it is expressed in immediately, generally significant forms of language (understood in the broadest sense of the word, including the language of drawings, diagrams, models, etc.), and (2) when it is transformed into an active form of man's activity with a real object (and not simply into a 'term' or 'utterance' as the material body of language). In other words the object proves to be idealised only when the faculty of actively recreating it has been created, relying on the language of words or drawings; when the faculty of converting words into deeds, and through deeds into things, has been created.

Spinoza understood this beautifully. With good reason he linked adequate ideas, expressed in the words of a language, precisely with ability to reproduce given verbal forms in real space. It was just there that he drew the distinction between a determination expressing the essence of the matter, i.e. the ideal image of the object, and nominal, formal definitions that fixed a more or less accidentally chosen property of the object, its outward sign. A circle, for example, could be defined as a figure in which lines drawn from the centre to the circumference were equal. But such a definition did not quite express the essence of a circle, but only a certain property of it, which property was derivative and secondary. It was another matter when the definition included the proximate cause of the thing. Then a circle should be defined as a figure described by any line one end of which was fixed and the other moved. This definition provided the *mode of constructing the thing* in real space. Here the *nomical definition* arose *together* with the *real action of the thinking body along the spatial contour of the object of the idea.* In that case man also possessed an adequate idea, i.e. an ideal image, of the thing, and not just signs expressed in words. That is also a materialist conception of the nature of the ideal. The ideal exists there where there is a capacity to recreate the object in space, relying on the word, on language, in combination with a need for the object, plus material provision of the act of creation.

Determination of the ideal is thus especially dialectical. It is that which is not, together with that which is, that which does not exist in the form of an external, sensuously perceived thing but at the same time does exist *as an active faculty of man.* It is being, which is, however, not-being, or the effective being of the external thing in the phase of its becoming in the activity of the subject, in the form of its inner image, need, urge, and aim; and therefore the *ideal being* of the thing is distinguished from its *real being*, and also from the bodily, material structures of the brain and language by which it exists 'within' the subject. The ideal image of the object is distinguished from the structure of the brain and language in principle by the fact that it is *the form of the external object*. It is also distinguished from the external object itself by the fact that it is objectified immediately not in the external matter of nature but in the organic body of man and in the body of language as a subjective image. The ideal is consequently the subjective being of the object, or its 'otherness', i.e. the being of one object in and through another, as Hegel expressed this situation.

The ideal, as the form of social man's activity, exists where the process of the transformation of the body of nature into the object of man's activity, into the object of labour, and then into the product of labour, takes place. The same thing can be expressed in another way, as follows: the form of the external thing involved in the labour process is 'sublated' in the subjective form of objective activity (action on objects); the latter is objectively registered in the subject in the form of the mechanisms of higher nervous activity; and then there is the reverse sequence of these metamorphoses, namely the verbally expressed idea is transformed into a deed, and through the deed into the form of an external, sensuously perceived thing, into a thing. These two contrary series of metamorphoses form a closed cycle: thing—deed—word—deed—thing. Only in this cyclic movement, constantly renewed, does the ideal, the ideal image of the thing exist.

The ideal is immediately realised in a symbol and through a symbol, i.e. through the external, sensuously perceived, visual or audible body of a word. But this body, while remaining itself, proves at the same time to be the being of another body and as such is its *'ideal being'*, its *meaning*, which is quite distinct from its bodily form immediately perceived by the ears or eyes. As a *sign*, as a *name*, a word has nothing in common with what it is the sign of. What is 'common' is only discovered in the act of transforming the word into a deed, and through the deed into a thing (and then again in the reverse process), in practice and the mastering of its results.

Man exists as man, as the subject of activity directed to the world around and to himself, from such time, and so long, as he actively produces his real life in forms created by himself and by his own labour. And labour, the real transformation of the world around and of himself, which is performed in socially developed and socially sanctioned forms, is just the process —beginning and continuing completely independent of thought—within which the ideal is engendered and functions as its metamorphosis, idealisation of reality, nature, and social relations is completed, and the language of symbols is born as the external body of the ideal image of the external world. In that is the secret of the ideal and in that too is its solution.

In order to make both the essence of the secret, and the means by which Marx resolved it, clearer, let us analyse the most typical case of the idealisation of actuality, or the act of the birth of the ideal, namely the phenomenon of price in political economy. 'The price, or the money form, of commodities is, like their form of value generally, distinct from their palpable and real bodily form. It is, that is to say, only an ideal or imaginary form.'[9] In the first place let ut note that price is an objective category and not a psycho-physiological phenomenon. Yet it is 'only an ideal form'. It is that which constitutes the materialism of the Marxian conception of price. Idealism on the contrary consists in affirming that price, since it is only an ideal form, exists solely as a subjective, psychic phenomenon, the interpretation that was given by none other than Bishop Berkeley, who wrote not only as a philosopher but also as an economist.

In making his critique of the idealist conception of money, Marx showed that price was the value of the product of man's labour expressed in money, for example, in a certain quantity of gold. But gold of itself, by its nature, was not money. It proved to be money because it performed a peculiar *social* function, the measure of value of all commodities, and as such functioned in the system of social relations between people

---

[9] Karl Marx. *Capital,* Vol. I, p 71.

in the process of the production and exchange of products; hence, too, the ideality of the form of price. Gold, while remaining itself in the process of circulation, nevertheless proved to be immediately the form of existence and movement of a certain 'other', represented and replaced that 'other' in the process of commodity-money circulation, and was its metamorphosis. 'As *price,* the commodity relates to money on one side as something existing outside itself, and secondly, it is *ideally* posited as money itself, since money has a reality different from it. . . . Alongside real money, there now exists the commodity as ideally posited money.'[10] 'After money is posited as a commodity in reality, the commodity is posited as money in the mind.'[11]

The ideal positing, or positing of the real product as the *ideal image of another product,* is accomplished during the circulation of the mass of commodities. It arises as a means of resolving the contradictions maturing in the course of the circulation process, and within it (and not inside the head, though not without the help of the head), as a means of satisfying a need that has become immanent in commodity circulation. This need, which appears in the form of an unresolved contradiction of the commodity form, is satisfied and resolved by one commodity 'being expelled' from their equal family and being converted into the immediately social standard of

---

[10] Karl Marx. *Grundrisse,* p 190.
[11] *Ibid.,* p 191.

the socially necessary expenditure of labour. 'The problem and the means of solution,' as Marx said, 'arise simultaneously.'[12]

In real exchange, before the appearance of money (before the conversion of gold into money), the following position had already taken shape: 'Intercourse in virtue of which the owners of commodities exchange their own articles for various other articles, and compare their own articles with various other articles, never takes place without leading the various owners of the various kinds of articles to exchange these for one special article in which the values of all the others are equated. Such a third commodity, inasmuch as it comes to function as equivalent for various other commodities, acquires, though within narrow limits, a generalised or social equivalent form.'[13] Thus the possibility and the necessity also arise of expressing the reciprocal exchange relation of two commodities through the exchange value of a third commodity, still without the latter entering directly into the real exchange but serving merely as the general measure of the value of the commodities really exchanged. And the 'third commodity', although it does not enter bodily into the exchange, is all the same involved in the act of exchange, since it is also present only *ideally,* i.e. in the idea, in the mind of the commodity-owners, in speech, on paper, and so on. But it is thus transformed into

---

12 Karl Marx. *Capital*, Vol. I, pp 63-64.
13 *Ibid.*, p 64.

a symbol and precisely into a symbol of the social relations between people.

All theories of money and value that reduce value and its forms to pure symbolics, to the naming of relations, to a conventionally or legally instituted sign, are associated with that circumstance. By the logic of their origin and structure they are organically related to those philosophers and logicians who, not being able to conceive the act of birth of the ideal from the process of social man's objective-practical activity, proclaim the forms of expression of the ideal in speech, in terms and statements, to be conventional phenomena, behind which, however, there stands something mystically elusive—be it the 'experience' of Neopositivists, the 'existence' of Existentialists, or the intuitively grasped, incorporeal, mystical 'eidetic being' of Edmund Husserl. Marx disclosed once and for all the whole triviality of such theories of the ideal, and of its reduction to a symbol or sign of immaterial relations (or connections as such, connections without a material substratum). 'The fact that commodities are only nominally converted in the form of prices into gold and hence gold is only nominally transformed into money led to the doctrine of the *nominal standard of money*. Because only imaginary gold or silver, i.e. gold and silver merely as money of account, is used in the determination of prices, it was asserted that the terms pound, shilling, pence, thaler, franc, etc., denote ideal particles of value but not weights of gold or silver or any form of materialised labour.'[14] Furthermore it was already easy to pass to the notion that the prices of commodities were merely terms for relations or proportions, pure signs.

Thus objective economic phenomena were transformed into simple symbols behind which there was hidden the will as their substance, representation as the 'inner experience' of the individual Ego, interpreted in the spirit of Hume and Berkeley. By exactly the same scheme modern idealists in logic convert terms and statements (the verbal envelope of the ideal image of the object) into simple names of relations in which the 'experiences' of the solitary individual are posited by the symbolising activity of language. Logical relations are transformed simply into the names of connexions (but of what with what is not known).

It must be specially stressed that the ideal transformation of a commodity into gold, and thus of gold into a symbol of social relations, took place both in time and in essence before the real conversion of the commodity into money, i.e. into hard cash. Gold became the measure of the value of commodities before it became the medium of circulation, and so functioned initially as money purely ideally. 'Money only circulates commodities which have already been *ideally* transformed into money, not only in the head

---

[14] Karl Marx. *A Contribution to the Critique of Political Economy*. Translated by S. W. Ryazanskaya (Progress Publishers, Moscow, 1970), p 76.

of the individual but in the conception held by society (directly, the conception held by the participants in the process of buying and selling).'[15]

That is a fundamentally important point of the Marxian conception not only of the phenomenon of price but also of the problem of the ideal, the problem of the idealisation of reality in general. The fact is that the act of exchange always posits an already formed system of relations between people mediated by things; it is expressed in one of the sensuously perceived things being transformed, without ceasing to function in the system as a separate, sensuously perceived body, into the *representative of any other body,* into the sensuously perceived body of an ideal image. In other words, it is the *external embodiment of another thing*, not its sensuously perceived image but rather *its essence*, i.e. the *law* of its existence within the system that in general creates the situation being analysed. The given thing is thus transformed into a symbol, the meaning of which remains all the time outside its immediately perceived image, in other sensuously perceived things, and is disclosed only through the whole system of relations of other things to it or, conversely, of it to all the others. But when this thing is really removed from the system it loses its role, i.e. its significance as a symbol, and is transformed once more into an ordinary, sensuously perceived thing along with other such things.

---

[15] Karl Marx. *Grundrisse*, p 187.

Its existence and functioning as a symbol consequently does not belong to it as such but only to the system within which it has acquired its properties. The properties attaching to it from nature therefore have no relation to its existence as a symbol. The corporeal, sensuously perceived envelope or 'body' of the symbol (the body of the thing that has been transformed into a symbol) is quite unessential, transient, and temporary for its existence as a symbol; the 'functional existence' of such a thing completely 'absorbs . . . its material existence', as Marx put it.[16] Furthermore, the material body of the thing is brought into conformity with its function. As a result the symbol is converted into a token, i.e. into an object that already means *nothing in itself* but only represents or expresses another object with which it itself has nothing in common (like the name of the thing with the thing itself). The dialectic of the transformation of a thing into a symbol, and of a symbol into a token, is also traced in *Capital* on the example of the origin and evolution of the money form of value.

The functional existence of a symbol consists precisely in its not representing *itself* but *another*, and in being a means, an instrument expressing the *essence of other sensuously perceived things*, i.e. their universal, socially-human significance, their role and function within the social organism. In other words, the function of a symbol consists in its being just the body of the ideal

---

[16] Karl Marx. *Capital*, Vol. I, p 110.

273

image of the external thing, or rather the law of its existence, the law of the universal. A symbol removed from the real process of exchange of matter between social man and nature also ceases in general to be a symbol, the corporeal envelope of the ideal image. Its 'soul' vanishes from its body because its 'soul' is in fact the objective activity of social man effecting an exchange of matter between humanised and virgin nature.

Without an ideal image man cannot in general exchange matter with nature, and the individual cannot operate with things involved in the process of social production. But the ideal image requires real material, including language, for its realisation. Therefore labour engenders a need for language, and then language itself.

When man operates with symbols or with tokens and not with objects, relying on symbols and tokens, he does not act on the ideal plane but only on the verbal plane. And it very often happens that, instead of discovering the real essence of things by means of terms, the individual sees only the terms themselves with their traditional meanings, sees only the symbol and its sensuously perceived body. In that case the linguistic symbol is transformed from an instrument of real activity into a fetish, blocking off with its body the reality that it represents. Then, instead of understanding and consciously changing the external world in accordance with its general laws expressed in the form of the ideal image, man begins to see and change only the verbal, terminological expression and thinks that, in so doing, he is changing the world itself.

This fetishisation of the verbal existence of the ideal was very characteristic of the Left Hegelian philosophy of the period of its decline, to which Marx and Engels drew attention at the time. It itself, and with it fetishisation of the system of social relations that it represents, proves to be the absolutely inevitable end of any philosophy that does not understand that the ideal is engendered and reproduced only through social man's objective-practical activity, and that it also only exists in that process. In the opposite case some form or other of fetishisation both of the external world and of symbolics develops.

It is very curious that no variety of fetishisation of the verbal-symbolic existence of the ideal embraces the ideal as such. Fetishisation registers the results of human activity but not man's activity itself, so that it embraces not the ideal itself but only its estrangement in external objects or in language, i.e. congealed products. That is not surprising; *the ideal as a form of human activity exists only in that activity,* and not in its results, because the activity is a constant, continuing negation of the existing, sensuously perceived forms of things, is their change and sublation into new forms, taking place in accordance with general patterns expressed in ideal forms. When an object has been created society's need for it is satisfied; the activity has petered out in its product, and the ideal itself has died.

An ideal image, say of bread, may arise in the imagination of a hungry man or of a baker. In the head of a satiated man occupied in building a house, ideal bread does not arise. But if we take society as a whole ideal bread, and ideal houses, are always in existence, and any ideal object with which man is concerned in the process of production and reproduction of his material life. In consequence of that all nature is idealised in man and not just that part which he immediately produces or reproduces or consumes in a practical way. Without a constant re-idealising of the real objects of human life activity, without their transformation into the ideal, and so without symbolisation, man cannot in general be the active subject of social production.

The ideal also appears as the product and form of human labour, of the purposive transformation of natural material and social relations effected by social man. The ideal is present only where there is an individual performing his activity in forms given to him by the preceding development of humanity. Man is distinguished from beasts by the existence of an ideal plane of activity. 'But what ... distinguishes the most incompetent architect from the best of bees, is that the architect has built a cell in his head before he constructs it in wax. The labour process ends in the creation of something which, when the process began, already existed in the worker's

276

imagination, already existed in an ideal form.'[17]

We must once more note that if the head is understood naturalistically, i.e. as a material organ of the separate individual's body, then there is no difference in principle, it transpires, between the architect and the bee. The wax cell that the bee builds also exists beforehand in the form of the pattern of the insect's activity programmed in its nerve centres. In that sense the product of the bee's activity is also given 'ideally' before its real performance. But the insect's forms of activity are innate in it, inherited together with the structural, anatomical organisation of its body. The form of activity that we can denote as the ideal existence of the product is never differentiated from the body of the animal in any other way than as some real product. The fundamental distinction between man's activity and the activity of an animal is this, that no one form of this activity, no one faculty, is inherited together with the anatomical organisation of the body. All forms of activity (active faculties) are passed on only in the form of objects created by man for man. The individual mastery of a humanly determined form of activity, i.e. the ideal image of its object and product, are therefore transformed in a special process that does not coincide with the objective moulding of nature (shaping of nature in objects). The form itself of man's activity is therefore transformed into a special object, into the object of special activity.

---

[17] Karl Marx. *Capital*, Vol. I, p 170.

When the ideal was defined above as the form of man's activity, that definition was, strictly speaking, incomplete. It characterised the ideal only according to its objectively conditioned content; but the ideal is only there where the form itself of the activity corresponding to the form of the external object is transformed for man into a special object with which he can operate specially without touching and without changing the real object up to a certain point. Man, and only man, ceases to be 'merged' with the form of his life activity; he separates it from himself and, giving it his attention, transforms it into an idea. Since man is given the external thing in general only insofar as it is involved in the process of his activity, in the final product—in the idea—the image of the thing is always merged with the image of the activity in which this thing functions.

That constitutes the epistemological basis of the identification of the thing with the idea, of the real with the ideal, i.e. the epistemological root of any kind or shade of idealism. True, the objectification of the form of activity as a result of which it becomes possible to take it as the form of the thing, and conversely the form of the thing as the product and form of subjective activity, as the ideal is still not, as a matter of fact, idealism. This real fact is only transformed into one variety or another of idealism or fetishism given certain social conditions, or more concretely given the spontaneous division of labour, in which the form of activity is forcibly imposed on the individual by social processes that are independent of him and not understood by him. The objectification (materialisation) of social forms of human activity characteristic of commodity production (commodity fetishism) is quite analogous to the religious alienation of active human faculties in ideas about gods. This analogy is realised quite clearly already within the limits of the objective-idealist view of the nature of the ideal. Thus the young Marx, still a Left Hegelian, noted that all the ancient gods possessed the same 'real existence' as money did. 'Did not the ancient Moloch reign? Was not the Delphic Apollo a real power in the life of the Greeks? Kant's critique means nothing in this respect. If somebody imagines that he has a hundred talers, if this concept is not for him an arbitrary, subjective one, if he believes in it, then these hundred imagined talers have for him the same value as a hundred real ones. . . . Real talers have the same existence that the imagined gods have. Has a real taler any existence except in the imagination, if only in the general or rather common imagination of man?'[18]

The real nature of this analogy, however, was only disclosed by him later, on the basis of the materialist conception of nature and money and religious images. The 'similarity' of commodity fetishism and religious estrangement is rooted in

<hr>

[18] Karl Marx. Doctoral Dissertation. In: Karl Marx and Frederick Engels. *Collected Works*, Vol. 1 (Lawrence & Wishart, London, 1975) p 104.

the real connexion of people's social ideas and their real activity, and the forms of practice, in the active role of the ideal image (notion). Up to a certain point man is able to change the form of his activity (or the ideal image of the external thing) without touching the thing itself, but only because he can separate the ideal image from himself, objectify it, and operate with it as with an object existing outside him. Let us recall once more the example of the architect, cited by Marx. The architect builds a house not simply in his head but by means of his head, on the plane of ideas on Whatman paper, on the plane of the drawing board. He thus alters his internal state, externalising it, and operating with it as with an *object distinct from himself.* In changing it he potentially alters the real house, i.e. changes it ideally, potentially, which means that he alters *one sensuously perceived object instead of another.*

In other words activity on the plane of representation, altering the ideal image of an object, is also sensuous objective activity transforming the sensuously perceived image of the thing to which it is directed. Only the thing altered here is special; it is only the objectified idea or *form of the person's activity taken as a thing.* That circumstance also makes it possible to slur over the fundamental, philosophical, epistemological difference between material activity and the activity of the theoretician and ideologist who directly alters only the verbal, token objectification of the ideal image.

A person cannot pass the ideal as such to another person, as the pure form of activity. One can observe the activity of a painter or an engineer as long as one likes, striving to catch their mode of action, the form of their activity, but one can thus only copy the external techniques and methods of their work but never the ideal image itself, the active faculty itself. The ideal, as the form of subjective activity, is only masterable through active operation with the object and product of this activity, i.e. through the form of its product, through the objective form of the thing, through its active disobjectification. The ideal image of objective reality therefore also only exists as the form (mode, image) of living activity, co-ordinated with the form of its object, but not as a thing, not as a materially fixed state or structure.

The ideal is nothing else than a concatenation of the general forms of human activity realised by individuals, which determine the will and aptitude of individuals to act as an aim and law. It is quite understandable that the individual realisation of the ideal image is always linked with some deviation or other, or rather with concretisation of the image, with its correcting in accordance with the specific conditions, new social needs, the peculiarities of the material, and so on. And so, it posits the capacity to correlate the ideal image consciously with real, not yet idealised actuality. In that case the ideal functions as a special object for the individual, and object that he can alter purposively in accordance with the needs (requirements) of his activity. When, on the contrary, the individual only masters the ideal image formally, as a rigid pattern and sequence of operations, without understanding its origin and links with real (not idealised) actuality, he proves incapable of taking a critical attitude to this image, i.e. as a special object differentiated from him. Then he merges with it, as it were, and cannot treat it as an object correlated with reality and alter it accordingly. In that case, strictly speaking, it is not the individual who operates with the ideal image but the dogmatised image that acts in and through the individual. Here it is not the ideal image that is a real function of the individual but, on the contrary, the individual who is a function of the image, which dominates his mind and will as an externally given formal scheme, as an estranged image, as a fetish, as a system of unarguable rules coming inevitably from somewhere out of the blue. The idealist conception of the nature of the ideal corresponds to just such a consciousness.

The materialist conception, on the contrary, will prove to be natural to the man of communist society in which culture will not be counterposed to the individual as something given to him from outside, something independent and alien, but will be the form of his own real activity. In communist society, as Marx showed, it will become immediately obvious that *all forms of culture are only forms of the activity of man himself*, which is only brought to light in the conditions of bourgeois society by a theoretical analysis dispelling the illusions inevitable under them. 'Everything that has a fixed form, such as the product, etc., appears as merely a moment, a vanishing moment, in this movement. . . . The conditions and objectifications of the process are themselves equally moments of it, and its only subjects are the individuals, but individuals in mutual relationships, which they equally reproduce and produce anew. The constant process of their own movement, in which they renew themselves even as they renew the world of wealth they create.'[19]

A consistently materialist conception of thought, of course, alters the approach to the key problems of logic in a cardinal way, in particular to interpretation of the nature of logical categories. Marx and Engels established above all that external world was not given to the individual as it was in itself simply and directly in his contemplation, but only in the course of its being altered by man: and that both *the contemplating man* himself and *the world contemplated* were products of history.

The forms of thought, too, the categories, were accordingly understood not as simple abstractions from unhistorically understood sensuousness, but primarily as universal forms of social man's sensuously objective activity reflected in consciousness. The real objective equivalent of logical forms was seen not simply in the abstract,

---

[19] Karl Marx. *Grundrisse*, p 712.

general contours of the object contemplated by the individual but in the forms of man's real activity transforming nature in accordance with his own ends: 'It is precisely *the alteration of nature by men*, not solely nature as such, which is the most essential and immediate basis of human thought, and it is in the measure that man has learned to change nature that his intelligence has increased.'[20] The subject of thought here already proved to be the individual in the nexus of social relations, the socially determined individual, all the forms of whose life activity were given not by nature, but by history, by the process of the moulding of human culture.

The forms of human activity (and the thought-forms reflecting them) are consequently laid down in the course of history independently of the will and consciousness of individuals, to whom they are counterposed as the forms of a historically developed system of culture, a system that does not develop at all according to the laws of psychology, since the development of social consciousness is not a simple arithmetic sum of psychic process but a special process governed in general and on the whole by the laws of development of society's material life. These laws not only do not depend on the will and consciousness of individuals but, on the contrary, also actively determine that will and consciousness. The separate individual does not develop the universal forms of human activity by himself, and cannot

---

[20] Frederick Engels. *Dialectics of Nature*, p 172.

do so, whatever the powers of abstraction he possesses, but assimilates them ready-made in the course of his own acquiring of culture, together with language and the knowledge expressed in it.

Psychological analysis of the act of reflexion of the external world in the individual head therefore cannot be the means of developing logic. The individual thinks only insofar as he has already mastered the general (logical) determinations historically moulded before him and completely independently of him. And psychology as a science does not investigate the development of human culture or civilisation, rightly considering it a premise independent of the individual.

While Hegel's recording of these facts led him to idealism, Marx and Engels, having considered the real (objective) prototype of logical definitions and laws in the concrete, universal forms and laws of social man's objective activity, cut off any possibility of subjectivist interpretation of the activity itself. Man does not act on nature from outside, but 'confronts nature as one of her own forces',[21] and his objective activity is therefore linked at every stage with, and mediated by, objective natural laws. Man 'makes use of the mechanical, physical, and chemical properties of things as means of exerting power over other things, and in order to make these other things subservient to his aims. . . . Thus nature becomes

---

[21] Karl Marx. *Capital*, Vol. I, p 169.

an instrument of his activities, an instrument with which he supplements his own bodily organs, adding a cubit and more to his stature, scripture notwithstanding'.[22] It is just in that that the secret of the *universality* of human activity lies, which idealism passes off as the consequence of reason operating in man: 'The universality of man appears in practice precisely in the universality which makes all nature his *inorganic body*—both inasmuch as nature is (1) his direct means of life, and (2) the material, the object, and the instrument of his life activity. Nature is man's *inorganic body*—nature, that is, insofar as it is not itself the human body.'[23]

The laws of human activity are therefore also, above all, laws of the natural material from which 'man's inorganic body', the objective (material) body of civilisation, is built, i.e. laws of the movement and change of the objects of nature, transformed into the organs of man, into moments of the process of production of society's material life.

In labour (production) man makes one object of nature act on another object of the same nature in accordance with their own properties and laws of existence. Marx and Engels showed that the logical forms and laws of man's action were the consequences (reflexion) of real laws of human actions on objects, i.e. of practice in all its

---

[22] Karl Marx. *Capital*, Vol. I, p 171.
[23] Karl Marx. Economic and Philosophic Manuscripts of 1844. *Op. cit.*, pp 275-276.

scope and development, laws that are independent of any thinking. Practice understood materialistically, appeared as a process in whose movement each object involved in it functioned (behaved) in accordance with its own laws, bringing its own form and measure to light in the changes taking place in it.

Thus mankind's practice is a fully concrete (particular) process, and at the same time a universal one. It includes all other forms and types of the movement of matter as its abstract moments, and takes place in conformity with their laws. The general laws governing man's changing of nature therefore transpire to be also general laws of the change of nature itself, revealed by man's activity, and not by orders foreign to it, dictated from outside. The universal laws of man's changing of nature are also universal laws of nature only in accordance with which can man successfully alter it. Once realised they also appear as laws of reason, as logical laws. Their 'specificity' consists precisely in their universality, i.e. in the fact that they are not only laws of subjective activity (as laws of the physiology of higher nervous activity or of language), and not only of objective reality (as laws of physics or chemistry), but also laws governing the movement both of objective reality and of subjective human life activity. (That does not mean at all, of course, that thought does not in general possess any 'specific features' worthy of study. As a special process possessing features specifically distinguishing it from the movement of objective reality, i.e. as a psycho-physiological faculty of the human individual, thought has, of course, to be subjected to very detailed study in psychology and the physiology of the higher nervous system, but not in logic). In subjective consciousness these laws appear as 'plenipotentiaries' of the rights of the object, as its universal, ideal image: 'The laws of logic are the reflections of the objective in the subjective consciousness of man.'[24]

[24] V. I. Lenin. Philosophical Notebooks. *Op. cit.*, p 183.

On the Coincidence of Logic with Dialectics and the Theory of Knowledge of Materialism

Like any other science logic is concerned with explaining · and systematising objective forms and patterns not dependent on men's will and consciousness, within which human activity, both material-objective and mental-theoretical, takes place. Its subject matter is *the objective laws of subjective activity.*

Such a conception is quite unacceptable to traditional logic since, from the standpoint of the latter, it unites the unjoinable, i.e. an affirmation and its negation, A and not-A, opposing predicates. For the subjective is not objective, and vice versa. But the state of affairs in the real world and in the science comprehending it also proves unacceptable to traditional logic, because in it the transition, formation, and transformation of things and processes (including into their own opposite) prove to be *the essence of the matter* at every step. Traditional logic is consequently inadequate to the real practice of scientific thought, and therefore has to be brought into correspondence with the latter.

Marx and Engels showed that science and practice, quite independently of consciously acquired logical notions, developed in accordance with the universal laws that had been described by the dialectical tradition in philosophy. It can (and in fact does) happen, even in situations when each separate representative of science involved in its general progress is consciously guided by undialectical ideas about thought. Science as a whole, through the clash of undialectical opinions mutually provoking and correcting one another, develops for all that in accordance with a logic of a higher type and order.

The theoretician who has succeeded finally in finding the concrete solution to some contentious problem or other has been objectively forced to think dialectically. Genuine logical necessity drives a road for itself in this case despite the theoretician's consciousness, instead of being realised purposively and freely. It therefore transpires that the greatest theoreticians and natural scientists, whose work has determined the main lines of development of science, have been guided as a rule by the dialectical traditions in logic. Thus Albert Einstein owed much to Spinoza, and Heisenberg to Plato, and so on.

Taking this conception as their starting point, Marx, Engels, and Lenin established that it was dialectics, and only dialectics, that was the *real logic* in accordance with which modern thought made progress. It was it, too, that operated at the 'growing points' of modern science, although the representatives of science were not wholly conscious of the fact. That was why logic as a science coincided (merged) not only with dialectics but also with *the theory of knowledge* of materialism. 'In *Capital* Marx applied to a single science logic, dialectics, and the theory of knowledge of materialism (three words are not needed; it is one and the same thing),' is how Lenin categorically formulated it.[1]

The problem of the relation of logic, the theory of knowledge, and dialectics occupied a special place in Lenin's work. One can say, without danger of exaggeration, that it forms the core of all his special philosophical reflexions, to which he returned again and again, each time formulating his conception and solution more succinctly and categorically.

In Lenin's reflexions, especially those arising in the course of critical rethinking of Hegelian structures, two themes are clearly distinguished: (1) the inter-relation between logic and epistemology; and (2) the conception of dialectics as a science that includes its own scientific, theoretical solution of problems that are traditionally isolated from it in the form of logic and the theory of knowledge. Reconstruction of the considerations that enabled Lenin to formulate the position of modern materialism (i.e. Marxism) so categorically is very important for the simple reason that no unanimous interpretation of his propositions has yet been reached in Soviet philosophy.

---

[1] V. I. Lenin. Philosophical Notebooks. *Op. cit.*, p 319.

Although the direct object of the critical analysis documented in the *Philosophical Notebooks* was first and foremost Hegel's conception, it would of course be a mistake to see in that book only a critical commentary on Hegel's works. Lenin was concerned, it goes without saying, not with Hegel as such but with the real content of problems that still preserve their urgent significance to this day. In other words Lenin undertook, in the form of a critical analysis of the Hegelian conception, a survey of the state of affairs in philosophy in his own day, comparing and evaluating the means of posing and resolving its cardinal problems. Quite naturally, the problem of scientific knowledge came to the fore, around which—and more clearly as time went on—all world philosophical thought revolved at the end of the nineteenth century and the beginning of the twentieth. Here is how Lenin depicted the aim of his investigations: 'The theme of logic. To be compared with present-day "epistemology".'[2]

The inverted commas enclosing the word 'epistemology' are not there quite by chance. The fact is that the isolation of a number of old philosophical problems in a special philosophical science (it is all the same whether we recognise it then as the sole form of scientific philosophy or as only of the many divisions of philosophy) is a fact of recent origin. The term itself came into currency only in the latter half of the nineteenth

---

[2] *Ibid.*, p 103.

century as the designation of a special science, of a special field of investigation that had not been sharply distinguished in any way in the classical philosophical systems, and had not constituted either a special science or even a special division, although it would be an error, of course, to affirm that knowledge in general and scientific knowledge in particular had only become the subject of specially close attention with the development of 'epistemology'.

The setting up of epistemology as a special science was associated historically and essentially with the broad spread of Neokantianism, which became, during the last third of the nineteenth century, the most influential trend in the bourgeois philosophical thought of Europe, and was converted into the officially recognised school of professorial, university philosophy, first in Germany, and then in all those areas of the world from which people came to the German universities hoping to study serious professional philosophy there. Neokantianism owed its spread not least to the traditional fame of Germany as the home of Kant, Fichte, Schelling, and Hegel.

Its special feature was not at all, of course, the discovery of knowledge as the central philosophical problem, but the specific form in which it was posed, which boiled down (despite all the disagreements among the various branches of this school) to the following: 'It is accepted to call the doctrine of knowledge, inquiring into the conditions by which indisputably existing knowledge becomes possible, and limits are established in accordance with these conditions up to which any knowledge whatsoever can be extended but beyond which there opens up the sphere of equally undemonstrable opinions, the "theory of knowledge" or "epistemology".... The theory of knowledge, of course, together with the tasks mentioned above, rightly poses itself yet other, and supplementary,' tasks. But if it wants to be a science making sense it must, above all, concern itself with explaining the problem of the existence or non-existence of boundaries to knowledge. . . .'[3]

The Russian Kantian A. I. Vvedensky, author of the definition just quoted, very accurately and clearly indicated the special feature of the science that 'it is accepted to call' epistemology in the literature of the Neokantian trend, and in all the schools that have arisen under its predominant influence. Dozens of similar formulations could be cited from the classical authors of Neokantianism (Rickert, Wundt, Cassirer, Windelband) and the work of such representatives of 'daughter' branches as Schuppe and Vaihinger.

The job of the theory of knowledge, consequently, was considered to be the establishment of 'limits of knowledge', boundaries that knowledge could not cross in any circumstances, or however high the development of the cognitive capacities

---

[3] A. I. Vvedensky. *Logika kak chast' teorii poznaniya* (Logic as Part of the Theory of Knowledge) (Moscow-Petrograd, 1923) p 29.

of a person or of humanity, or of the technique of scientific experiment and research. These 'limits' differentiated the sphere of what was knowable in principle from that of what was in principle unknowable, extralimital, 'transcendent'. They were not determined at all by the limitation of human experience in space and time (in that case extension of the 'sphere of experience' would constantly widen them, and the problem would boil down simply to differentiation between what was already known and what was not yet known but was, in principle, knowable), but by the eternal and immutable nature of man's psycho-physiological peculiarities through which all external influences were refracted (as through a prism). These 'specific mechanisms', by which alone the external world was given to man, were those that generated the 'limit' beyond which lay what was in principle unknowable. What was unknowable in principle proved to be nothing more nor less than the real world lying outside man's consciousness, as it was 'before its appearance in consciousness'. In other words 'epistemology' was distinguished as a special science in this tradition only on the grounds of *a priori* acceptance of the thesis that human knowledge was not knowledge of the external world (i.e. existing outside consciousness) but was only a process of the ordering, organisation, and systematisation of facts of 'inner experience', i.e. ultimately of the psycho-physiological states of the human organism, absolutely dissimilar to the states and events of the external world.

That meant that any science, be it physics or political economy, mathematics or history, did not tell us anything (and could not) about just how matters stood in the external world, because in fact it described only facts arising within ourselves, the psycho-physiological phenomena illusorily perceived as a sum of external facts.

For the sake of special proof of this thesis a special science 'epistemology' was created that concerned itself exclusively with the 'inner conditions' of knowledge and purged them carefully of any dependence whatsoever on the effect of 'external conditions', above all of a 'condition' such as the existence of an external world with its own objective laws.

'Epistemology' was thus distinguished as a special science counterposed to 'ontology' (or 'metaphysics'), and not at all as a discipline investigating the real course of human knowledge of the surrounding world; quite the contrary, it was born as a doctrine postulating that every form of knowledge without exception was not a form of knowledge of the surrounding world but only a specific schema of the organisation of the 'subject of knowledge'.

From the standpoint of this 'theory of knowledge' any attempt to interpret existing knowledge as knowledge (understanding) of the surrounding world was impermissible 'metaphysics', 'ontologisation' of purely subjective forms of activity, an illusory attributing of determinations of the subject to 'things in themselves', to the world outside consciousness.

By 'metaphysics' and 'ontology' then was meant not so much a special science of 'the world as a whole', a universal scheme of the world, as the whole aggregate of real, so-called 'positive' sciences (physics, chemistry, biology, political economy, history, and so on). So that the main fervour of Neokantian 'epistemologism' proved to be directed precisely against the idea of a scientific world outlook, of a scientific understanding of the world realised in the real sciences themselves. A 'scientific world outlook', according to this view, was an absurdity, nonsense, since 'science' (read: the whole aggregate of natural and social sciences) in general knew nothing about the world outside consciousness and did not speak of it. Under the scornful term 'metaphysics' Neokantians therefore in fact refuse the laws and patterns discovered and formulated by physics, chemistry, biology, political economy, history, etc., any philosophical significance as a world outlook. From their point of view metaphysics could not be a 'science', and science (read again: the aggregate of all sciences) could not and had no right to play the role of 'metaphysics', i.e. to lay claim to an objective meaning (in the materialist sense of the term) for its statements. A world outlook therefore also could not be scientific, because it was the connected aggregate of views of the world within which man lived, acted, and thought, and science was not in a position to unite its achievements in a world outlook without thereby falling into difficulties that were unresolvable for it, into contradictions.

This had already, allegedly, been demonstrated once and for all by Kant. It was impossible to build a world outlook from the data of science. But why not, precisely?

Because the very principles of knowledge, which were the conditions for the possibility of any scientific synthesis of notions into concepts, judgments, and inferences, i.e. into categories, at the same time also proved to be the conditions of the impossibility of achieving a full synthesis of all scientific ideas into the body of a connected, united, and non-contradictory picture of the world. And that, in the language of Kantians, meant that a world outlook built on scientific principles (or simply a scientific world outlook) was impossible in principle. In a scientific world outlook (and not by chance, not from lack of information, but of the necessity inherent in the very nature of thought expressed in categorial schemas) there were always flaws of contradictions cracking it to bits that were unconnectable with one another without flagrant breach of the supreme principle of all analytical judgments, the principle of contradiction in scientific determinations.

Man could unite and connect the isolated fragments of the scientific picture of the world into a higher unity in one way only, by breaking his own supreme principles; or, what was the same thing, by turning unscientific schemas of the coupling of ideas in a united whole into the principles of synthesis, since the latter had no relation with the principle of contradiction, but were the principles of faith and opinion, dogmas that were equally undemonstrable and uncontrovertible scientifically, and were acceptable solely according to irrational whims, sympathy, conscience, etc., etc. Only faith was capable of synthesising the fragments of knowledge into a united picture at those points where all attempts to do so by means of science were doomed to failure. Hence the slogan specific to all Kantians of the uniting of science and faith, of the logical principles of the construction of a scientific picture of the world and of irrational precepts (logically undemonstrable and incontrovertible), compensating the powerlessness organically built into the intellect to accomplish the highest synthesis of knowledge.

Only within the limits described above could the meaning of the Kantian posing of the problem of the relation of logic to the theory of knowledge be understood. Logic as such was interpreted by all Kantians as *part of the theory of knowledge.* Occasionally this 'part' was given the main significance and it almost swallowed the whole (for example, in the variants of Cohen and Natorp, Cassirer and Rickert, Vvedensky and Chelpanov), and occasionally it was relegated to a more modest place, subordinated to the other 'parts' of the theory of knowledge; but logic was always 'part'. The theory of knowledge was broader, because its job was wider, since reason (understanding) was not the sole, though the most important, means of processing the data of sensations, perceptions, and ideas into the form of knowledge, into concepts and a system of concepts, into science. Logic, therefore, in the Kantian interpretation, never covered the whole field of the problems of the theory of knowledge; beyond it lay an analysis of processes effected by other aptitudes, that is to say, perception, and intuition, and memory, and imagination, and many others. Logic, as the theory of discursive thought, which moved in rigorous determinations and in strict accord with rules clearly realisable and formulatable, only partly did the job of the theory of knowledge, only through analysis of its own object, singled out from the whole complex of cognitive faculties. The main job of the theory of knowledge, however, thus also remained logic's chief task, i.e. to establish the limits of knowledge and clarify the inner limitedness of the possibilities of thought in the course of constructing a world outlook.

Logic therefore had neither the least connection nor least relation with understanding of the real world of 'things in themselves'. It was applicable solely to things already realised (with or without its involvement), i.e. to the psychic phenomena of human culture. Its special task was rigorous analysis of the already available images of consciousness (transcendental objects), i.e. their resolution into simple components, expressed in strictly defined terms, and the reverse operation, the synthesis or linking together of the components into complex systems of determinations (concepts, systems of concepts, theories) again by the same rigorously established rules.

Logic must also demonstrate that real discursive thought was incapable of leading knowledge beyond the limits of existing consciousness, or of crossing the boundaries dividing the 'phenomenal' world from the world of 'things in themselves'. Thought, if it were logical, could not concern itself with 'things in themselves', and had no right to. So that, even within the boundaries of knowledge, thought was assigned in turn a limited field of legitimate application, within which the rules of logic were binding and obligatory.

The laws and rules of logic were inapplicable to the images of perception as such, to sensations, to ideas, to the phantoms of mythologised consciousness, including in that the idea of God, of the immortality of the soul, and so on. But they did, and had to, serve as filters, as it were, retaining these images at the boundaries of scientific knowledge. And only that. To judge whether these images were true in themselves, whether they played a positive or a negative role in the body of spiritual culture, thought oriented on logic had neither the possibilities nor the right. In fact there was not and could not be a rationally substantiated, scientifically verified position in relation to any image of consciousness if it arose before and independently of the special logical activity of the mind, before and outside science. In science, inside its specific limits defined by logic, the existence of such images was inadmissible. Beyond its limits their existence was sovereign, outside the jurisdiction of reason and comprehension and therefore morally and epistemologically inviolable.

Considering the special features of the Kantian interpretation of the relation of logic and epistemology, one can understand the close attention that Lenin paid to Hegel's solution of this problem. In Hegel's understanding of the matter logic as a whole and in full, without irrational vestiges, embraced the whole field of the problems of knowledge and left no images of contemplation or fantasy outside its boundaries. It included their examination as external products (realised in the sensuously perceived material) of the real force of thought, because they were thought itself, only embodied not in words, judgments, and conclusions, deductions and inferences, but in *things* (actions, events, etc.) sensibly opposed to the individual consciousness. Logic merged here with the theory of knowledge because all other cognitive faculties were considered as *forms of thought*, as thinking that had not yet attained an adequate form of expression, had not yet matured to it.

Here we come up against the extreme expression, as it were, of Hegel's absolute idealsm, according to which the whole world, and not only the cognitive faculties, was interpreted as alienated or estranged (embodied) thought that has not yet arrived at itself. With that, of course, Lenin as a consistent materialist could not agree. It is very indicative, however, that Lenin formulated his attitude to the Hegelian solution very cautiously: 'In this conception [i.e. Hegel's—*EVI*],

logic coincides with the *theory of knowledge.*
This is in general a very important question.'[4]

We have succeeded, it seems, in demonstrating just why, in the course of Lenin's reading of Hegel's logic, this problem appeared more and more clearly to him to be 'very important', and perhaps the most important of all; why Lenin's thought returned to it again and again, in circles as it were, each time becoming more and more definite and categorical. The fact is that the Kantian conception of logic, generally accepted at the time, as part of the theory of knowledge, by no means remained an abstract, philosophical, theoretical construction. The Kantian theory of knowledge defined the limits of the competence of science in general, leaving the most acute problems as regards world outlook beyond its limits, and declaring them 'transcendental' for logical thought, i.e. for theoretical knowledge and solution. But in this case the union of scientific investigation and faith in the corpus of a world outlook would be not only permissible but necessary. And it was in fact under the banner of Kantianism that the revisionist stream (the principles of which had been laid down by Eduard Bernstein and Conrad Schmidt) surged forward in the socialist movement. The Kantian theory of knowledge was directly oriented here on 'uniting' 'rigorous scientific thought' (the thinking of Marx and Engels, according to Bernstein, was not strictly scientific because it

---

[4] V. I. Lenin. Philosophical Notebooks. *Op. cit.*, p 175.

was marred by foggy Hegelian dialectics) with 'ethical values' and undemonstrable and irrefutable faith in the transcendental postulates of the 'good', of 'conscience' of 'love of one's neighbour' and of the whole 'human race' without exception, and so on and so forth.

The harm done to the working class movement by the propagation of 'higher values' was not, of course, the talk about conscience being good and lack of conscience bad, or about love of the human race being preferable to hatred of it. The harm of the Kantian idea of uniting science with a system of 'higher' ethical values consisted in principle in its orienting theoretical thought itself along lines other than those along which the teaching of Marx and Engels had been developed. It plotted its own, Kantian strategy of scientific research for social-democratic theoreticians and confused ideas on the main line of development of theoretical thought and on the lines along which theoretical solution of the real problems of modern times could and should be sought. The Kantian theory of knowledge turned theoretical thinking not to analysis of the material, economic relations between people that form the foundation of the whole pyramid of social relations, but to the elaborating of far-fetched 'ethical' constructions, morally interpretable policies, and social psychology of the Berdyaev kind, and to other things, which were interesting but absolutely useless (if not harmful) to the working class movement.

The orientation of theoretical thought not on

the logic of *Capital* but on moral-fictional harping on the secondary, derivative defects of the capitalist system in its secondary, superstructural storeys, led to the decisive, dominant trends of the new, imperialist stage of the development of capitalism escaping the notice of the theoreticians of the Second International; not because they lacked talent, but rather because of a petty-bourgeois class orientation and a false epistemological position.

In this respect the fate of Rudolf Hilferding and H. W. C. Cunow was very characteristic. Insofar as they tried to develop Marx's political economy by means of the 'latest' logical devices, rather than of dialectics, it inevitably degenerated into a superficial classificatory description of contemporary economic phenomena, i.e. into a quite uncritical acceptance of them, into an apologia. This path led directly to Karl Renner and his *Theory of the Capitalist Economy*, the Bible of Right-wing socialism, which was already linked, as regards its method of thinking and logic of investigation, with vulgar positivist epistemology. Renner's philosophical credo was as follows: '...Marx's *Capital*, written in an age far removed from us, with a quite different way of thinking, and a manner of exposition not worked out to the end, with every new decade increases the reader's difficulties.... The style of writing of the German philosophers has become foreign to us. Marx came from a very philosophical age. Science today no longer proceeds deductively (not only in research but also in presentation), but rather inductively; it starts from experimentally established facts, systematises them and so by degrees arrives at the level of abstract concepts. For an age that is so accustomed to think and to read, the first section of Marx's principal work presents sheer insuperable difficulty.'[5]

The orientation on 'modern science' and the 'modern way of thinking', already begun with Bernstein, turned into an orientation on the idealistic and agnostic vogue interpretations of 'modern science', on Humean-Berkeleian and Kantian epistemology. Lenin saw that quite clearly. From the middle of the nineteenth century bourgeois philosophy frankly moved 'back to Kant', and further back to Hume and Berkeley; and Hegel's logic, despite all its absolute idealism, was more and more clearly depicted as the pinnacle of the development of all pre-Marxian philosophy in the field of logic understood as the theory of the development of scientific knowledge, *as the theory of knowledge*.

Lenin repeatedly stressed that it was only possible to *move forward* from Hegel along one line and one line only, that of a materialist reworking of his achievements, because Hegel's absolute idealism had really exhausted all the possibilities of idealism as a principle for understanding thought, knowledge, and scientific consciousness. But, because of certain circumstances lying outside science, only Marx and Engels had been

---

5 Karl Renner. *Die Wirtschaft als Gesamtprozess und die Sozialisierung* (Berlin, 1924) p 5.

able to take that line. It was closed to bourgeois philosophy; and the slogan 'Back to Kant' was imperiously dictated by the fear aroused in the bourgeoisie's ideologists by the social perspectives opened up from the heights of the dialectical view of thought. From the moment the materialist view of history appeared, Hegel was seen by bourgeois consciousness as none other than the 'spiritual father' of Marxism. That had a considerable grain of truth, too, for Marx and Engels had disclosed the genuine sense of Hegel's main achievement, dialectics, and demonstrated not only the constructive, creative power of its principles, understood as the principles of man's rational attitude to the world, but also their revolutionary, destructive force.

Why then did Lenin, while fighting Hegel's absolute idealism, began to join sides with him more and more just at that point where the idealism seemed in fact to become *absolute*? For surely the conception of logic as a science embracing in its principles not only human thought but also the real world outside consciousness was linked with panlogism, with the interpretation of the forms and laws of the real world as alienated forms of thought, and thought itself as the absolute force and power organising the world?

The fact is that Hegel was and remains the sole thinker before Marx who consciously introduced practice into logic with full rights as the criterion both of truth and of the correctness of the operations that man performs in the sphere of the verbal, symbolic explication of his psychic states. In Hegel logic became identified with the theory of knowledge precisely because man's practice (i.e. realisation of the aims of the 'spirit' in sense objects, in natural, physical material) was brought into the logical process as a phase, was looked upon as thought in its external revelation, in the course of checking its results through direct contact with 'things in themselves'.

Lenin traced the development of Hegel's corresponding ideas with special scrupulousness. '... The practice of man and of mankind is the test, the criterion of the objectivity of cognition. Is that Hegel's idea? It is necessary to return to this,' he wrote.[6] And returning to it, he wrote confidently, and quite categorically: '... Undoubtedly, in Hegel practice serves as a link in the analysis of the process of cognition, and indeed as the transition to objective ("absolute", according to Hegel) truth. Marx, consequently, clearly sides with Hegel in introducing the criterion of practice into the theory of knowledge: see the Theses on Feuerbach.'[7]

In appearing as a practical act thought included *things outside consciousness* in its movement, and then it turned out that the 'things in themselves' were subordinated to the dictates of thinking man and obediently moved and changed

---

[6] V. I. Lenin. Philosophical Notebooks. *Op. cit.*, p. 211.
[7] *Ibid.*, p. 212.

according to laws and schemas dictated by his thought. Thus not only did the 'spirit' move according to logical schemas, but also the world of 'things in themselves'. Logic consequently proved to be precisely a theory of knowledge of *things also*, and not solely a theory of the self-knowledge of the spirit.

Formulating the 'rational kernel' of Hegel's conception of the subject matter of logic, Lenin wrote: 'Logic is the science not of external forms of thought, but of the laws of development "of all material, natural and spiritual things", i.e., of the development of the entire concrete content of the world and of its cognition, i.e., the sum-total, the conclusion of the *History* of knowledge of the world.'[8]

There is no such a formulation, and furthermore no such a *conception* of the subject matter of logic in Hegel himself. In this passage Lenin did not simply translate Hegel's thought 'into his own words', but reworked it materialistically. Hegel's own text, in which Lenin discovered the 'rational kernel' of his conception of logic, does not sound at all like that. Here it is: 'The indispensable basis, the Concept, the Universal, which is Thought itself—in so far, that is, as in using the word *Thought* one can abstract from the idea—this cannot be regarded as a *merely* indifferent form which is attached to some content.

---

[8] V. I. Lenin. Philosophical Notebooks. *Op. cit.*, pp 92-93.

But these thoughts of all natural and spiritual things [Only these words are found in Lenin's formulation—*EUI*] even the substantial content, are yet such as to possess manifold determinations and to contain the distinction between Soul and Body, between a concept and its respective reality; the deeper basis is the soul in itself, the pure concept, which is the very core of objects, their very life-pulse, as it is the core and pulse of subjective thinking itself. To bring into clear consciousness this *logical* character which gives soul to mind and stirs and works in it, this is our problem."[9]

The difference between Hegel's formulation and Lenin's is one *of principle*, because there is nothing in Hegel about the development of natural things, and could not even be. It would therefore be a gross error to think that the definition of logic as the science of the laws of development of all material and spiritual things is only Hegel's idea transmitted by Lenin, or even simply cited by him. It is nothing of the sort; it is *Lenin's own idea*, formulated, by him in the course of a critical reading of Hegel's words.

Hegel's logic is also his theory of knowledge for the reason that the science of thought was inferred by him from an investigation of the history of the spirit's self-knowledge, and thus of

---

[9] *Hegel's Science of Logic*, Vol. I, p 45.

the world of natural things, since the latter were considered moments of the logical process, schemas of thought, concepts, alienated in natural material.

Logic is also the theory of knowledge of Marxism, but for quite another reason, because the forms themselves of the activity of the 'spirit'— the categories and schemas of logic—are inferred from investigation of the history of humanity's knowledge and practice, i.e. from the process in the course of which thinking man (or rather humanity) cognises and transforms the material world. From that standpoint logic also cannot be anything else than a theory explaining the universal schemas of the development of knowledge and of the transformation of the material world by social man. *As such it is also a theory of knowledge*; any other, definition of the tasks of a theory of knowledge inevitably leads to one version or another of the Kantian conception.

In no case, accoring to Lenin, logic and the theory of knowledge were two different sciences. Even less could logic be defined as part of the theory of knowledge. The *logical* determinations of thought therefore included exclusively universal categories and laws (schemas) of the development of the objective world in general cognised in the course of the millenia of the development of scientific culture and tested for objectivity in the crucible of social man's practice, schemas common to both natural and social-historical development. Being reflected in social consciousness, in mankind's spiritual culture, they functioned as active logical forms of the work of thought, and logic was a systematic, theoretical depiction of the universal schemas, forms, and laws of the development of nature *and* of society, *and* of thought itself.

In this conception, however, logic (i.e. the materialist theory of knowledge) was fully merged without residue in *dialectics*. And once more there were not two sciences, however 'closely linked' with one another, but one and the same science, one in subject matter and its stock of concepts. And this, Lenin stressed, was not 'an aspect of the matter', but 'the essence of the matter'. In other words, unless logic was understood simultaneously as the *theory of knowledge*, it could not be truly understood.

So logic (the theory of knowledge) and dialectics, according to Lenin, were in a relationship of full identity, full coincidence of subject matter and stock of categories. Dialectics had no subject matter distinct from that of the theory of knowledge (logic), just as logic (the theory of knowledge) had no object of a study that would differ in any way from the subject matter of dialectics. In the one and in the other it was a matter of universal forms and laws of development in general that were reflected in consciousness precisely in the shape of logical forms and laws of thought through the determination of categories. And because categories as schemas of the synthesis of experimental data in concepts had a quite objective significance, the same significance also attached to the 'experience' processed with their aid, i.e. to science, the scientific picture of the world, the scientific outlook.

'Dialectics *is* the theory of knowledge of (Hegel and) Marxism,' Lenin wrote in his notes 'On the Question of Dialectics', in which he summed up the vast job he had done in several years of hard work on critically reworking the Hegelian conception of logic in a materialist way. 'This is the "aspect" of the matter (it is not "an aspect" but the *essence* of the matter) to which Plekhanov, not to speak of other Marxists, paid no attention.'[10] That categorical conclusion, hardly admitting of any other interpretation than a literal one, must not be considered as a phrase dropped by chance, but as a real resume of all Lenin's understanding of the problem of the relationship of dialectics, logic, and the theory of knowledge of modern materialism.

In the light of the foregoing, attempts to interpret their relation in the body of Marxism in such a way that dialectics is transformed into a special category treating 'pure forms of being', and logic and the theory of knowledge into special sciences connected with dialectics but not, however, merged with it, and devoted exclusively to the 'specific' forms of the reflexion of this ontology in men's consciousness—the one (epistemology) being devoted to the 'specific' forms of knowledge and the other (logic) to the 'specific'

---

10 V. I. Lenin. Philosophical Notebooks. *Op. cit.*, p 362.

forms of discursive thought—proved to be bankrupt (and in no way linked with Lenin's conception).

The idea whereby logic is distinguished from dialectics as the particular from the general and therefore studies just that 'specific feature' of thought from which dialectics digresses, is based on a simple misunderstanding, on neglect of the fact that the 'specific nature' of the forms and laws of thought consists precisely in their universality.

Logic as a science is not at all interested in the 'specific features' of the thinking of the physicist or chemist, economist or linguist, but only in those universal (invariant) forms and laws within which the thinking of any person flows, and of any theoretician, including the logician by profession, who specially thinks about thought. From the angle of materialism, therefore, logic also investigates forms and laws that equally govern both thinking about the external world and thinking about thought itself, and is thus the science of the universal forms and patterns of thought and reality; so that the statement that logic must study the 'specific forms' of the movement of thought as well as the universal ones (common to thought and being), in fact ignores the historically formed division of labour between logic and psychology, depriving psychology of its subject matter, and throwing onto logic a task that is too much for it.

To understand logic as a science distinguished from dialectics (though closely connected with it) means to understand both logic and dialectics incorrectly, and not in a materialist way; because logic, artificially separated from dialectics, is inevitably converted into a description of purely subjective methods and operations, i.e. of forms of activities depending on the will and consciousness of people, and on the peculiarities of the material, and therefore ceases to be an objective science. While dialectics, counterposed to the process of the development of knowledge (thought), in the form of a doctrine about 'the world as a whole', in the form of 'world schematics' is just as inevitably converted into a collection of extremely general statements about everything on earth and not about anything in particular (something of the sort of that 'everything in nature and society is interconnected', or that 'everything develops' and even 'through contradictions', and so on).

Dialectics, understood so, is tacked on to the real process of cognition in a purely formal way, through examples 'confirming' one and the same general proposition over and over again. But it is clear that such a formal superimposition of the general onto the particular does not deepen our understanding of either the general or the particular by a single jot, while dialectics is transformed into a dead scheme. Lenin therefore quite justly considered the transformation of dialectics into a sum of examples as the inevitable consequence of not understanding it as the logic and theory of knowledge of materialism.

Being the science of the universal forms and patterns within which any process, either objective or subjective, takes place, logic is a rigorously defined system of special concepts (logical categories) reflecting the stages ('steps') consecutively passed through in the formation of any concrete whole (or correspondingly of the process of its mental-theoretical reproduction). The sequence of the development of the categories in the body of a theory has an objective character, i.e. does not depend on the will and consciousness of people. It is dictated primarily by the objective sequence of the development of empirically based theoretical knowledge,[11] in the form of which, the objective sequence of the real historical process, purged of its disruptive fortuities and of the historical form, is reflected in people's consciousness.

Logical categories are thus directly stages in distinguishing the world, i.e. of cognising it, and nodal points helping to cognise and master it.[12]

In explaining this view Lenin remarked on the general sequence of the development of logical categories: 'First of all impressions *flash by,* then *Something* emerges—afterwards the concepts of *quality* (the determination of the thing or the phenomenon) and *quantity* are developed. After that study and reflection direct thought to the

---

[11] See Frederick Engels. *Dialectics of Nature,* p 239.
[12] See V. I. Lenin. Philosophical Notebooks, *Op. cit.,* p 93.

cognition of identity—difference—Ground—Essence versus phenomenon—causality, etc. All these moments (steps, stages, processes) of cognition move ... from subject to object, being tested in practice and arriving through this test at truth.'[13] 'Such is actually the *general course* of all human cognition (of all science) in general. Such is the course also of *natural science* and *political economy* (and history).'[14] The *movement* of scientific cognition, Lenin said, was the nub.[15]

Logical categories are stages (steps) in cognition developing the object in its necessity, in the natural sequence of the phases of its own formation, and not at all man's technical devices imposed on the subject like a child's bucket on sandpies. Not only do the determinations of each of the logical categories therefore have an objective character, i.e. determine the object and not simply the form of subjective activity, but the sequence in which the categories appear in the theory of thought also has the same necessary character. It is impossible to determine necessity or purpose strictly scientifically, on an objective basis, before and independently of the scientific determination of identity and difference, quality and measure, etc., just as it is impossible to understand capital and profit scientifically unless

---

[13] V. I. Lenin. Philosophical Notebooks, *Op. cit.*, p 319.
[14] *Ibid.*, p 318.
[15] *Ibid.*, p 87.

their 'simple components'—commodity and money—have previously been analysed, and just as it is impossible to understand the complex compounds of organic chemistry while their constituent chemical elements are unknown (not identified by analysis).

In outlining a plan for systematic treatment of the categories of logic, Lenin noted: 'If Marx did not leave behind him a *Logic* (with a capital 'L'), he did leave the *logic* of *Capital*, and this ought to be utilised to the full in this question.'[16] Moreover, one can only distinguish the logical categories underlying the theory of political economy from the movement of the theory by basing oneself on the best (dialectical) traditions in the development of logic as a science. 'It is impossible completely to understand Marx's *Capital*, and especially its first chapter, without having thoroughly studied and understood the *whole* of Hegel's *Logic*.'[17] 'In his *Capital*,' Lenin wrote further, 'Marx first analyses the simplest, most ordinary and fundamental, most common and everyday *relation* of bourgeois (commodity) society, a relation encountered billions of times, viz. the exchange of commodities. In this very simple phenomenon (in this "cell" of bourgeois society) analysis reveals *all* the contradictions (or the germs of *all* the contradictions) of modern society. The subsequent exposition shows us the development (*both* growth *and* movement) of

---

16 *Ibid.*, p 319.
17 *Ibid.*, p 180.

318

these contradictions and of this society in the ε [summation—*Ed.*] of its individual parts, from its beginning to its end.

'Such must also be the method of exposition (or study) of dialectics in general (for with Marx the dialectics of bourgeois society is only a particular case of dialectics).'[18]

---

[18] V. I. Lenin, Philosophical Notebooks, *Op. cit.*, pp 360-361.

Contradiction as a Category
of Dialectical Logic

Contradiction as the concrete unity of mutually exclusive opposites is the real nucleus of dialectics, its central category. On that score there cannot be two views among Marxists; but no small difficulty immediately arises as soon as matters touch on 'subjective dialectics', on dialectics as the logic of thinking. If any object is a living contradiction, what must the thought (statement about the object) be that expresses it? Can and should an objective contradiction find reflection in thought? And if so, in what form?

Contradiction in the theoretical determinations of an object is above all a fact that is constantly being reproduced by the movement of science, and is not denied by dialectics or metaphysics, by materialists or idealists. The point that they dispute is something else, namely: what is the relationship of the contradiction in thought to the object? In other words, can there be a contradiction in true, correct thought?

The metaphysical logician tries to demonstrate the inapplicability of the dialectical law of the coincidence or concurrence of opposites, which amounts to their identity, to the very process of thought. Such logicians are occasionally prepared even to recognise that the object can, in agreement with dialectics, be by itself inwardly contradictory. The contradiction is in the object but must not be in the ideas about it. The metaphysician, however, still cannot permit himself in any way to recognise the truth of the law that constitutes the nucleus of dialectics, in relation to the logical process. The principle of contradiction is transformed into an absolute, formal criterion of truth, into an indisputable *a priori* canon, into the supreme principle of logic.

Some logicians strive to substantiate this position, which it is difficult to call other than eclectic, by citing the practice of science. Any science, when it comes up against a contradiction in determinations of an object, always strives to resolve it. In that case does it not act in accordance with the recipes of metaphysics, which holds that any contradiction in thought is inadmissible, and something that must be got rid of somehow or other? The metaphysician in logic interprets similar moments in the development of science in such a way. Science, he says, always strives to avoid contradictions, but in dialectics there is an opposite tendency.

The view under consideration is based on a misunderstanding, or rather simply on ignorance of the important historical fact that dialectics was born just where metaphysical thought (i.e. thinking without knowing or desiring to know any other logic than formal logic) finally became caught up in the logical contradictions it had brought to light just because it persistently and consistently observed the ban on any kind of contradiction whatsoever in determinations. Dialectics as logic is the means of resolving these contradictions, so that it is stupid to accuse it of an itch to pile up contradictions. It is irrational to see the cause of the illness in the coming of the doctor. The question can only be whether dialectics is successful in curing the contradictions into which thought falls, in fact, as a result of a most rigorous metaphysical diet that unconditionally forbids any contradiction. And if it is successful, just why is it?

Let us turn to the analysis of a striking example, a typical case of how mountains of logical contradictions have been piled up just by means of absolutised formal logic, and rationally resolved only by means of dialectical logic. We have in mind the history of political economy, the history of the disintegration of the Ricardian school and the rise of Marx's economic theory. The way out of the blind alley of the theoretical paradoxes and antinomies into which the Ricardian school had got was found, as we know, only by Karl Marx, and was found precisely by means of dialectics as logic.

That Ricardo's theory contained a mass of logical contradictions was not discovered by Marx at all. It was plainly seen by Malthus, and Sismondi, and McCulloch, and Proudhon. But only Marx was able to understand the real character of the contradictions of the labour theory of value. Let us, following Marx, consider one of them, the most typical and acute, the antinomy of the law of value and the law of the average rate of profit.

David Ricardo's law of value established that living human labour was the sole source and substance of value, an affirmation that was an enormous advance on the road to objective truth. But profit was also value. In trying to express it theoretically, i.e. through the law of value, a clear logical contradiction was obtained. The point was that profit was new, newly created value, or rather part of it. That was an indisputably true analytical determination. But only new labour produced new value. How, however, did that tie up with the quite obvious empirical fact that the quantity of profit was not determined at all by the quantity of living labour expended on its production? It depended exclusively on the quantity of capital as a whole, and in no case on the size of that part that went on wages. And it was even more paradoxical that the higher the profit the less living labour was consumed during its production.

In Ricardo's theory the law of the average rate of profit, which established the dependence of the scale of profit on the quantity of capital as a whole, and the law of value, which established that only living labour produced new value, stood in a relation of direct, mutually exclusive contradiction. Nevertheless, both laws determined one and the same object (profit). This antinomy was noted with spiteful delight in his day by Malthus.

Here then was a problem that it was impossible to resolve on the principles of formal logic. And if thought had arrived here at an antinomy, and had landed in a logical contradiction, it was difficult to blame dialectics for it. Neither Ricardo nor Malthus had any idea of dialectics. Both knew only the Lockian theory of understanding and the logic (and that formal) corresponding to it. Its canons were indisputable for them, and the only ones. This logic justified a general law (in this case the law of value) only when it was demonstrated as an immediately general empirical rule under which all facts whatsoever were subsumed without contradiction.

It was found that there was in fact no such relationship between the law of value and the forms of its manifestation. As soon as one tried to treat profit theoretically (i.e. to understand it through the law of value), it suddenly proved to be an absurd contradiction. If the law of value was universal, profit was impossible in principle. By its existence it refuted the abstract universality of the law of value, the law of its own particular existence.

Ricardo, the creator of the labour theory of value, was primarily concerned with the accord of the theoretical statements with the object. He soberly, and even cynically, expressed the real state of affairs; and the latter, riddled with unresolvable antagonisms, was naturally presented in thought as a system of conflicts, antagonisms, and logical contradictions. This circumstance, which bourgeois theoreticians regarded as evidence of the weakness and ir :ompleteness of his theory, was evidence rather of the contrary, of its strength and objectivity.

When Ricardo's disciples and successors no longer made correspondence of theory to the object their chief concern, but rather agreement of the developed theoretical determinations with the requirements of formal logical consistency, with the canons of the formal unity of theory, the labour theory of value began to disintegrate. Marx wrote of James Mill: 'What he tries to achieve is formal, logical consistence. The *disintegration* of the Ricardian school "therefore" begins with him.'[1]

In fact, as Marx showed, the general law of value stood in a relation of mutually exclusive contradiction with the empirical form of its own manifestation, with the law of the average rate of profit. That was *a real contradiction of a real object*. And it was not surprising that, in trying to subsume the one law directly and immediately under the other, a logical contradiction was obtained. But when, nevertheless, they continued trying to make value and profit agree directly and *without contradiction*, they then obtained a problem that was, in Marx's words, 'much more difficult to solve than that of squaring the circle. . . . It is simply an attempt to present that which does not exist as in fact existing'.[2]

---

[1] Karl Marx. *Theories of Surplus-Value,* Part III, p 84.
[2] *Ibid.,* p 87.

The metaphysically thinking theoretician, coming up against such a paradox, inevitably interprets it as the result of mistakes committed earlier in thought, in the working out and formulation of the universal law. And he naturally seeks a solution of the paradox by way of a purely formal analysis of the theory, by making the concepts more precise, by correcting expressions, and so on. *A propos* of this approach to solving the problem Marx wrote: 'Here the contradiction between the general law and further developments in the concrete circumstances is to be resolved not by the discovery of the connecting links but by directly subordinating and immediately adapting the concrete to the abstract. This moreover is to be brought about by a *verbal fiction*, by changing *vera rerum vocabula*. (These are indeed "verbal disputes", they are "verbal", however, because real contradictions, which are not resolved in a real way, are to be solved by phrases.)'[3]

When the general law contradicts the empirically common position of things the empiricist immediately sees the way out in altering the formulation of the general law in such a fashion that the empirically general will be directly subsumed under it. At first glance that is how it ought to be; if thought contradicts the facts, then the thought should be altered so as to bring it into line with the general phenomena immediately given on the surface. In fact, this way is theore-

---

[3] Karl Marx. *Theories of Surplus-Value*, Part III, pp 87-88.

tically false, and by taking it the Ricardian school arrived at complete rejection of the labour theory of value. The general law revealed by Ricardo was sacrificed to crude *empeiria* (experience), but the crude empiricism was inevitably converted into a 'false metaphysics, scholasticism, which toils painfully to deduce undeniable empirical phenomena by simple formal abstraction directly from the general law, or to show by cunning argument that they are in accordance with that law'.[4]

Formal logic, and the metaphysics that made it an absolute, knew only two ways of resolving contradictions in thought. The first was to adjust the general law to the directly general, empirically obvious, state of affairs. That, as we have seen, brought about loss of the concept of value. The second way was to represent the internal contradiction, expressed in thinking as a logical contradiction, as an external contradiction of two things, each of which was, in itself, non-contradictory, a procedure known as reducing the internal contradiction to a contradiction 'in different relations or at a different time'. It was done as follows. Profit could not be explained from value without contradiction? Well, what of it! There was no need to persist in a one-sided approach; one must admit that profit originated in reality not only from labour but also from

---

[4] Karl Marx. *Theories of Surplus-Value*, Part I. Translated by Emile Burns (Progress Publishers, Moscow, 1969) p 89.

many other factors. It was necessary to take the role of land, and of machines, and of supply and demand, and of many, many other things into account. The point, they said, lay not in the contradictions but in the fullness. So the famous triune formula of vulgar economics was born: 'Capital—interest; land—rent; labour—wages'. There was no logical contradiction there, it is true; it had disappeared, but with it, too, had disappeared the theoretical approach to things in general.

The conclusion was obvious; not every means of resolving the contradictions led to *development* of the theory. The two ways outlined above signified a solution such as was identical with converting the theory into empirical eclecticism. Because theory in general existed only where there was a conscious and principled striving to understand all the separate phenomena as necessary modifications of one and the same general, concrete substance, in this instance the substance of value, of living human labour.

The only theoretician who succeeded in resolving the logical contradictions of the Ricardian theory so as to bring about not disintegration but real *development* of the labour theory of value was, of course, Karl Marx. What did his dialectical materialist method of resolving the antinomy consist in? First of all, we must state that the real contradictions discovered by Ricardo did not disappear in Marx's system. Futhermore, they were presented in it as *necessary* contradictions of the object itself, and not at all as the result of mistakenness of the idea, or of inexactitudes in determinations. In the first volume of *Capital*, for example, it is demonstrated that surplus value is exclusively the product of that part of capital which is expended on wages and converted into living labour, i.e. variable capital. The proposition in the third volume, however, reads: 'However that may be, the outcome is that surplus-value springs simultaneously from all portions of the invested capital.'[5]

Between the first and the second propositions a whole system was developed, a whole chain of connecting links; between them, nevertheless, there was preserved a relationship of mutually exclusive contradiction banned by formal logic. That is why vulgar economists triumphantly declared, after the appearance of the third volume of *Capital*, that Marx had not fulfilled his pledge, that the antinomy of the labour theory of value remained unresolved by him and that the whole of *Capital* was consequently nothing more than speculative, dialectical hocus-pocus.

The general is thus also contradicted in *Capital* by its own particular manifestation, and the contradiction between them does not disappear just because a whole chain of mediating links has been developed between them. On the contrary, this actually demonstrates that the antinomies of the labour theory of value are not logical ones at all but real contradictions in the object, correctly expressed by Ricardo, though not understood by

---

[5] Karl Marx. *Capital*, Vol. III, p 36.

him. In *Capital* these antinomies are not done away with at all as something subjective, but prove to be understood, i.e. have been *sublated* in the body of a deeper and more concrete theoretical conception. In other words, they are *preserved* but have lost the character of logical contradictions, having been converted into abstract moments of the concrete conception of economic reality. And there is nothing surprising in that; any concrete, developing system includes contradictions as the principle of its self-movement and as the form in which the development is cast.

So let us compare how the metaphysician Ricardo and the dialectician Marx understood value. Ricardo, of course, did not analyse value by its form. His abstraction of value, on the one hand, was incomplete, and on the other was formal, and for that reason was untrue. In what, then, did Marx see the fullness and pithiness of the analysis of value that was missing in Ricardo? First, in value being a living, concrete contradiction.

Ricardo showed value only from the aspect of its substance, i.e. took labour as the substance of value. As for Marx, he (to use an expression from Hegel's *Phenomenology of Mind*) understood value not only as substance but also as subject. Value was represented as the substance-subject of all the developed forms and categories of political economy; and with that conscious dialectics in this science began. Because the 'subject' in Marx's conception (in this case he employed the terminology of the *Phenomenology of Mind*) is reality developing through its own internal contradictions.

But let us look a little closer at Marx's analysis of value. First of all it investigates the direct, moneyless exchange or barter of commodity for commodity. In exchange, in the course of which one commodity is replaced by another, value is only manifested, is only expressed; and in no case is it created. It is manifested as follows: one commodity plays the role of relative value, and the other, counterposed to it, the role of equivalent. 'In one expression of value, one commodity cannot simultaneously appear in both forms. These forms are polar opposites, are mutually exclusive.'[6]

The metaphysician will no doubt be delighted to read that two mutually exclusive economic forms cannot simultaneously be combined in one commodity! But can one say that Marx was refuting the possibility of the coincidence of mutually exclusive determinations in the object and in its conception? Rather the contrary. The fact is that we are not yet concerned with the *concept* of value, with value as such. The passage cited crowns the analysis of the *form of the revelation* of value. Value itself still remains a mysterious and theoretically unexpressed essence of each of the commodities. On the surface of phenomena it really appears as if two abstract, one-sided forms of its revelation are visible. But value itself does

---

[6] Karl Marx. *Capital,* Vol. I, p 19.

not coincide with either of these forms, or with their simple, mechanical unity. It is a third something, something lying deeper. In relation to its owner, for example, linen as a commodity appears only in the relative form of value; and in that same relation it cannot be simultaneously an equivalent.

But matters appear so only from an *abstract, one-sided* angle. For the owner of linen is absolutely equal to the owner of a coat, and from the position of the latter the relation under consideration proves directly the opposite, so that we do not have two different relations, but *one concrete objective relation, a mutual relation* of two commodity owners. From the *concrete* standpoint each of the two commodities—linen and coat—*mutually* measures the other's value and also *mutually* serves as the material in which it is measured. In other words each mutually presupposes that the equivalent form of value is realised in the other commodity, the very form in which the latter can no longer be because it is in the relative form.

In other words the exchange really being completed presupposes that *each of the two* commodities mutually related in it simultaneously takes on both economic forms of the revelation of value in itself, both measuring its own value and serving as the material for expressing the value of the other commodity. And if, from the abstract, one-sided point of view, each of them is only in one form, and functions as relative value in one relation and as equivalent in the other, from the concrete aspect, i.e. in fact, each of the commodities is *simultaneously* and, moreover, *within one and the same relation* in both mutually exclusive forms of the expression of value. If the two commodities do not mutually recognise each other as equivalents, exchange simply cannot take place. If, however, exchange does take place, that means that the two polarly excluded forms of value are combined in each of the two commodities.

What you get, then, says the metaphysician, is that Marx contradicts himself. How can he say that two polar forms of the expression of value cannot be combined in one commodity, and then state that in real exchange they are all the same so combined? The answer is that concrete examination of things refutes the result obtained by the abstract, one-sided approach to them, and shows it to be untrue. The truth of commodity exchange is just that a relation is realised in it that is absolutely impossible from the angle of an abstract, one-sided view.

Something else is discovered in the form of the contradiction under consideration, as analysis shows, and that is the absolute content of each of the commodities, its value, the *inner* contradiction of value and use-value. 'Thus the contrast between use-value and value hidden away within the commodity,' Marx wrote, 'has an outward and visible counterpart, namely the relation between two commodities, the relation in which the commodity whose value is to be expressed counts only as use-value, whereas the commodity in terms of which value is to be expressed counts only as exchange-value. The simple value form of a commodity is, therefore, the simple phenomenal form of the inherent contrast (within the commodity) between use-value and value.'[7]

From the aspect of logic this point is extraordinarily instructive. The metaphysician, coming up against the fact of the coincidence of contradictory determinations in a concept, in the statement of a thing, sees in it a false theoretical expression and strives to turn the internal contradiction into an external contradiction of two things, each of which, in his view, is internally non-contradictory, into a contradiction 'in various relations or at a different time'. Marx acted quite the contrary. He showed that the inner contradiction hidden in each of the interrelated things was only outwardly manifested in a contradiction of an external order.

As a result value was presented as an inner relation of a commodity *to itself*, outwardly revealed through the relation to another commodity. The other commodity played only the role of a mirror in which the inwardly contradictory nature of the commodity that expressed its value was reflected. In philosophical terms, the external contradiction was presented only as a phenomenon and the relation to the other commodity (as mediated through this relation) as the relation of the commodity to itself. The *inner* relation, the

---

[7] Karl Marx. *Capital*, Vol. I, p 33.

relation to itself, was also value as the absolute economic content of each of the mutually related commodities.

The metaphysician always strives to reduce the internal relation to an external one. For him a contradiction in 'one relation' is an index of the abstractness of knowledge, an index of the confusion of different planes of abstraction, and so on, and an external contradiction is a synonym of the 'concreteness' of knowledge. For Marx, on the contrary, it was an index of the one-sidedness and superficiality of knowledge when an object was presented in thought simply as an external contradiction, signifying that only the outward form of the manifestation of an internal contradiction had been caught, instead of the contradiction itself. Dialectics obliges one always to see, behind a thing's relation to another thing, its own relation to itself, its own inner relation.

The difference between dialectics and metaphysics does not consist at all in the former's recognising only inner contradictions and the latter's recognising only external ones. Metaphysics really always tries to reduce the inner contradiction to a contradiction 'in different relations', denying it objective significance. Dialectics by no means reduces the one to the other. It recognises the objectivity of both. The point, however, does not lie in reducing an external contradiction to an inner one, but in *deriving* the former from the latter and thus comprehending the one and the other in their objective necessity. Dialectics moreover does not deny the fact that an inner contradiction always appears in phenomena as an external one.

The immediate coincidence of mutually exclusive economic determinations (value and use-value) in *each* of the two commodities meeting in exchange is also the true theoretical expression of the essence of simple commodity exchange. And this essence is value. From the logical aspect the concept of value (in contrast to the outward form of its manifestation in the act of exchange) is characterised by its being presented as an immediate contradiction, as the direct coincidence of two forms of economic existence that are polar opposites.

Thus, what was effected in the real act of exchange was impossible from the angle of abstract (formal, logical) reason, namely, the direct or immediate identification of opposites. This was the theoretical expression of the real fact that direct commodity exchange could not be completed smoothly, without collisions, without conflicts, without contradictions and crises. The point was that direct commodity exchange was not in a position to express the socially necessary measure of the expenditure of labour in the various branches of social production, i.e. value. And value therefore remained, within the limits of the simple commodity form, an unresolved and unresolvable antinomy. In it the commodity *had to be, yet could not be,* in the two polar forms of expression of value, and consequently real exchange by value was impossible. But it did happen somehow, and consequently both polar forms of value were somehow combined in each commodity. There was no way out of the antinomy. Marx's contribution was precisely that he understood that, and expressed it theoretically.

Insofar as exchange through the market remained the sole and universal form of the social exchange of things, the antinomy of value found its solution in the movement of the commodity market itself. The market created the means for resolving its own contradictions. So money was born. Exchange became not direct and unmediated, but mediated—through money; and the coincidence of mutually exclusive economic forms in a commodity came to an end, as it were, since it was split into two 'different relations', into an act of sale (which transformed use-value into value) and an act of purchase (which converted value into use-value). The two antinomic acts, mutually exclusive in their economic content, already did not coincide immediately but were completed at a different time and in different parts of the market.

The antinomy seemed at first glance to be resolved by all the rules of formal logic; but the semblance was purely external. In fact the antinomy had not disappeared at all, but had only acquired a new form of expression. Money did not become absolutely pure value, and the commodity thus pure use-value. Both commodity and money were fraught, as before, with an inner contradiction that was expressed, as before, in thought in the form of a contradiction in determinations; once again, moreover, the contradiction was unresolved and unresolvable, and revealed itself in the clearest way, though only from time to time, precisely in crises, and then making itself felt the more strongly.

'The only commodity is money,' says the commodity owner at times when this contradiction does not show on the surface. 'The only money is commodities,' he asserts in a directly opposite way during a crisis, refuting his own abstract statement. Marx's theoretical, but concrete, thinking showed that the inner opposition of the economic determinations of money existed at every fleeting second, even when they were not manifested in an obvious, visible way but were hidden in commodities and in money, when everything was apparently going swimmingly and the contradiction seemed resolved once and for all.

In theoretical determinations of money the antinomy of value brought out earlier was preserved; in them it formed the 'simple essence' both of commodities and of money, although on the surface of phenomena it proved to be annulled, broken down into two 'different relations'. But these relations, like the direct exchange of commodity for commodity, formed on inner unity that was preserved in all its acuteness and tension in both commodities and money, and consequently also in theoretical determinations of the one and of the other. As before, value remained an internally contradictory relation of a commodity to itself, which was no longer revealed, though, on the surface through a direct relation to another commodity of the same sort, but through its relation to money. Money now functioned as the means by which the mutual, reciprocal transformation of the two originally exposed poles of the expression of value (value and use-value) was effected.

From that angle the whole logical structure of *Capital* was traced out from a new and very important aspect. Any concrete category was presented as a metamorphosis through which value and use-value passed during their reciprocal transformations into one another. The forming of the capitalist, commodity system appears in Marx's theoretical analysis as a complicating of the chain of connecting links through which the poles of value, mutually attracting and at the same time excluding each other, have to pass. The path of the reciprocal transformation of value and use-value becomes longer and longer, and more and more complicated, and the tension between the poles increases.

The relative and temporary resolution of the tension takes place through crises, and its final resolution is through socialist revolution.

That approach to things immediately gave thought an orientation in the analysis of any form of economic relation. In fact, just as the commodity market found a relative resolution of its objective contradictions in the birth of money, so the theoretical determinations of money in *Capital* served as a means of relatively resolving the theoretical contradiction revealed in the analysis of the simple form of value. Within the limits of the simple form the antinomy of value remained unresolved and fixed in thought as a contradiction in the concept. Its sole true logical resolution consisted in tracing how it was resolved objectively in practice in the course of the movement itself of the commodity market. And the movement of the investigating thought consisted in revealing this new reality that developed by virtue of the impossibility of resolving the objective contradiction originally disclosed.

Thus the very course of theoretical thought became not a confused wandering but a rigorous, purposive process, in which thinking used empirical facts to find the conditions and data that were lacking for solution of a clearly formulated task, of problem. Theory therefore appeared as a process of the constant resolution of problems pushed to the fore by the investigation of the empirical facts itself.

Investigation of the commodity-money circulation led to an antinomy. As Marx wrote: 'Turn and twist as we may, the sum total remains the same. If equivalents are exchanged, then no surplus value is created; and if non-equivalents are exchanged, still no surplus value is created. Circulation, the exchange of commodities, does not create value.'[8] So, he concluded, capital could not arise from circulation, just as it could not arise outside it. It 'must simultaneously take place in the sphere of circulation and outside the sphere

---

[8] Karl Marx. *Capital*, Vol. I, p 150.

of circulation. Such are the conditions of the problem. That is the nut we have to crack!'⁹

Marx's way of posing the problem was not at all fortuitous and was not simply a rhetorical device. It was linked with the very essence of the dialectical method of developing theory, following the development of the actual object. The solution of the question corresponds to the posing of it. The problem arising in thought in the form of a contradiction in the determination could only be resolved if the theoretician (and the real owner of money) was 'lucky enough to find somewhere within the sphere of circulation, to find in the market, a commodity whose use-value has the peculiar quality of being a source of value; a commodity whose actual consumption is a process whereby labour is embodied, and whereby therefore value is created'.¹⁰

Objective reality always develops through the origin within it of a concrete contradiction that finds its resolution in the generation of a new, higher, and more complex form of development. Within the initial form of development, the contradiction is unresolvable. When expressed in thought it naturally appears as a contradiction in the determinations of the concept that reflects the initial stage of development. And that is not only correct, but is the sole correct form of movement

---

⁹ *Ibid.*, p 153. (Marx actually used the Latin tag *Hic Rhodus, hic salta!*, which the Pauls rendered here as 'That is the nut we have to crack!'—*Tr.*)
¹⁰ *Ibid.*, p 154.

of the investigating mind, although there is a contradiction in it. A contradiction of that type in determinations is not resolved by way of refining the concept that reflects the given form of development, but by further investigating reality, by discovering another, new, higher form of development in which the initial contradiction finds its real, actual, empirically established resolution.

It was not fortuitous that the old logic passed this very important logical form over as a 'question'. For the real questions, the real problems that arise in the movement of the investigating mind, always rise before thought in the form of contradictions in the determination, in the theoretical expression of the facts. The concrete contradiction that arises in thought also leads toward a further and, moreover, purposive examining of the facts, toward the finding and analysing of just those facts that are lacking for solving the problem and resolving the given theoretical contradiction.

If a contradiction arises of necessity in the theoretical expression of reality from the very course of the investigation, it is not what is called a logical contradiction, though it has the formal signs of such but is a logically correct expression of reality. On the contrary, the logical contradiction, which there must not be in a theoretical investigation, has to be recognised as a contradiction of terminological, semantic origin and properties. Formal analysis is also obliged to discover such contradictions in determinations; and the principle of contradiction of formal logic applies fully to them. Strictly speaking it relates to the use of terms and not to the process of the movement of a concept. The latter is the field of dialectical logic. But there another law is dominant, the law of the unity or coincidence of opposites, a coincidence, moreover, that goes as far as their identity. It is that which constitutes the real core of dialectics as the logic of thought that follows the development of reality.

The Problem of the General in Dialectics

The category of the general or universal occupies an extremely important place in the body of dialectical logic. What is the general or universal? Literally, in the meaning of the word, it is relating to *all*, i.e. to all individua, in the form of the limitless multitude of which the world within which we live and about which we speak presents itself to us at first glance. That is all the unquestionable, very likely, that can be said about the general, equally acceptable to everyone.

Without going into the philosophical disagreements about the general or universal, one can note that the term 'common' (or rather 'general' or 'universal') is used very ambigously in the living language, indeterminately, and relates not only to different objects or meanings that do not coincide with one another, but also to directly opposite ones that are mutually exclusive. Any large dictionary (e.g. the *Shorter Oxford Dictionary*) contains a dozen such meanings. At the extremes of the spectrum, moreover, there are meanings such as can scarcely be considered consistent or compatible. 'Common' is used even for two objects, let alone all, both for what appertains to each of them (like the biped nature or mortality of both Socrates and Caius, or like the velocity or speed of an electron and of a train) and cannot exist separately from the relevant individua in the form of a separate 'thing', and for what exists precisely outside the individua in the form of a special individuum, namely a common ancestor, a common field (i.e. one for two (or all)), a common motor vehicle or entry, a common (mutual) friend or acquaintance, and so on and so forth.

One and the same word, or one and the same sign, obviously does *not* serve just for one and the same thing. Whether one sees in that the imperfection of natural language or on the contrary considers it the superiority of the flexibility of a living language over the rigidity of the definitions of an artificial language, the fact itself remains a fact and one, moreover, that is often encountered and therefore calls for explanation.

But then the quite reasonable question arises, whether or not it is possible to find something common between two extreme, mutually exclusive meanings of the world 'common' (or 'general') in the living language, equally sanctioned by usage, to find the *basis* of the fact of the divergence of meanings. In the interpretation that is sanctioned as the 'sole correct one' by the tradition of formal logic, it is impossible to discover such a common attribute as would form part of the definition of two polar meanings of 'common' ('general'). Nevertheless, it is clear that here, as in many other cases, we are dealing with related words which, like human relatives, although they have nothing in common between them, all with equal right bear one and the same surname.

This relationship between the terms of natural language was once brought out by Ludwig Wittgenstein as quite typical in the following example: Churchill-A has a family likeness to Churchill-B in attributes a, b, c; Churchill-B shares attributes b, c, d with Churchill-C; Churchill-D has only a single attribute in common with Churchill-A, while Churchill-E and Churchill-A have not a single one in common, nothing except the name.

The image of a common ancestor, however, of a progenitor, cannot be reconstructed by abstracting those attributes, and only those, that are genetically preserved by all his (or her) descendants. There simply are no such attributes. But there is a community of name, recording a common origin.

It is the same with 'common' ('general') as a term. The original meaning of the word also cannot be established by a purely formal union of attributes, uniting all the offspring-terms into one family, into one class, because (to continue the analogy) Churchill-Alpha would have to be represented as an individuum who was simultaneously both brunette and blonde (not-brunette), both gangling and dwarfish, both snub-nosed and hook-nosed, and so on.

But there, of course, the analogy ends, because the position with related terms is rather different. The ancestor, as a rule, does not die but continues to live alongside all its offspring as an individuum among other individua, and the problem consists in discovering among the *existing separate individua* the one that was born before the others and therefore could have given birth to all the rest.

Among the attributes of a common ancestor who continues to live among his descendants, one has to presuppose a capacity to give birth to something which is opposite to itself, i.e. a capacity to give birth both to the gangling (in relation to itself) and the dwarfish (again in relation to itself). The common ancestor, consequently, can be representable as an individuum of medium height with a straight nose, and ash-grey locks, i.e. to 'combine' *opposing* determinations (if only potentially) in himself, to combine both the one and the other, directly opposite determinations *in himself*, like a solution or mixture. Thus the colour grey can be fully represented as mixture of black and white, i.e. as simultaneously white and black. There is nothing incompatible in that with the 'common sense' that Neopositivists like to enlist as an ally against dialectical logic.

But it is just here that the two incompatible positions in logic, and in understanding of the general (universal), take shape—that of dialectics and the completely formal conception. The latter has no desire to admit into logic the idea of *development* organically linked (both in essence and in origin) with the concept of *substance,* i.e. the principle of the *genetic community* of phenomena that are at first glance quite heterogeneous (insofar as no abstract, common attributes can be discovered among them).

It was thus that Hegel saw the point of departure of the paths of dialectical thought (in his terminology 'speculative') and purely formal thought; and in that connection he highly values Aristotle's relevant statement: 'As to what concerns more nearly the relation *of the three souls,* as they may be termed (though they are incorrectly thus distinguished), Aristotle says of them, with perfect truth, that we need look for no one soul in which all these are found, and which in a definite and simple form is conformable with any of them. This is a profound observation, *by means of which truly speculative thought marks itself out from the thought which is merely logical and formal* [my italics—*EUI*]. Similarly among figures only the triangle and the other definite figures, like the square, the parallelogram, etc., are truly anything; for what is common to them, the universal figure [or rather the 'figure in general'—*EUI*], is an empty thing of thought, a mere abstraction. On the other hand, the triangle is the first, the truly universal figure, which appears also in the square, etc., as the figure which can be led back to the simplest determination. Therefore, on the one hand, the triangle stands alongside of the square, pentagon, etc., as a particular figure, but—and this is Aristotle's

348

main contention—it is the truly universal figure [or rather the 'figure in general'—*EUI*]. ... Aristotle's meaning is therefore this: an empty universal is that which does not itself exist, or is not itself species. All that is universal is in fact real, in that by itself, without further change, it constitutes its first species, and when further developed it belongs, not to this, but to a higher stage.'[1]

If we look at the problem of the determination of the general as a universal (logical) category from this angle, or at the problem of the theoretical reconstruction of the common ancestor of a family of related meanings seemingly having nothing in common, there is some hope of resolving it.

The stand of formal logic, oriented on finding the abstract, common element in every single representative of one class (all having one and the same name) yields nothing in this instance. The general in this sense cannot be found here, and cannot for the reason that there actually is no such thing, not in the form of attribute or determination actually common to all the individua, in the form of a resemblance proper to each of them taken separately.

It is quite clear that the concrete (empirically obvious) essence of the link uniting the various individua in some 'one', in a *common* multitude or plurality, is by no means posited and expres-

---

[1] *Hegel's Lectures on the History of Philosophy,* Vol. II, pp 185-186.

sed in an abstract attribute common to them, or in a determination that is equally proper to the one and the other. Rather such unity (or community) is created by the attribute that one individuum possesses and another does not. And the absence of a certain attribute binds one individuum to another much more strongly than its equal existence in both.

Two absolutely equal individuals, each of which has the very same set of knowledge, habits, inclinations, etc., would be absolutely uninteresting to one another, and the one would not need the other. They would simply bore each other to death. It is nothing but a simple doubling of solitariness. The general is anything but continuously repeated similarity in every single object taken separately and represented by a common attribute and fixed by a sign. The universal is above all the regular connection of two (or more) particular individuals that converts them into moments of one and the same concrete, real unity. And it is much more reasonable to represent this unity as the aggregate of *different,* separate moments than as an indefinite plurality of units indifferent to one another. Here the general functions as the law or principle of the connection of these details in the make-up of some whole, or totality as Marx preferred to call it, following Hegel. Here analysis rather than abstraction is called for.

If we return to the question of the genetic community of the different (and opposing) meanings that the term 'common' or 'general' ('universal') has acquired in the evolution of the living language, the problem seemingly boils down to recognising that among them which can confidently be considered as the progenitor-meaning, and then to tracing why and how the initial meaning, first in time and immediately simple in essence, was broadened so as to embrace something opposite, something that was not originally intended at all. Since it is difficult to suspect our remote ancestors of an inclination to invent 'abstract objects' and 'constructions', it is more logical (it would seem) to consider the original meaning the one that the term 'common' still preserves in such expressions as 'common ancestor' and 'common field'. Philological research provides evidence, incidentally, in favour of that view. 'What would old Hegel say in the next world,' Marx wrote with satisfaction to Engels, 'if he heard that the *general* [*Allgemeine*] in German and Norse means nothing but the common land [*Gemeinland*], and the particular, *Sundre, Besondere,* nothing but the separate property divided off from the common land? Here are the logical categories coming damn well out of "our intercourse" after all.'[1]

It is quite understandable that if we have in mind here the originally simple, 'truly general' meaning of the word, as Hegel would have said, then it is impossible to discover in the idea according to which the general (universal) precedes

---

[1] Karl Marx and Frederick Engels. *Selected Correspondence* (International Publishers, New York, 1936) pp 236-237.

the individual, the separate, the particular, the isolated, or exclusive, both in essence and in time, even a hint of the refined mysticism that permeates the corresponding views of Neoplatonists and mediaeval Christian scholasticism, whereby the universal is made a synonym of the idea, being considered from the very beginning as the word, as *logos*, as something incorporeal, spiritualised, purely mental. On the contrary, the universal in its original meaning appears distinctly in the mind, and therefore in the language expressing it, as a synonym of a quite corporeal substance, in the form of water, fire, tiny uniform particles ('indivisibles'), and so on. Such a notion may be considered naive (though in fact it is far from being so naive), crudely sensual, 'too materialistic', but there is not the slightest tendency to, or trace of, mysticism in it.

It is therefore quite absurd to press the accusation that is constantly advanced against materialism by its opponents, the accusation of a disguised Platonism that is immanently linked, as it were, with the thesis of the *objective reality* of the universal. If, of course, one takes the view from the very beginning (but why—we do not know) that the universal is the idea, and only the idea, then not only do Marx and Spinoza turn out to be 'cryptoplatonists' but also Thales and Democritus.

One is forced to evaluate the identification of the universal with the idea (as the initial thesis of any system of philosophical idealism) as an axiom accepted quite without proof, as the purest prejudice inherited from the Middle Ages. Its vitality is not fortuitous but is linked with the really immense role that the word and the verbal 'explication' of the idea have played and play in the moulding of intellectual culture. From that, too, arises the illusion that the universal allegedly has its actual existence (its reality) only and exclusively in the form of *logos*, in the form of the meaning of a word, term, or linguistic sign. Since philosophical consciousness specially reflecting on the universal is concerned from the very beginning with its verbal expression, the dogma of the identity of the universal and the sense (meaning) of a word also begins to seem a natural premise, and the soil on which it grows, and the air that it breathes, to be something self-evident.

We would note in passing that the prejudice described here, read as absolute truth by modern Neopositivists, also seemed such to Hegel, who is not a favourite with them. Hegel, too, candidly suggested that materialism was impossible as a philosophical system on the grounds that philosophy was the science of the *universal,* and the universal was the idea, just the idea, and only the idea, and could not be anything else. He had the immense advantage over the latest devotees of this prejudice that he understood thought itself much more profoundly. Thus it was Hegel himself who thoroughly undermined the prestige of the prejudice that consisted in identifying thought and speech; but he returned a prisoner to it by a roundabout route since, though he did not consider the word the sole form of the being there of an idea, it retained the significance of the *first* form of its being for him, both in time and in essence. Hegel, and this was typical of him in general, first smashed the old prejudice, and then restored it to all its rights by means of a cunningly clever dialectical apparatus.

The radical, materialist rethinking of the achievements of his logic (dialectics) carried through by Marx, Engels, and Lenin, was linked with affirmation of the *objective reality of the universal*, not at all in the spirit of Plato or Hegel, but rather in the sense of a law-governed connexion of material phenomena, in the sense of the law of their being joined together in the composition of some whole, in the context of a self-developing totality or aggregate, all the components of which were related as a matter of fact not by virtue of their possessing one and the same identical attribute, but by virtue of a unity of genesis, by virtue of their having one and the same common ancestor, or to put it more exactly, by virtue of their arising as diverse modifications of one and the same substance of a *quite material* character (i.e. independent of thought and word).

Uniform phenomena therefore do not necessarily possess anything like a 'family resemblance' as the sole grounds for being counted as one class. The *universal* in them may be outwardly expressed much better in the form of differences, even of opposites, that make the separate phenomena complement one another, components of a whole, of some quite real, organic aggregate, and not an amorphous plurality of units taken together on the basis of a more or less chance attribute. On the other hand, the universal, which manifests itself precisely in the particularities, in the individual characteristics of all the components of the whole without exception, also exists in itself as a particular alongside other isolated individua derived from it. In that there is nothing even remotely mystical; a father often lives a very long time side by side with his sons. And if he is not present, he *was* once, of course, i.e. must be definitely thought of in the category of 'being there'. The genetically understood universal does not simply exist, naturally, in the ether of the abstract, in the elements of the word and idea; and its existence in no way abolishes or belittles the reality of its modifications and of the separate individua derived from it and dependent on it.

In Marx's analysis of capital the concept of the universal that we have briefly described plays a most important methodological role. 'To the extent that we are considering it here, as a relation distinct from that of value and money, capital is *capital in general,* i.e. the incarnation of the qualities which distinguish value as capital from value as pure value or as money. Value, money, circulation, etc., prices, etc., are presupposed, as is labour, etc. But we are still concerned neither with a *particular* form of capital, nor with an *individual capital* as distinct from other individual capitals, etc. We are present at the process of its becoming. This dialectical process of its becoming is only the ideal expression of the real movement through which capital comes into being. The later relations are to be regarded as developments coming out of this germ. But it is necessary to establish the specific form in which it is posited at a *certain* point. Otherwise confusion arises.'[3]

Here there is very clearly brought out that relation between value and capital which Hegel, in the passage cited above, discovered between a triangle and a square, pentagon, etc., and, moreover, in a dual sense. (1) The concept of value in general is in no case defined here through the aggregate of the abstract, general attributes that one may want to discover in the composition of all its special forms (i.e. commodities, labour power, capital, rent, interest, etc., etc.) but is achieved by way of the most rigorous analysis of one single, quite specific, and actually existing relation between people, the relation of the direct exchange of one commodity for another. In the analysis of this value reality, reduced to its simplest form, the universal determinations of value are brought out that are later met (reproduced) at higher levels of development and analysis as abstract, general determinations of money, and labour power, and capital.

(2) If we are concerned with defining capital in general, then, as Marx specially remarked, we must take the following point of principle into account, which has 'more of a logical than an

---

[3] Karl Marx. *Grundrisse*, p 310.

economic character'.[4] '...Capital in general, as *distinct* from the particular real capitals, is itself a *real* existence. This is recognised by ordinary economics, even if it is not *understood*, and forms a very important moment of its doctrine of equilibrations, etc. For example, capital in this *general form*, although belonging to individual capitalists, in its *elemental form* as capital, forms the capital which accumulates in the banks or is distributed through them, and, as Ricardo says, so admirably distributes itself in accordance with the needs of production.[5] Likewise, through loans, etc., it forms a level between the different countries. If it is therefore e.g. a law of capital in general that, in order to realise itself, it must posit itself doubly, and must realise itself in this double form, then e.g. the capital of a particular nation which represents capital *par excellence* in antithesis to another will have to lend itself out to a third nation in order to be able to realise itself. This double positing, this relating to self as to an alien, becomes damn real in this case. While the general is therefore on the one hand only a mental (*gedachte*) mark of distinction (*differentia specifica*), it is at the same time a *particular* real form alongside the form of the particular and individual.'[6] It is 'the same also in algebra,' Marx

---

[4] *Ibid.*, p 450.

[5] D. Ricardo. *On the Principles of Political Economy* (London, 1821) p 139 (Marx's footnote).

[6] Karl Marx. *Grundrisse*, pp 449-450. [There is a footnote in the *Grundrisse* at this point (cf. Hegel. *Science of Logic*, p 600. Translated by A. V. Miller, London, 1969):

continued. 'For example, a, b, c, are numbers as such; in general; but then again they are whole numbers as opposed to a/b, b/c, c/b, c/a, b/a, etc., which latter, however, presuppose the former as their general elements'.[7]

The situation of the dialectical relation between the general (universal) and the particular, the individual, by virtue of which the general cannot in principle be revealed in the make-up of the particular individuals by formal abstraction (by way of identifying the similar or identical in them) can be most vividly demonstrated by the example of the theoretical difficulties connected with the concept 'man', with the definition of the essence of man, the solution of which was found by Marx, basing himself precisely on a dialectical understanding of the problem of the general.[8] '...The essence of man is no abstraction inherent in each separate individual. In its reality it is the *ensemble* (aggregate) of social relations,'[9] as Marx aphoristically formulated his conception in the famous theses on Feuerbach.

Here one clearly sees not only the sociological principle of Marx's thinking, but also its logical principle. Translated into the language of logic, his aphorism means that it is useless to seek the general determinations expressing the essence of

'This universal action contains the three moments: universality, particularity, and individuality.'—*Tr.*]

[7] *Ibid.*, p 450.

[8] See E. V. Ilyenkov. *Dialektika abstraktnogo i konkretnogo v 'Kapitale' Marksa* (The Dialectics of the Abstract and Concrete in Marx's 'Capital') (Moscow, 1960).

[9] Karl Marx. Theses on Feuerbach. *Op. cit.*, p 198.

a class, be it the human race or some other genus, in a series of the abstract, general attributes possessed by each member of the given class taken separately. The essence of human nature in general can only be brought out through a scientific, critical analysis of the 'whole aggregate', the 'whole ensemble', of man's social and historical relations to man, through concrete investigation and understanding of the patterns within which the process of the birth and evolution both of human society as a whole and of the separate individual has taken place and is taking place.

The separate individual is only human in the exact and strict sense of the word, insofar as he actualises—and just by his individuality—some ensemble or other of historically developed faculties (specifically human forms of life activity), some fragment or other of a culture formed before and independently of him, and mastered by him during upbringing (the moulding of the person). From that angle the human personality can rightly be considered as an individual embodiment of culture, i.e. of the universal in man.

Universality so understood is by no means a silent, generic 'sameness' of individuals but reality repeatedly and diversely broken up within itself into particular (separate) spheres mutually complementing each other and in essence mutually dependent on each other and therefore linked together by bonds of community of origin no less firm and no less flexible than the organs of the body of a biological specimen developed from one and the same egg cell. In other words, theoretical, logical determination of the concrete universality of human life can consist solely in disclosing the necessity with which the diverse forms of specifically human life activity develop one from the other and in interaction of the one on the other, the faculties of social man and his corresponding needs.

The materialist conception of the essence of man sees (in full agreement with the data of anthropology, ethnography, and archaeology) the universal form of human life in labour, in the direct transformation of nature (both external and his own) that social man brings about with the help of tools made by himself. That is why Marx felt such sympathy to Benjamin Franklin's famous definition (quoted in Boswell's *Life of Johnson*) of man as a tool-making animal: a tool-making animal and only therefore also a thinking animal, talking, composing music, obeying moral norms, and so on.

The definition of man in general as a tool-making animal is a typical example in which the Marxian conception of the universal as the concretely universal is seen most clearly of all, and also the Marxian conception of its relation to the particular and the individual. From the standpoint of the canons of formal logic this definition is much too concrete to be universal, for under it such undoubted members of the human race as Mozart or Leo Tolstoy, Raphael or Kant cannot be subsumed.

Formally such a definition applies only to a narrow circle of individuals, to the workers in engineering works, say, or workshops. Even workers who do not make machines (or tools) but only use them, formally do not come within the scope of this definition. The old logic therefore rightly regarded it not as a universal but exclusively as a particular definition, not as a definition of man in general but of a particular profession.

The general (concretely universal) stands opposed to the sensuously given variety of separate individuals primarily not as a mental abstraction but as their own *substance*, as a concrete form of their interaction. As such it also *embodies* or includes the whole wealth of the particular and individual in its concrete determinateness and that not simply as the possibility of development but as its necessity. The conception of the general and of its paths of scientific realisation described here is by no means the monopoly of philosophical dialectics. Science, in its real historical development, unlike its depiction in the epistemological and logical constructions of Neopositivists, always begins, more or less consistently, from such a concept of the universal, and that often in spite of the conscious logical precepts and maxims that its representatives profess. This circumstance is clearly traceable in the history of the concept 'value', a universal category of political economy.

The abstraction of value in general and the word that records it are as old as market relations. The Greek *axia*, the German *Werth*, and so on were not created by Sir William Petty, or

Adam Smith, or Ricardo. Every merchant and peasant of all ages used 'value' or 'worth' for everything that could be bought or sold, everything that cost something, or was worth something.

And if the theoretical political economists had tried to work out a *concept* of value in general, guided by the recipes that purely formal, nominalistly oriented logic still suggests to science, they would never, of course, have done so. Here it has not been a matter at all, from the very beginning, of the bringing out of the abstractly general, of the similar that each of the objects possesses, which general word usage long ago united in the term 'value' (in that case it would simply introduce order into the notions that any shopkeeper uses, and the matter would be limited to simple 'explication' of the shopkeeper's notions about value, to a simple, pedantic enumeration of the attributes of those phenomena to which the word 'value' is opposite, and no more; and the whole exercise would amount simply to clarification of the scope of the term's applicability). The whole point, however, is that the classical political economists posed the question quite differently, so that the answer to it proved to be a *concept,* i.e. an awareness of the real generality. Marx pointed out clearly the essence of their posing of the question.

The first English economist Sir William Petty arrived at the concept of value by the following reasoning: 'If a man can bring to London an ounce of Silver out of the Earth in Peru *in the same time* that he can produce a Bushel of Corn, then one is the natural price of the other. ...'[10]

Let us note in passing that in the reasoning adduced here the term 'value' is absent in general, 'natural price' being spoken of. But we are present here right at the birth of the fundamental *concept* of all subsequent science of the production, distribution, and accumulation of wealth. Here the concept also expresses (reflects) (like Hegel's example of the triangle) such a real phenomenon given in experience as (being quite particular among other particulars) at the same time proves to be universal and represents value in general.

The classical political economists spontaneously groped out the way of determining value in its general form; but in retrospect, having already formed the relevant concept, they tried to 'verify' it in accordance with the canons of logic, relying on Locke's notions about thought and the universal, which led them into a number of paradoxes and antinomies. The general, when they tried to 'justify' it by analysis of its own particular variants, like profit and capital, was not only not confirmed, but was directly refuted by them, contradicted by them.

Only Marx succeeded in establishing the reason for the origin of the various paradoxes, and

---

[10] Sir William Petty. *A Treatise of Taxes and Contributions* (London, 1667); cited by Karl Marx in *Theories of Surplus-Value*, Part I, p 356.

so the way out; and he did so just because he was guided by dialectical notions of the nature of the general and its inter-relations with the particular and the individual. The reality of the universal in nature is a law, but a law in its reality (as is shown, in particular, by modern natural science, e.g. the physics of the microworld) is not realised as some abstract rule by which the movement of each single particle taken separately would be governed, but only as a *tendency* manifesting itself in the behaviour of a more or less complex ensemble of individual phenomena, through the breach and negation of the universal in each of its separate (individual) manifestations. And thought is forced willy-nilly to take that circumstance into account.

The general determinations of value (of the law of value) are worked out in *Capital* in the course of an analysis of one example of the concreteness of value, historically the first and therefore logically the simplest, i.e., the direct exchange or barter of one commodity for another, with the most rigorous abstraction of all other individual forms (developed on its basis), namely money, profit, land rent, and so on. Marx saw the shortcoming of Ricardo's analysis of value precisely in his not being able, when examining the problem of value in its general form, to forget profit. That is why Ricardo's abstraction proved *incomplete* and so *formal*.

Marx himself obtained a solution of the problem in general form because all the subsequent formations—not only profit but also even money

—were taken as not existent at the start of the analysis. Only direct exchange or barter without money was analysed; and it was immediately clear that such a raising of its individual to the general differed in principle from the act of simple, formal abstraction. Here the *peculiarities* of the simple commodity form, specifically distinguishing it from profit, land rent, interest, and other individual forms of value, were not thrown away as something inessential; quite the contrary, their theoretical expression coincided with the determination of value in its general form.

The incompleteness of Ricardo's abstraction, and the formality linked with it, consisted precisely in its being formed on the one hand through his inability to abstract it from the existence of other developed forms of value, and on the other hand through his abstracting of the *peculiarities* of direct commodity exchange. The general was thus taken in the end as completely isolated from the particular and separate, and ceased to be its theoretical expression. That is what distinguishes the dialectical conception of the general from the purely formal conception.

The distinction between Marx's dialectical *materialist* conception, however, and the interpretation given the general in Hegel's idealistic dialectics is no less important. And it is important to bring this out clearly for the reason that their conceptions are too often equated in Western literature. Yet it is quite obvious that the orthodox Hegelian interpretation of the general, despite all its dialectical value, comes close, on a decisive point of principle and not just in details, to that very metaphysical view that Hegel himself had so strongly undermined the authority and influence of. This comes out particularly clearly in the concrete applications of the principles of Hegelian logic to the analysis of real, earthly problems.

The point is as follows. When Hegel explains his 'speculative' conception of the general in opposition to the 'purely formal' on the example of geometrical figures (treating the triangle as 'the figure in general') it may seem at first glance that here was the logical schema in ready-made form that enabled Marx to cope with the problem of the general determination of value. Actually, it would seem that Hegel saw the difference between genuine universality and purely formal abstraction in the truly general's itself existing in the form of the particular, i.e. as an empirically given reality existing in time and space (outside men's heads) and perceived in contemplation.

According to Hegel, the general *as such,* in its strict and exact sense, exists exclusively in the ether of 'pure thought' and in no case in the space and time of external reality. In that sphere we are dealing only with a number of particular alienations, embodiments, hypostasies of the 'genuinely general'.

That was why the definition of man as a tool-making animal would have been quite unacceptable to Hegelian logic, and logically incorrect.

For the orthodox Hegelian, as for any representative of the formal logic criticised by him (a very notable unanimity!), Franklin's definition (and Marx's) was much too concrete to be general or universal. In the production of tools Hegel saw not the basis of everything human in man, but only one, though important, manifestation of his *thinking* nature. In other words the idealism of the Hegelian interpretation of the general leads to the very same result as the metaphysical interpretation he so disliked.

When Hegelian logic is taken in its pristine form as the means of evaluating the movement of thought in the first chapters of *Capital*, the whole movement seems 'illegitimate' and 'illogical'. The Hegelian logician would be right, from his angle, if he were to say of Marx's analysis of value that there was no general determination of this category in it, that Marx only 'described' but did not theoretically 'deduce' the determination of one *special, particular* form of the realisation of value in general, because that, like any truly general category of human life activity, was a form immanent in the 'rational will' and not in man's external being, in which it was only manifested and materialised.

So Hegelian logic, despite all its superiority over formal logic, could not and cannot be taken into the armoury of materialistically oriented science without any essential amendments, and without a radical purging of all traces of idealism. For idealism did not remain something 'external' for logic at all, but orientated the very logical sequence of thought. When Hegel spoke, for example, of the *transitions* of opposing categories (including the general and the particular), the schema of the examination then and there received a one-way character. In the Hegelian schema there could be no place, say, for the transition that Marx discovered in the determinations of value, the transformation of the singular or individual into the general. With Hegel only the general had the privilege of alienating itself in forms of the particular and the singular, while the singular always proved to be a product, a particular 'modus' of universality (and therefore poor in content).

The actual history of economic (market) relations testified, however, in Marx's favour, demonstrating that the form of value in general was by no means always the *general* form of the organisation of production. It *became* the general, but up to a certain point (and for very long) it remained a particular relation happening from time to time between people and things in production. Only capitalism made value (the commodity form of the product) the general form of the interrelations of the components of production.

This transition of the individual and chance into the general was not at all rare in history, but was even rather the rule. It has always happened in history that phenomena that subsequently became general arose first precisely as individual exceptions to the rule, as anomalies, as something particular and partial. Hardly anything really new can arise in any other way.

It is in the light of that, that the rethinking to which the Hegelian dialectical conception of the general was subjected by Marx and Lenin must be understood. While preserving all the dialectical moments noted by Hegel, materialism deepened and broadened its conception, transforming the category of the general or universal into the most important category of the logic of concrete investigation of concrete, historically developing phenomena.

In the context of the materialist conception of the dialectics of history and the dialectics of thought, the Hegelian formulas sound differently from on the lips of their creator, having lost all mystical colouring. The general includes and embodies in itself the whole wealth of details, not as the 'idea' but as a quite real, particular phenomenon with a tendency to become general, and developing 'from itself' (by virtue of its inner contradictions) other just as real phenomena, other particular forms of actual movement. And there is not a trace of any of the Platonic-Hegelian mystique in that.

CONCLUSION

Quite understandably we have not undertaken the task here of giving a systematic exposition of Marxist-Leninist logic. That is beyond the powers of a single person, and can scarcely be done within the space of one book. We have simply tried to throw some light on a number of the conditions and premises for further work in that direction, which we consider should be a collective effort.

We think, however, that only by taking the conditions formulated above into account can such a work be successful, i.e. lead to the creation of a capital work which could rightly bear one of three titles: *Logic, Dialectics,* or *The Theory of Knowledge* (of the modern, materialist world outlook); and which could take as its epigraph Lenin's words: 'Three words are not needed: it is one and the same thing.'

The creation of a Logic understood as a system of categories, of course, constitutes only one stage. The next step would have to be the realisation, actualisation of the logical system in a concrete scientific investigation, because the end product of all work in the field of philosophical dialectics is the resolution of the concrete problems of concrete sciences. Philosophy alone cannot achieve this 'end product'; that calls for an alliance of dialectics and concrete scientific research, understood and realised as the business-like collaboration of philosophers and natural scientists, of philosophy and social and historical fields of knowledge. But in order for dialectics to be an equal collaborator in concrete scientific knowledge, it 'must' first develop the system of its own specific philosophical concepts, from the angle of which it could display the strength of critical distinction in relation to actually given thought and consciously practised methods.

It seems to us that this conclusion stems directly from the analysis we have presented here, and that this conception corresponds directly to Lenin's ideas both in the field of philosophical dialectics and on the plane of the inter-relations of the latter and the other branches of scientific knowledge. It appears to us that, in the conception set out above, logic does become an equal collaborator with the other sciences, and not their servant, and not their supreme overseer, not a 'science of sciences' crowning their system as just another variety of 'absolute truth'. Understood as logic philosophical dialectics becomes a necessary component of the scientific, materialist world outlook, and no longer claims a monopoly realisation of that outlook, or a monopoly in relation to the 'world as a whole'. The scientific world outlook can only be described by the whole system of modern sciences. That system also includes philosophical dialectics, and without it cannot claim either fullness or scientism.

The scientific world outlook that does not include philosophy, logic, and the theory of knowledge, is as much nonsense as the 'pure' philosophy that assumes that it alone is the world outlook, taking on its shoulders a job that can only be done by a whole complex of sciences. Philosophy is also the logic of the development of the world outlook, or, as Lenin put it, its 'living soul'.